INTERPROFESSIONAL COLLABORATION
IN SOCIAL WORK PRACTICE

INTERPROFESSIONAL COLLABORATION IN SOCIAL WORK PRACTICE

Karin Crawford

Los Angeles | London | New Delhi
Singapore | Washington DC

SAGE Publications Ltd
1 Oliver's Yard
55 City Road
London EC1Y 1SP

SAGE Publications Inc.
2455 Teller Road
Thousand Oaks, California 91320

SAGE Publications India Pvt Ltd
B 1/I 1 Mohan Cooperative Industrial Area
Mathura Road
New Delhi 110 044

SAGE Publications Asia-Pacific Pte Ltd
33 Pekin Street #02–01
Far East Square
Singapore 048763

Library of Congress Control Number: 2010940734

British Library Cataloguing in Publication data

A catalogue record for this book is available from the British Library

ISBN 978–1–84920–427–9
ISBN 978–1–84920–428–6 (pbk)

Typeset by C&M Digitals (P) Ltd, Chennai, India
Printed in India at Replika Press Pvt Ltd
Printed on paper from sustainable resources

CONTENTS

LIST OF FIGURES

ABOUT THE AUTHOR

Dr. Karin Crawford is a Principal Teaching Fellow and Faculty Director of Teaching and Learning at the University of Lincoln. Karin is a fellow of the Higher Education Academy and a registered social worker. Prior to moving into higher education, Karin gained substantial practice experience in both health and social care, as a practitioner and manager. This experience spanned statutory, voluntary and private sectors and included general nursing, social work, policy development and the management of both adult and children's care management services. More recently, Karin has experience of working in other European countries in areas related both to teaching and learning, social work, and research in health and social care. Karin's research work and publications relate to both health and social care subject-related research and pedagogic-related research. Principally she uses qualitative, narrative approaches to further understanding of the experience of individuals' life trajectories. Karin teaches on undergraduate and postgraduate social work programmes and supervises a number of doctoral students working on educational research. Karin is particularly interested in the development and facilitation of learning through open, distance part-time learning and using technology to aid learning.

PART 1

UNDERSTANDING COLLABORATIVE PRACTICE

1

INTRODUCING INTERPROFESSIONAL COLLABORATIVE PRACTICE

Chapter summary

When you have worked through this chapter, you will be able to:

- Understand the overall purpose, aims, scope and features of this book.
- Recognise how the book is aligned with a range of national standards related to professional social work practice.
- Be familiar with how the book is structured and the brief content of each chapter.
- Be aware of the key themes that underpin the whole book.
- Understand the range of terms, words and phrases used to describe aspects of working together.

INTRODUCTION

This introductory chapter will provide you with an overview of the whole book, laying out its purpose, aims and scope through an outline of the structure and key themes. This chapter will also identify how the contents of the book are related to key national standards for practice and social work education. Also, to inform your studies through the book, this chapter includes discussion about the different terminology employed to describe similar aspects of working together in social work practice; the language, terms and discourse we use are significant to how we understand

and interpret the world around us. As an introduction to your learning across the book, this chapter can be likened to a course induction process.

Interprofessional Collaboration in Social Work Practice is, as they say, everyone's business. The transition from a position of multi-professionalism, where there are many people from different disciplines working in isolation, to a state of interprofessionalism, where those professionals work collaboratively, is not as straightforward as it may sound: it impacts on everyone involved and everyone involved influences the progress. Written primarily for social work students and practitioners, although having relevance across the wider range of stakeholders, this book explores the issues, benefits and challenges that interprofessional collaborative practice can raise, with a particular emphasis on its impact on social work practice.

BOOK PURPOSE, AIMS, SCOPE AND FEATURES

As long ago as 1959, following an inquiry into the role, recruitment and training of social workers, the Younghusband Report stated that:

> People do not normally feel part of a team unless they appreciate the effect of the combined operation, and the working method and function of each member. The elements in good team-work are, therefore, an administrative structure which facilitates co-operation, good working relationships between different types of officer and departments, and opportunities for regular meetings and discussion at all levels. (Younghusband 1959: 35)

Through the chapters of this book, you will read about how interprofessional collaborative practice has continued to be a policy and practice imperative. The book provides discussion and activities to help you learn about and reflect upon the ways in which collaborative working across professional and agency boundaries can impact upon the experiences of service users, carers and practitioners. Taking a broad, inclusive view of all aspects of social work and social care practice, this book emphasises the significance of social work as a profession in the collaborative environment. Your study through these chapters will help you look at the way social work and social work care agencies develop a professional and an agency culture and how this can both impede and assist working across organisational boundaries. It therefore encourages you to develop your skills as a critical, reflective interprofessional social worker.

The book requires you to critically examine the political, legal, social and economic context of interprofessional practice, exploring consistencies and contradictions evident in policy and procedure, through an analysis of their influence on the reality of professional practice. Within this, the background of current collaborative working practices, the continuities and changes will be considered. A principal theme throughout your reading will be the impact of interprofessional and collaborative working practices on the experiences of, outcomes for, and participation of service users and carers. Through concepts of participation and empowerment, the book will examine changes in the balance of power and influence between service providers and service users. Within an exploration of related research and theoretical models, you will critically examine the tensions inherent in interprofessional practice so as to be able to identify frameworks and components that typify effective collaboration.

This book focuses on relationships at different levels: between organisational or structural levels, interprofessional or interdisciplinary, and the individual levels of practice within the 'helping professions'. Whilst it has a focus on 'what this means' for social work practice, you should be aware that collaborative working is not only limited to health and social care, but can involve a vast range of 'stakeholders'. The term 'stakeholders' refers to any person who may have an interest or be affected by the relevant practice or service. As you study the materials in this text and work through the various activities and questions, it is important that you keep this range of possible 'stakeholders' in mind. To help you start thinking about the people and organisations you might work with in social work practice, take a moment to work through Activity 1.1.

Activity 1.1

- Think broadly about your knowledge and, if you have it, experience of social work practice. Make a list of all the different individuals, professions and organisations that might be considered to be 'stakeholders' – those who have an interest in, or are affected by, social work services and practice.

Whilst this activity is useful if you work through it on your own, it becomes even more interesting and expansive if you have the opportunity to work together with other students or colleagues from practice.

COMMENT

You are likely to have a long list of people and organisations, which may differ from another student as the lists may reflect different experiences and different knowledge of practice. I imagine that you may have started by including service users, carers and perhaps volunteers, local communities and neighbourhoods more widely. You are likely then to have moved on to think about various professions such as nurses, midwives, school teachers, careers advisors, probation officers, police officers, general practitioners (GPs) and so on. You may also have thought about the many organisations involved, ranging from statutory agencies such as local authorities, probation services and various National Health bodies, to private profit-making services, social enterprises, voluntary or charitable groups (some of which are small, local agencies, while others might be affiliated to national groups), and user-led organisations. There are also wider national bodies, such as government departments and national research institutions. This is also not to forget the role of agencies and individuals who provide education and training for the various

Individuals	Role or interest	Professionals	Role or interest	Organisations	Role or interest
Service user	Participant and recipient of services; controller of own services	General Practitioner (GP)	Health and medical assessment and services	Primary Care Trust	Community-based services to meet health and social care needs
Carer	Provides informal care and support	Housing Manager	Manages local housing services and tenancy arrangements	Local Authority Social Services	Services, advice and support for vulnerable people
Continue completing this table with your own examples					

Figure 1.1   Identifying the stakeholders in the interprofessional, collaborative environment

professions, not only in universities and colleges, but also from private and voluntary organisations. One way to try and represent the massive scope of this is to tabulate them. Figure 1.1 shows the beginnings of a table setting this out. As you will see, I have added columns to identify the role or interest that the person or organisation has in practice. You could complete the table by adding your list to it and completing the additional columns.

However you undertake this activity, it will help you become more aware of the people and organisations you might collaborate with and the potential scope of interprofessional practice. You are encouraged to keep your notes from this activity, as you may need to refer back to them later as you work through this book. Whilst it is not possible in a book of this size to examine each of these many aspects of interprofessional collaboration, throughout the book I acknowledge the range of settings where collaborative working practices are being embedded. Through case studies, reflective activities, research examples and further reading, all of which focus on different areas and levels of practice, you will develop transferable knowledge, skills and awareness of values relevant across all practice contexts, to support you as you develop as an interprofessional social worker. Furthermore, with regard to the scope of this book, you will find that, as far as possible, the materials and concepts relate to social work practice across the four countries of the United Kingdom, however the legislation discussed is largely English.

Given the fast pace of political and policy change, though, and the increasingly differing approaches that the devolved governments are developing, Chapter 2 of this book offers a broad overview of the context for collaborative practice with many suggestions and references that you might explore for more knowledge on specific contemporary issues for each country. Beyond Chapter 2, the book explores concepts, theories, research and practices which are broadly applicable, not only across professional and organisational boundaries, but, crucially, geographical boundaries as well.

In each chapter, you will have the opportunity to further your learning and understanding through interacting with a range of features, which as you have read above, include activities and reflective practice questions, followed by my own thoughts and comments on the issues that might be raised as you undertake the tasks. There are also case studies, annotated further reading with links to relevant Internet Web pages and ideas of ways in which you might take your learning further. Please note that there are ongoing changes in governmental structures and the Internet sources that reflect them, references to the Department for Children, Schools and Families and Every Child Matters websites may be sourced through the Department for Education at http://www.education.gov.uk. At the end of the book, you will find a Glossary of terms and abbreviations. This is not an exhaustive list as I have defined and explored many terms throughout the text, but you may find this useful if you are seeking a succinct definition of a particular concept discussed in the chapters. It is my intention that by working through this book and engaging with the interactive experience I offer you, you will build up a portfolio of notes, diagrams, reflective records and tables that will support your further learning and development. Finally, to support your learning through this book and to provide educators and tutors with additional materials to support you, this book has a companion website (www.sagepub.co.uk/crawford).

ALIGNMENT WITH THE NATIONAL STANDARDS

As you study the contents of the chapters in this book, your learning and development will be closely associated with the national requirements for social work practice as set out in the National Occupational Standards for Social Work (TOPSS UK Partnership 2002), the Common Core of Skills and Knowledge for the children and young people's workforce (CWDC 2010) and the General Social Care Council Codes of Practice for Social Care Workers (GSCC 2002). The approach taken across the text is also related to the academic subject benchmark statements for social work (Quality Assurance Agency 2008), which set out the nature and characteristics of social work education at Bachelor's (with honours) degree level. It is important to note that national standards and requirements of this nature are always subject to change, as social work education and practice is continually under review. Therefore, whilst the overall themes are always likely to be relevant, as a student or practitioner, you should ensure that you are aware of the most current principles and standards for social work practice and education. One way to start achieving this is to work through Activity 1.2.

Activity 1.2

- For the first part of this activity, select to focus on either the National Occupational Standards for Social Work, the Common Core of Skills and Knowledge for the children and young people's workforce, the GSCC Codes of Practice for Social Care Workers or the academic subject benchmark statements for social work.
- Using the links and references provided in this section of the chapter, examine the full details of the area you have chosen.
- As you examine the range of statements, make a note of those that you feel have relevance or support interprofessional collaborative practice. You could use a table or grid to do this.

When you have examined one area of these national standards, it is recommended that you work through this activity, drawing on each of the other areas. If you have the opportunity to carry out this activity with colleagues, you could each take a different area and then come together to compare your findings.

COMMENT

On completion of Activity 1.2, you should have a comprehensive list of national requirements for social work that pertain to collaborative working practice. You will also have furthered your knowledge and understanding of these fundamental imperatives for social work practice and education. You could now compare your findings with my work on this, as I detail below the statements from each of the areas that, in my view, address interprofessional collaborative practice.

NATIONAL OCCUPATIONAL STANDARDS FOR SOCIAL WORK

The National Occupational Standards for Social Work (TOPSS UK Partnership 2002 at http://www.skillsforcare.org) are set out in 'key roles', each of which is broken down into units. The chapters of this book all have relevance against the six key roles of the standards, which are as follows:

Key Role 1:   Prepare for, and work with individuals, families, carers, groups and communities to assess their needs and circumstances

Key Role 2:   Plan, carry out, review and evaluate social work practice with individuals, families, carers, groups and communities and other professionals

Key Role 3:   Support individuals to represent their needs, views and circumstances

Key Role 4:   Manage risk to individuals, families, carers, groups, communities, self and colleagues

Key Role 5:   Manage and be accountable, with supervision and support, for your own social work practice within your organisation

Key Role 6:   Demonstrate professional competence in social work practice

Amongst the detail within these key roles, examples from units and elements under Key Roles 5 and 6 are of particular relevance to your learning in this book:

Key Role 5 – Unit 14: Manage and be accountable for your work

14.1 Manage and prioritise your workload within organisational policies and priorities
14.2 Carry out duties using accountable professional judgement and knowledge-based social work practice
14.3 Monitor and evaluate the effectiveness of your programme of work in meeting the organisational requirements and the needs of individuals, families, carers, groups and communities
14.4 Use professional and managerial supervision and support to improve your practice

Key Role 5 – Unit 17: Work within multi-disciplinary and multi-organisational teams, networks and systems

17.1 Develop and maintain effective working relationships
17.2 Contribute to the identifying and agreeing the goals, objectives and lifespan of the team, network or system
17.3 Contribute to evaluating the effectiveness of the team, network or system
17.4 Deal constructively with disagreements and conflict within relationships

Key Role 6 – Unit 18: Research, analyse, evaluate, and use current knowledge of best social work practice

18.1 Review and update your own knowledge of legal, policy and procedural frameworks
18.2 Use professional and organisational supervision and support to research, critically analyse, and review knowledge-based practice
18.3 Implement knowledge-based social work models and methods to develop and improve your own practice

Key Role 6 – Unit 21: Contribute to the promotion of best social work practice

21.2 Use supervision and organisational and professional systems to inform a course of action where practice falls below required standards
21.3 Work with colleagues to contribute to team development

COMMON CORE OF SKILLS AND KNOWLEDGE FOR THE CHILDREN AND YOUNG PEOPLE'S WORKFORCE (CWDC)

The 'common core', as it is known, was revised and updated in 2010 (CWDC 2010 at http://www.cwdcouncil.org), with a renewed emphasis on strengthening integration and collaborative practice. With a focus on work with children and young people, the common core sets out six areas of expertise that all practitioners should have. This framework 'underpin[s] multiagency and integrated working, professional standards, training and qualifications across the children and young people's workforce' (CWDC 2010: 2). The six key areas are:

- effective communication and engagement with children, young people and families;
- child and young person development;
- safeguarding and promoting the welfare of the child or young person;

- supporting transitions;
- multi-agency and integrated working;
- information sharing.

GENERAL SOCIAL CARE COUNCIL CODES OF PRACTICE FOR SOCIAL CARE WORKERS

> The Code of Practice for Social Care Workers is a list of statements that describe the standards of professional conduct and practice required of social care workers as they go about their daily work. (GSCC 2002)

The codes state that as a social care worker, you must:

- Protect the rights and promote the interests of service users and carers;
- Strive to establish and maintain the trust and confidence of service users and carers;
- Promote the independence of service users while protecting them as far as possible from danger or harm;
- Respect the rights of service users whilst seeking to ensure that their behaviour does not harm themselves or other people;
- Uphold public trust and confidence in social care services; and
- Be accountable for the quality of their work and take responsibility for maintaining and improving their knowledge and skills.

One of the aspects included within this last point is 'recognising and respecting the roles and expertise of workers from other agencies and working in partnership with them' (GSCC 2002: point 6.7).

ACADEMIC SUBJECT BENCHMARK STATEMENTS FOR SOCIAL WORK (QUALITY ASSURANCE AGENCY)

The academic subject benchmark statements for social work (Quality Assurance Agency (QAA)) relate to honours degrees in social work and are set out in the explicit context that:

> Social work programmes are expected to prepare students to work as part of the social care workforce, working increasingly in integrated teams across and within specialist settings in adult health, mental health and children's services; interprofessionally alongside professionals in the National Health Service (NHS), schools, police, criminal justice and housing, and in partnership with service users and carers. Increasingly, practice is outcome-focused. (QAA 2008: 2)

The document from the Quality Assurance Agency for Higher Education that I refer to here, also sets out in some detail the regulatory and contemporary context for social work education in each of the four countries that make up the United Kingdom. You will find this a useful source if you want more detail about one specific country. The chapters of this book have been written to support your learning in the context of these academic standards. The subject benchmarks are lengthy and detailed, so I have had to be particularly selective here, but have drawn out a few of the most pertinent extracts for you:

3.7 Contemporary social work increasingly takes place in an inter-agency context, and social workers work collaboratively with others towards interdisciplinary and cross-professional objectives. Honours degree programmes as qualifying awards are required to help equip students with accurate knowledge about the respective responsibilities of social welfare agencies, including those in the public, voluntary/independent and private sectors, and acquire skills in effective collaborative practice.

4.2 At honours level, the study of social work involves the integrated study of subject-specific knowledge, skills and values and the critical application of research knowledge from the social and human sciences, and from social work (and closely related domains) to inform understanding and to underpin action, reflection and evaluation. Honours degree programmes should be designed to help foster this integration of contextual, analytic, critical, explanatory and practical understanding.

4.3 … Social work, both as occupational practice and as an academic subject, evolves, adapts and changes in response to the social, political and economic challenges and demands of contemporary social welfare policy, practice and legislation.

4.6 … honours undergraduates must learn to … work in partnership with service users and carers and other professionals to foster dignity, choice and independence, and effect change.

4.7 The expectation that social workers will be able to act effectively in such complex circumstances requires that honours degree programmes in social work should be designed to help students learn to become accountable, reflective, critical and evaluative. This involves learning to: think critically about the complex social, legal, economic, political and cultural contexts in which social work practice is located; work in a transparent and responsible way, balancing autonomy with complex, multiple and sometimes contradictory accountabilities (for example, to different service users, employing agencies, professional bodies and the wider society); acquire and apply the habits of critical reflection, self-evaluation and consultation, and make appropriate use of research in decision-making about practice and in the evaluation of outcomes.

5.1 During their degree studies in social work, honours graduates should acquire, critically evaluate, apply and integrate knowledge and understanding in the following … core areas of study.

5.1.1 The relationship between agency policies, legal requirements and professional boundaries in shaping the nature of services provided in interdisciplinary contexts and the issues associated with working across professional boundaries and within different disciplinary groups.

5.1.2 The significance of interrelationships with other related services, including housing, health, income maintenance and criminal justice (where not an integral social service).

Reproduced with permission from www.qaa.ac.uk/academicinfrastructure/benchmark/statements/socialwork08. asp © The Quality Assurance Agency for Higher Education, 2008.

BOOK STRUCTURE

This book is set out in two parts: Part 1, made up of Chapters 1, 2 and 3, sets the context, background and theoretical approaches to exploring and understanding interprofessional collaborative practice; Part 2, made up Chapters 4, 5, 6, 7 and 8, examines practice within the context of the collaborative environment set out in Part 1 of the book. As the core chapters that make up the second, practice-orientated part of the book, Chapters 4 to 7 move from examining the individual perspective (service users, carers, social workers, other practitioners), through the wider whole profession perspective in Chapter 6, to organisational issues in Chapter 7. The final chapter, Chapter 8, turns the 'spotlight' back to you and an individual social work perspective on ways to develop and enhance practice for interprofessional collaborative working.

CHAPTER 2

Studying Chapter 2 will further your understanding of the political, policy, social and economic imperatives that drive collaborative working and organisational change in the statutory, voluntary and independent sectors. Through an exploration of the history of working together, lessons learnt from public inquiries and Serious Case Reviews, political drivers, legislative and policy initiatives, this chapter sets the contemporary context for interprofessional collaboration in social work practice.

CHAPTER 3

Your study through this chapter will enable you to examine and apply theoretical frameworks and models that assist understanding and analysis of the interrelationships between professionals and organisations in practice. The chapter provides an overview of some examples of relevant theories, as well as research findings that have provided frameworks to support our knowledge of barriers and drivers, tensions and contradictions for practice in the collaborative environment. The theories, models and frameworks explored in this chapter provide the theoretical underpinning for the second part of the book, where these concepts and their application for practice are revisited through examples and case studies.

CHAPTER 4

Whilst the whole of this book has a central focus on developing your skills and knowledge with regard to working in collaboration, particularly with service users and carers, Chapter 4, the first chapter of the second part of the book, specifically explores the experience of service users. It also considers the changing position, status and role of service users and carers, particularly where this influences participation in collaborative work. Following on from Chapter 3, this chapter shows how the theoretical explanations introduced might aid an understanding of collaborative relationships with service users and carers. The particular example of the personalisation agenda, also known as 'self-directed support', provides an interesting vehicle for a discussion towards the end of Chapter 4, about how collaborative practice and local partnerships might respond to new ways of working, offering choice, control and opportunities for social inclusion.

CHAPTER 5

The focus in this chapter is your developing practice as an interprofessional social worker. Chapter 5 examines what collaborative practice can mean for the individual practitioner. Again, drawing on theories to aid understanding, the chapter tackles issues of professional identity and the skills and attributes needed for effective interprofessional practice. Here, you will also learn about examples of interprofessional practice, particularly examples of assessment processes, examining the ways in which, as a social worker, you will work with others to assess needs and circumstances. The particular examples are the Common Assessment Framework for Children and Young People (DfES 2006), and the Common Assessment Framework for Adults (DoH 2007, 2009b), which builds on the Single Assessment Process (SAP) (DoH 2004), and the Care Programme Approach (CPA) in Mental Health (DoH 2008).

CHAPTER 6

Following the 'seeds sown' in Chapter 5, you will further your understanding of the complexity of professionalism by exploring issues of professional identity, power and professional culture in Chapter 6. This chapter addresses the question of what all this means for social work and for social work practice. Hence, whilst acknowledging the range of professionals and stakeholders involved in collaborative work, Chapter 6 maintains a consistent aim to expose the implications for professional social work and the contribution of the profession to the collaborative venture. Within this, the chapter considers how practitioners learn and work together in teams and networks.

CHAPTER 7

Your learning in Chapter 7 centres on the organisational context of interprofessional collaborative social work. The chapter explores how organisations are responding to the collaborative 'agenda' by highlighting different approaches to working together at agency or organisational levels. The examples of integrated care services and the place of user-led organisations are given particular attention in Chapter 7. Furthermore, building on a discussion about professional cultures in Chapter 6, Chapter 7 looks at organisational cultures and the position of leaders and managers in driving collaborative practices forward. The chapter closes by discussing how interprofessional practice might be evaluated at the organisational level and providing some evaluative research examples to support your understanding.

CHAPTER 8

In the final chapter in the book, the key themes emerging from across the first seven chapters are summarised. Indeed, Chapter 8 is structured to reflect those themes. Additionally, this final chapter aims to focus your learning on how you can further develop as a consequence of your studies of this text. It is intended that, after working through this chapter, you will be able to critically evaluate and reflect on the implications of collaboration, cooperation and integrated working on your individual practice. Thus, here you will consolidate your learning through a range of reflective practice questions, activities and practical tasks, supported by strategies, guidance and tools that will assist you in taking your learning forward beyond this text and into interprofessional social work practice. As you work through the book, the activities and further reading, you are encouraged to keep notes on areas that you can identify where you consider your skills and knowledge can be further developed with regard to interprofessional practice.

KEY THEMES

As you read and study this book, you will become aware of recurrent key themes that are threaded throughout the text of each chapter. These themes are:

- The experience and participation of service users and carers in the collaborative environment.
- The place, contribution and significance of social work as a profession in the collaborative environment.
- The skills, knowledge, research and values that will underpin your effective interprofessional practice, including ways in which you might source ongoing development and support.

As stated above, these emergent themes are drawn together to provide the structure for the final chapter of this book.

TERMINOLOGY AND DISCOURSE

The words, phrases and terms that are used to describe ways of working are socially constructed, which means they reflect the values, interests and ideals of society. Indeed, Carnwell and Carson (2009) take this further in stating that the choice of terminology is often determined by policy. Additionally, these words tend to have particular meanings or associations that result in them influencing understanding,

rather than reflecting what we might really want to convey. In that w
and phrases we choose can influence our assumptions, behaviours, v
standings and practice. Also, it is possible to form a range of different
meanings and ideas around the same word or phrase. For these reasons,
out on your studies through this text, it is imperative that from the begin   ₒ, you,
as the reader, examine the different ways in which working closely with others in
social work practice is described and labelled, and are aware of the interpretations
being applied.

This book has been given the title *Interprofessional Collaboration in Social Work Practice* and much discussion and thought went into the formulation of that title.

Activity 1.3

Think about the terms 'interprofessional' and 'collaboration':

- Write out your own definitions of these terms. You are advised not to use dictionaries or Internet searches for this, but to write your own ideas of what might or might not be included in these concepts.
- Make a list of some of the other words or terms which might be used to describe similar concepts.

In the literature and through the Web pages, you will see a range of terms used. I imagine that your list for the second part of the activity is quite lengthy and may include, for example, partnership working, collaboration, integrated working, seamless service, joint working, working across organisations, interprofessional working, interagency working, multiagency working, interdisciplinary working and possibly many others. You will find many of these terms explained further in the Glossary of terms and abbreviations at the end of this book. Arguably, the preferred term has changed over time, with 'collaborative working' being the current 'favoured' term and that which is most commonly found. You may find it helpful to remember this issue when you are making library and Internet searches, as you may need to use a range of words in order to source relevant and appropriate materials.

Whilst, of course, purely indicative, it is interesting to note, for example, that at the time of writing this book, a Google search for the 'exact phrase' 'collaboration in health and social care' achieved 66,200 hits, whilst a similar search for the 'exact phrase' 'interprofessional working in health and social care' achieved 9,060 hits. However, I have chosen the terms 'interprofessional' and 'collaboration' as I believe they reflect the processes and skills needed to ensure effective 'liaising and negotiating across differences such as organisational and professional boundaries', which is one of the Quality Assurance Agency's social work subject benchmarks (QAA 2008: 13). It is useful, though, to consider what other authors have to say and the definitions and critique that they offer.

It is suggested that the term 'partnership' indicates a formalised approach, something that emanates from policy and legislation; whilst collaboration is more active, practice-led and the process of 'partnership in action' (Whittington 2003a: 16). Carnwell and Carson (2009) add that 'partnership' is an entity, an arrangement or how something is, whereas 'collaboration' is an activity or what people do. Partnership is also seen as being able to embrace all levels across the scale or range of activity in practice:

> Partnership can be considered as the process and integration as the outcome. This also reflects the reality of a continuum of partnership working: tentative collaboration between specific individuals at one end of the spectrum, through formalised joint delivery, to combination into a single agency, full integration, at the other. Partnership working therefore becomes an umbrella term for all degrees of inter-agency working short of merger. (Petch 2008: 2)

You will learn more about the concept of partnership, particularly that which is formed with service users, in Chapter 4 of this book. The Integrated Care Network (2004) suggests a continuum from 'fragmentation' of services between and within organisations, through 'partnership' and finally 'integration', which is defined as 'the integration of organisations of services into single entities ... which allow(s) potential for greater transparency between partners and enhanced benefits for service users' (Integrated Care Network 2004: 13). You will learn more about different service configurations and integrated services in Chapter 7 of this book.

Following consideration of dictionary definitions and the use of the terms in recent health and social care policy documents, Carnwell and Carson define partnership as:

> A shared commitment, where all partners have a right and an obligation to participate and will be affected equally by the benefits and disadvantages arising from the partnership. (Carnwell and Carson 2009: 7)

Activity 1.4

Consider Carnwell and Carson's (2009) definition of partnership given above:

- How much does the approach and process described reflect your views, and if you have them, your experiences from practice?
- Write down in a few sentences what the implications of this definition are for the participation of service users in the environment of collaborative and integrated practice.

You may feel that this is as an ideal definition of partnership, rather than reflecting the reality of collaborative working in practice. The definition is interesting, if perhaps broad. Crucially, though, there are some key words in this definition from Carnwell and Carson (2009: 7), particularly the notions of rights and obligations, benefits and disadvantages. Assuming that there is common agreement that service users and carers are considered to be partners in practice, then these concepts may be helpful in enabling you to analyse service users' and carers' experiences of collaborative practice and partnership working. Importantly, 'collaboration and partnership are closely congruent with user-centred social work values' (Whittington 2003a: 32). You will return to this later in the book, with a particular focus on the experiences of service users and carers in Chapter 4.

What seems undisputed in the literature is that there is a 'lexicon of terms' (Quinney 2006: 11) and that the term chosen, the scope and meanings attributed to it need to be made explicit within the context of its usage. One way of achieving this is to consider theoretical frameworks and models that assist us in understanding and analysing the complex interrelationships in practice. This will be the focus of Chapter 3 of this book.

CONCLUSION

I hope that you enjoy your studies on interprofessional collaboration as you move through this book. This first chapter has given you a 'flavour' of the range and scope of the book, its overall structure, aims, themes and approach. In summary here, it is evident that whilst at the highest level of generality, the objectives of care and support services are likely to be agreed, there are questions and debates about definition, ideologies, philosophies, strategies and methods:

> The difficulty is that whilst it takes thirty seconds or so to say 'and there shall be co-ordination between the various forms of provision', the actual, day-to-day carrying-out of this co-ordination is a different kettle of fish ... behind an apparently rational statement is the whole range of human intractability, incompetence, power politics, greed and negativity, together with, of course, sweet reasonableness, great imagination, creativity, generosity and altruism. (Gillett 1995, cited in Hornby and Atkins 2000: 17)

2

THE CONTEXT
OF COLLABORATIVE
PRACTICE

Chapter summary

When you have worked through this chapter, you will be able to:

- Describe the historical and political context of collaborative practice.
- Analyse the legal and policy context of collaborative practice.
- Evaluate the social and economic context of collaborative practice.
- Consider the changing experience of service users and carers.

INTRODUCTION

In the first chapter of this book, you have explored the concepts and terminology associated with interprofessional collaboration in social work practice. In this second chapter, you will develop your understanding of how these concepts came to be embedded within contemporary policy and professional practice. This chapter and the following chapter, which explores ways of understanding interprofessional practice, set the foundation and context for your later studies in Part 2 of this book, where more specific areas of practice and perspectives are considered. Hence, Chapter 2 provides an overview of the background within which the contemporary developments in practice are taking place.

As noted in the previous chapter, whilst the concepts and discussion throughout this book relate to social work practice across the four countries of the United Kingdom, the legislation discussed is predominantly English. In acknowledgement of the increasing pace of devolution, the chapter includes suggestions and references that you might explore for specific contextual knowledge relevant to each country.

Reflective practice question 2.1

Before you start reading the sections of this chapter, reflect on your developing professional practice. Drawing on your increasing knowledge and any relevant experience to date, make a list of the key issues that you can think of that set the 'backdrop' or context for changes and drivers towards increasingly collaborative working practices.

COMMENT

When other students have previously responded to this question, they have been surprised at how much knowledge and understanding they already have, which is 'surfaced' by such reflection. Some students focus on developing a list of legislation or policies that they are aware of, such as Every Child Matters (DfES 2003) or the Mental Health Act 2007 or the White Paper *Our health, our care, our say* (DoH 2006). Others have included literature, research or theory covered in previous modules of learning, such as examples used from their practice learning. Some lists will include drivers related to the position of service users and carers, for example the changing status of user organisations and the importance given to meaningful participation. Many students included high-profile public inquiries, for instance the inquiry following the death of Victoria Climbié (Laming 2003) or Baby P(eter) (Laming 2009). This chapter will explore these relevant and important facets of the context of collaborative practice. These examples lay testament, not only to the strength and depth of the knowledge and understanding that you already have, but also to the complex interaction of factors that influence professional practice in contemporary society.

At this point, as you embark on studying this chapter, you may consider that the range of imperatives and contextual detail discussed under different headings and sections are presented as if they are separate factors. However, they are set out in this way only to give structure and clarity to the written text. In professional practice, these issues are interdependent, being implemented and experienced through complex interactions, which will be the focus of later chapters in the book. In particular, this chapter aims to draw attention to some of the implications of the political, legal, policy, social and economic contexts for strategy, agencies, communities and individuals.

As with many 'knotty issues' related to social work practice, the concept of working together in collaboration appears, at first, to be quite straightforward, readily understood, taken-for-granted and 'good practice'. However, the reality is that these ideas and ways of practising have not always been part of the vocabulary and have not necessarily been implemented in a way that has ensured effective best practice at all times. Yet, whilst working together has not always been 'on the agenda', it remains true that these are not totally new concepts; there is evidence of continuity amongst seemingly ubiquitous change. As you read the first section of this chapter, which explores the background and development of the current collaborative environment for social work practice, you may notice how some of those continuities are exposed.

THE HISTORICAL AND POLITICAL CONTEXT

Social work practice and the interprofessional environment in which it operates have been influenced and shaped by history and the political ideologies through which they have evolved. To examine how interprofessional collaboration has emerged and why it has been given such emphasis and importance latterly, it is necessary to understand the historical context of practice. Exploring the early establishment of the welfare state is a useful starting point. Sir William Beveridge is often attributed with being the founder of the British Welfare State, setting out his ideals in the Beveridge Report (1942). Beveridge identified five areas of social need at that time, known as the 'five giants' of idleness, want, ignorance, squalor and disease. Whilst the language of the time may feel uncomfortable, the underlying concerns or needs, which we might now refer to as unemployment, poverty, education, homelessness and health, continue to be significant political and social imperatives (Quinney 2006). Furthermore, it is interesting to note that Beveridge talked about 'co-operation' and considered that 'co-operation between public and voluntary agencies ... is one of the special features of British public life' (Beveridge 1948, cited in Powell and Glendinning 2002: 4). At this time, a Labour government passed a range of legislation that set foundational frameworks for education, social care and the health service. Political ideology, the postwar social and economic climate and 'principles of collective action, paternalism and pragmatism' can be seen to lie beneath these developments at that time (Quinney 2006: 18).

Alongside this, different disciplinary groups were developing and 'taking ownership' or control of different aspects of service provision. At this time, the National Health Service Act 1946 set in place a tripartite structure. This structure included hospital and specialist services employing their own 'almoners', who are often considered as being the first 'social workers', general practitioners' services as independent contractors, and local authority health services employing 'Medical officers of health' with responsibility for public health and community services. Thus, it can be seen that welfare provision was potentially fragmented and duplicated. By 1948, new children's departments had been established, although the later Seebohm Report (1968) recommended that the differences between children's and adult services be reduced by placing them all under amalgamated local authority social services departments. This 'unification of services in new departments, breaking down fragmentation of service' (Horner 2009: 92), 'reflected a strong move to integration' (Loxley 1997: 11), and arguably led to the 'first comprehensive approach to local authority social services' (Petch 2008: 16). You may notice, with regard to issues of continuity and change, that in more recent times, this position is being reversed.

Changes in the political environment, particularly at the national level, serve to draw attention to how political ideologies underpin the policy and legislative drivers (discussed later in the chapter) and contribute to setting the frame for collaborative practice. For many writers, it is not until the 1980s and the major political changes brought about by the Conservative government under Prime Minister Margaret Thatcher that significant imperatives and moves towards collaborative practice unfolded (Barrett et al. 2005). Concerns about a chronic lack of coordination and the failure of joint planning arrangements were made explicit through, for example, the Audit Commission (1986) report, *Making a reality of community care*. The consequence arguably being that a more policy, statutory driven and hence mandatory environment for collaboration began to emerge. Subsequently, the Griffiths Report (1988), a Green Paper, led to the White Paper, *Caring for people: Community care in the next decade and beyond* (DoH 1989),[1] and the National Health Service and Community Care Act 1990 which required health and local authorities to produce and publish jointly 'Community care plans'.

The Act also set in place quasi-markets, encouraging the growth of a plurality of providers, with the individual as consumer, within an environment where the commissioning role (purchasers) was clearly differentiated from the delivery of services (providers). Thus, whilst exhorting the need for improved coordination, the Conservative government at this time set care and support within the context of competition, with clear tensions between the two:

> Co-operation is not compatible with competition between people and agencies striving to win and survive in a pure deregulated market, because co-operation implies trust and a willingness to share information and resources. (Loxley 1997: 11)

The Conservatives' rational goal or consumerist model emphasised the need for control, planning, goal-setting, customer-driven services, productivity, effectiveness and efficiency. It was deemed to offer a greater degree of flexibility and responsiveness, with all agencies and professionals focusing on the needs and choices of those who use services, including providing users with more information about the services and options available to them. Yet, the tension between collaboration and competition seen in earlier approaches, alongside the lack of resources, rationing, charging for services and unclear assessment procedures, resulted in a myriad of challenges for the management of quasi-markets (Johnson 1999).

---

[1]A separate White Paper was published for Northern Ireland, *People first: Community care in Northern Ireland for the 1990s* (DHSS 1990).

Whittington (2003a: 32) suggests that collaboration and partnership 'became instruments of policy under the Conservatives, especially in community care in the early 1990s, later taking a central place in the New Labour government's "modernisation" of public services'. With the aim of 'bringing down the "Berlin Wall" between health and social care (Glasby 2003), the concepts of collaboration, interprofessional and integrated working at all levels became a recurrent and emphasised theme in the policies of the New Labour government elected in 1997 (Powell and Glendinning 2002). In parallel with these developments, public sector organisations have seen the increasing influence of private sector management approaches which are highly hierarchical, efficiency and accountability driven – known as 'new public management'. The political approach adopted by the New Labour government has been labelled as the 'third way', being characterised by a commitment to the principles of greater social justice and public participation, alongside continuing confidence in the merits of the free market, entrepreneurship, enterprise and wealth creation, with the state having a key role in social change. 'Third way' politics set out to modernise service provision; in part this was to happen through effective joint working, which has been viewed as a change in political direction from the Conservative focus on internal markets and competition, with 'whole systems' developing through partnerships (Loxley 1997; Whittington 2003a). Yet, the perception that partnership working will provide a panacea for practice, responsively meeting individuals' needs across society, should be critiqued, questioned and analysed (Lymbery and Millward 2009: 169).

Activity 2.1

- From your learning so far in this chapter and utilising additional sources, such as those listed at the end of the chapter, consider the political context of collaborative social work practice as driven by the principles and values of the 'third way'.
- Identify and note any potential tensions or contradictions with regard to interprofessional collaboration that arise from your understanding of this approach. Ensure that you record the references to the sources of your ideas.

COMMENT

Effectively, Activity 2.1 requires you to begin a critique of the political context of collaborative practice as set out by New Labour's 'third way', albeit a rather one-sided critique in that you are asked to focus on tensions and contradictions. You were asked to keep a note of the references to your source materials as it is only by doing so that your critique will be academically robust.

Clarke and Glendinning (2002: 41), writing in the third chapter of the edited book detailed in the Further Reading section at the end of this chapter, state that 'partnerships are located on a somewhat unsteady footing within New Labour's "Third Way"'. Similarly, White and Harris (2001: 24), referring specifically to adult community care, consider that 'the Third Way's integrationist agenda' presents significant 'complexity to be faced by workers on the ground'. One of the core tensions, raised by Clarke and Glendinning (2002: 41), is the problematic relationship between 'partnership and performance'. You may have identified from your reading, the challenges of an approach that, whilst denouncing right-wing neoliberalism, has a strong 'new public management' emphasis on regulation, performance, audit and measurable indicators which commonly scrutinise single agencies, yet aim to promote cross-organisational, interprofessional 'whole systems' models of joint working:

> Partnerships have to deal with the traditional tensions of working across organisational, budgetary, contractual and professional boundaries, and must overcome some of the less helpful dynamics that are also intrinsic to the 'modernisation' of pubic services. (Clarke and Glendinning 2002: 41)

You may also have noted that the 'third way' political ideology values the free market. Thus, whilst arguably there is a move away from competition and internal markets, the emphasis on market models has not 'gone away' and the uneasy tensions and contradictions between notions of collaboration and competition discussed earlier in the chapter remain evident. For example, within adult community care, particularly care management services, the 'purchaser–provider split', quasi-markets, eligibility criteria, budgetary constraints and procedural requirements negate the 'progressive potential of partnership' (White and Harris 2001: 28).

It is clear from this overview that politics is characterised by change and continuity, and in 2010, the political landscape of the UK changed with the election of a coalition government with Conservative and Liberal Democrat politicians cooperating to develop policy and legislation and run the country. At the time of writing this text, it was too early in the coalition's formation to predict the likely impact of its policies for interprofessional practice. Suffice it to say that there is already evidence of changing structures, the abolition of some quangos, notions of reduced bureaucracy and, above all, substantial financial reductions that will have an effect on all aspects of professional practice.

Given that political developments can be seen to inform significantly the context for collaborative social work, it is important to be mindful that the four countries that make up the United Kingdom are developing increasingly divergent approaches, policies and priorities in respect of health and social care. Within this, there may also be very specific geographical or cultural influences, for example 'political developments involving the Republic of Ireland, Northern Ireland and Great Britain have given a major impetus to co-operation across the Irish border, in aspects of social and economic well-being' (Heenan and Birrell 2005: 63). Further, political change, organisational restructuring and reform are not only a feature of UK welfare services. Research into European integrated care policies provides evidence that 'fragmentation is persistent in European health and social care systems' (Mur-Veeman et al. 2008: 172), with reform being high on the political agendas of many European countries (Thompson and Mathias 1997). It is suggested that the background to these changes lay in emerging demands for improved choice and quality of service provision, and enhanced job opportunities and reward (Thompson and Mathias 1997: 203). Furthermore, at arguably the most macro, structural level, internationally, the World Health Organization (WHO) has, within broader concerns about the global workforce for health, set out a policy for 'working together within and across countries' which argues that:

> By working together through inclusive stakeholder alliances – global as well as national – problems that cross sectors, interest groups and national boundaries can be tackled: limited expertise can be pooled, and opportunities for mutual learning, sharing and problem-solving can be seized. (WHO 2006: 147)

Adding to this in a later publication, the WHO argue that, 'Interprofessional education and collaborative practice can positively contribute to some of the world's most urgent health challenges' (WHO 2010: 14).

This section of the chapter has shown that in the current political context the 'drive for partnership working has become a familiar feature of much recent policy', although the implementation of these policies and whether they have resulted in desirable change for service users is perhaps still to be questioned (Petch 2008: 32). It is to these policy matters that this chapter now turns.

THE LEGAL AND POLICY CONTEXT

Making the links to your learning about the historical and political context of collaborative practice, this section will consider 'recent history' with regard to legal and policy developments that have shaped contemporary collaborative practice across children's services and services for all adults and mental health services. As set out in Chapter 1, whilst the chapter will make necessary and appropriate reference to these specific areas of practice, it also acknowledges that policy imperatives towards interprofessional collaboration can be actively seen in operation across all areas and aspects of social work practice. If you have a particular area of practice interest, however, you will find it very useful and developmental to consider whether and how policy and legislative initiatives in other areas of practice are of relevance, or are sometimes paralleled in your setting. For example, Glasby and Littlechild (2004), in their third chapter, set out the legal context of changes to the professional 'landscape' for services working with older people, yet much of the content relates to adult services more broadly, with some aspects relevant to health and social care services 'across the board'.

One example to consider is the process of assessment. For older people, there has been much work on the development of a Single Assessment Process (known as SAP) (DoH 2004). More recently, following a commitment outlined in the White Paper *Our health, our care, our say* (DoH 2006), there have been consultations and piloting of a Common Assessment Framework (CAF) across all adults, which aims to improve information sharing across organisations for multidisciplinary assessment, care and support planning. There are clear parallels with developments in assessment processes for professionals working with children, their families and carers, notably the Common Assessment Framework (DfES 2006). These examples are considered in more detail in Chapter 5. Therefore, as you study this section of the chapter, you are encouraged to reflect and make notes on where there are similarities and differences in the legal and policy contexts of collaborative practice across different practice settings.

Dowling et al. (2004: 309) state that partnership working has 'become a central feature of British social welfare reform since 1997'. They consider that:

> It is difficult to find a contemporary policy document or set of good practice guidelines that does not have collaboration as the central strategy for the delivery of welfare. The message is clear: the pressure to collaborate and join together in partnership is overwhelming. Partnership is no longer simply an option; it is a requirement. (Dowling et al. 2004: 309)

It is not my intention here, nor do I believe it would be helpful, to list all the policies and laws that mention collaboration; if I did, you would probably stop reading at this point! Instead, my aim is to draw your attention to some of the more significant policy and legislative drivers that influence the way in which social work is currently practised in the interprofessional arena and to alert you to ways in which you can further explore specific areas.

New Labour's overarching 'Modernisation Agenda' was first set out in the White Papers, *The new NHS: Modern, dependable* (DoH 1997a) and *Modernising social services* (DoH 1998). Within these documents, the government set out a new duty of partnership requiring local services to work together. The government aimed at:

> fostering a new spirit of flexible partnership working which move[d] away from sterile conflicts over boundaries to an approach where this wasted time and effort is directed positively towards working across them. (DoH 1998: paragraph 6.3)

During the same period, the government set out a range of initiatives to foster new local ways of working, such as Health Action Zones, New Deal for Communities, Sure Start and Education Action Zones. Also, at a broad strategic, community level, Local Strategic Partnerships were proposed under the Local Government Act 2000, bringing together key partners such as local government, private, business, community and voluntary sectors to address, not only social care, health and education, but also wider priorities.

More specifically, at this time, the Health Act 1999 (later strengthened in the NHS Act 2006) opened new possibilities for agencies to cooperate and potentially overcome some of the financial barriers. These are discussed later in the chapter within the section that explores the economic context of collaborative practice. Following the Health Act, the NHS Plan (DoH 2000a) and the Health and Social Care Act 2001 furthered the requirement for partnership, making it possible for the use of financial flexibilities to be enforced and introducing the authorisation for the establishment of care trusts. These statutes set out to enable change, at one and the same time, through mandatory requirements and incentive-driven approaches, which, it is argued, reflect 'neither outright central compulsion, nor an overwhelming vote of confidence in local discretion' (Glasby 2003: 974).

To drive forward greater integration between the health, social care, housing and other key agencies, a requirement for Joint Investment Plans was set out (DoH 1999*a*). Addressing a range of priorities, these plans demonstrate how, at the level of agencies and communities, collaboration has resulted in assessment of specific areas of local need and joint planning to meet shortfalls in services through a partnership approach to identifying the investment and reinvestment needed. More recent examples of a similar multiagency forum approach are Local Safeguarding Boards. For children, board membership is set out in the Children Act 2004. Both children's and adult board memberships include a range of key local agencies which are charged with wide-ranging duties: from commissioning to providing safe services, from developing and reviewing policies to protecting individuals, but overall having to work effectively together to safeguard children and adults in their locality.

Alongside these examples of legislation, policy and agency level practices that have been shaping the broader context of social work practice, further imperatives have been influencing specific practice areas. The chapter now moves on to outline briefly some examples of policy drivers related to practice with children and their families, work with adults and older people, and finally some of the other specific practice settings within these broader age-defined areas.

The Children Act 1989 set the statutory ground for interagency collaboration across work with children and their families. This was followed by policy guidance on 'working together', which has been continually updated. The most recent iteration of this guidance was published in 2010 (DCSF 2010) to reflect the Children Act 1989, the Children Act 2004, Lord Laming's Progress Report (2009) and the government's response to that report (DCSF 2009*b*). During the 1990s and into the first part of the new century, a raft of initiatives that aimed to promote the development of interprofessional and multiagency services to provide preventative 'low-level' support to children and families across health, social care and education, were published (see, for example, Children's Fund (2000) as outlined by Ofsted (2003); and Sure Start as proposed by DfEE (1998)). These policies set out to engage with a range of 'cross-cutting' issues such as poverty, social exclusion, educational attainment and community safety (you may recall from the previous section of the chapter that similar issues were set out in the Beveridge Report (1942) as being the main areas of social need when the welfare state was first established); it being acknowledged here that to address them, more than one agency or discipline was needed.

Taking what might be argued as being a similar 'cross-cutting' approach, the Children Act 2004 relates to all services which children may access, including more specialist services for children with additional needs. According to the Department for Children, Schools and Families website:

> The overall aim (of the Children Act 2004) is to encourage integrated planning, commissioning and delivery of services as well as improve multi-disciplinary working, remove duplication, increase accountability ... .
> (http://www.dcsf.gov.uk/childrenactreport/)

The Act provides the legal underpinning for 'Every Child Matters' (DfES 2003), which was a response to the Laming Inquiry (2003) into the death of Victoria Climbié, discussed later in this chapter. The Every Child Matters website is a useful source of up-to-date information, including White Papers, strategy and policy documents, case studies and research outcomes (DfES 2003). The wealth of information available on these Web pages is testament to the complexity of the policy context of interprofessional practice with children and their carers. One example of many that you may find useful to read through is the booklet *Making it happen: Working together for children, young people and families* (DCSF 2008*b*), which explores information sharing and multiagency working and suggests that 'we need to continue to break down traditional barriers, and the bureaucracy that goes with them' (DCSF 2008*b*: 9).

The policy context of interprofessional collaborative practice in social work continues to develop and change as, following another highly publicised child death, that of Baby P(eter) (discussed later in the chapter), Lord Laming was asked by the secretary of state to report on progress on safeguarding since his 2003 report. This report (Laming 2009) led to the publication of a response in the form of an action plan to deliver 'a step change in the arrangements to protect children from harm' (DCSF 2009*b*: 1). You are encouraged to read the full document, but may wish to focus particularly on paragraphs 57–91 (pp. 18–27), which address many issues related to collaborative practice on 'the frontline', for example the reform of social work and the Integrated Children's System.

The legal and policy context of interprofessional social work practice with adults, older people and their carers can be seen to reflect many of the same aspirations as those articulated in the imperatives outlined above. The NHS Plan (DoH 2000*a*) included the concept of care trusts as new single health and social care organisations to 'prevent patients – particularly old people – falling in the cracks between the two services or being left in hospital when they could be safely in their own home' (DoH 2000*a*: 5). After extensive national 'listening events' and consultation, this was followed by the White Paper *Our health, our care, our say: A new direction for community services* (DoH 2006), which set out a plan for further modernisation across health and social care. One of the key themes in the White Paper is integration and joint working. Whilst many of the proposed changes are outlined at strategy and management levels, they cannot be implemented without significant developments in practice at both team and individual levels (which are discussed in Part 2 of this book). The White Paper is supported by a plethora of additional documents and reports that further emphasise partnership working in enabling improved outcomes in health and well-being, with greater choice, control and participation for service users. In 2008, taking the concept of 'integration' further, the Department of Health launched a two-year pilot programme to evaluate a range of models of integrated care. An introductory guide giving an overview of each of the pilot projects can be downloaded at http://www.dhcarenetworks.org.uk_library/Resources/ICP/ICP-intro.pdf (DoH 2009*c*). Another Green Paper for England, *Shaping the future of care together* (HMG 2009), reviews care provision and funding and continues the emphasis on effective 'joined-up working'.

In addition to the arguably generic laws and policies that tend to relate either to children or to adults, regardless of specific needs, there has recently been a recognition of the need to collaborate across service areas. Following a review of 'families at risk', the Social Exclusion Task Force (2008: 7) states that: 'in a system that "thinks family", both adults' and children's services join up around the needs of the family … '. The Think Family initiative states that services would:

- 'Have no "wrong door"
- Look at the whole family
- Build on family strengths
- Provide support tailored to need.' (Social Exclusion Task Force 2008: 7)

Further to this, the context of collaborative social work practice within particular service areas is shaped by a further layer of legislation and policy. If you are interested in collaborative work from a mental health services perspective, you could, for example, explore the Mental Health National Service Framework (DoH 1999b), discussed below, the Mental Health Act 2007 and the Care Programme Approach (DoH 2008) as a starting point.

On the other hand, social work with people who have learning difficulties has been significantly transformed by a White Paper *Valuing people: A new strategy for learning disability for the 21st century* (DoH 2001a). This is particularly evident through the development of partnership boards, set out in Chapter 9 of the White Paper. These locality-based interagency boards are responsible for overseeing joint planning and commissioning of integrated and inclusive services. To support this partnership work, the Department of Health published *Keys to partnership* (DoH 2002a), and, more recently, *Valuing people now: A new three-year strategy for people with learning disabilities* (DoH 2009d), which offers specific practical guidance and support on building partnerships within learning disability services.

Interprofessional collaboration, including some specific partnership initiatives, has been given further impetus through National Service Frameworks (NSF), which set standards, principles and objectives to improve health and social care services nationally. Each NSF addresses a particular service area. Examples of frameworks which are of specific interest to social work practice are the NSF for Older People (DoH 2001b), the NSF for Mental Health (DoH 1999b), and the NSF for Children, Young People and Maternity Services (DfES/DoH 2004). If you are interested in collaborative practice in one of these areas of social work, then you should familiarise yourself with the relevant framework. Each of these frameworks includes requirements for improved collaboration. Some references and examples are shown in Figure 2.1.

As stated earlier, this section of the chapter aimed to highlight some of the key policy and legislative influences on collaborative social work practice. It would not have been possible or useful for me to provide a comprehensive policy list here, particularly as so many policies and laws are specific to particular areas of practice, however you will find it helpful to spend some time investigating the policy and legal context of your own area of practice interest and/or experience.

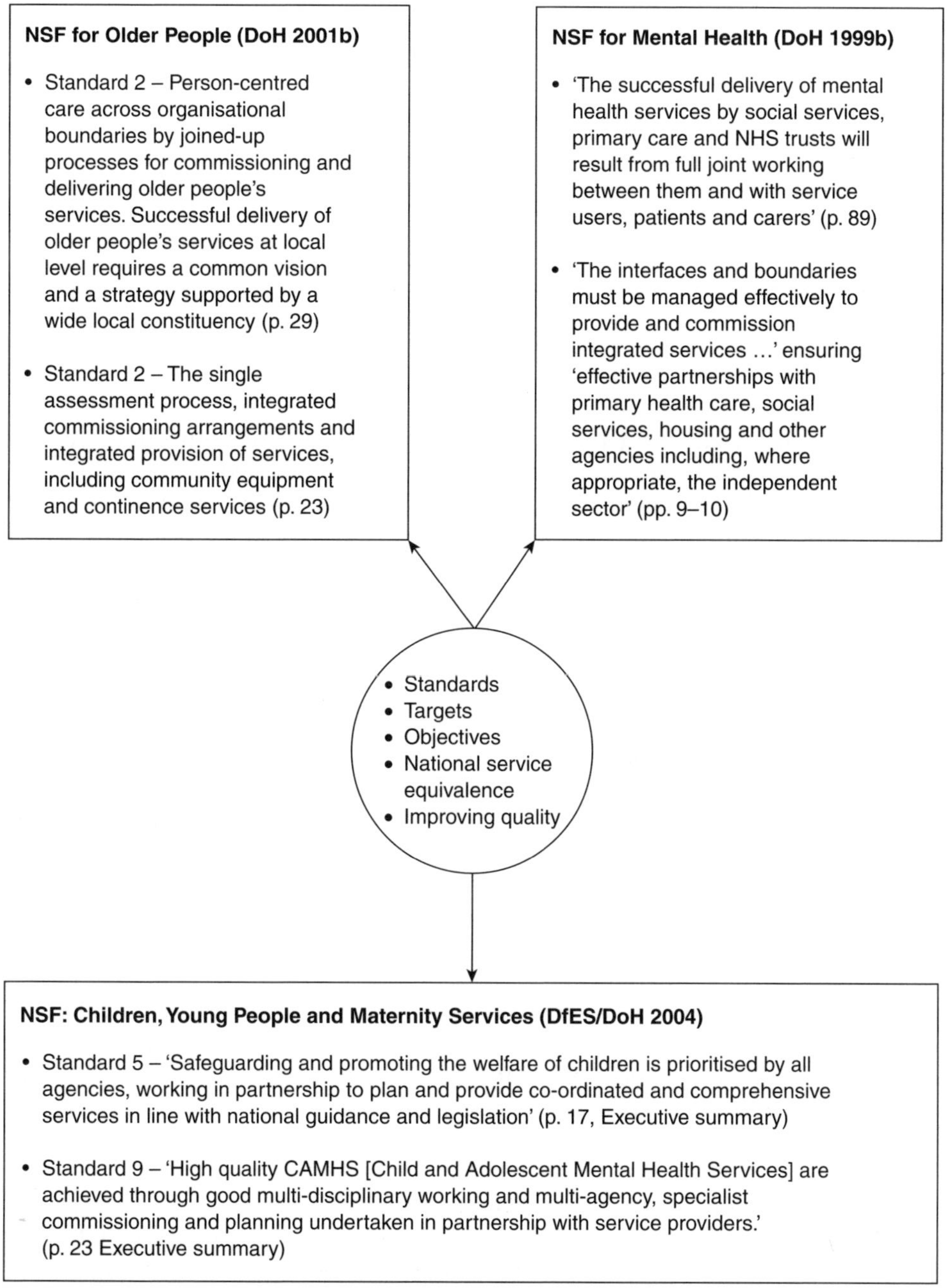

NSF for Older People (DoH 2001b)

- Standard 2 – Person-centred care across organisational boundaries by joined-up processes for commissioning and delivering older people's services. Successful delivery of older people's services at local level requires a common vision and a strategy supported by a wide local constituency (p. 29)

- Standard 2 – The single assessment process, integrated commissioning arrangements and integrated provision of services, including community equipment and continence services (p. 23)

NSF for Mental Health (DoH 1999b)

- 'The successful delivery of mental health services by social services, primary care and NHS trusts will result from full joint working between them and with service users, patients and carers' (p. 89)

- 'The interfaces and boundaries must be managed effectively to provide and commission integrated services …' ensuring 'effective partnerships with primary health care, social services, housing and other agencies including, where appropriate, the independent sector' (pp. 9–10)

- Standards
- Targets
- Objectives
- National service equivalence
- Improving quality

NSF: Children, Young People and Maternity Services (DfES/DoH 2004)

- Standard 5 – 'Safeguarding and promoting the welfare of children is prioritised by all agencies, working in partnership to plan and provide co-ordinated and comprehensive services in line with national guidance and legislation' (p. 17, Executive summary)

- Standard 9 – 'High quality CAMHS [Child and Adolescent Mental Health Services] are achieved through good multi-disciplinary working and multi-agency, specialist commissioning and planning undertaken in partnership with service providers.' (p. 23 Executive summary)

Figure 2.1 Interprofessional collaboration: Examples from National Service Frameworks (NSFs)

Activity 2.2

Using the material you have studied so far in this chapter and the texts referred to, if they are available to you, alongside any other relevant materials you may have, attempt to represent diagrammatically (perhaps a timeline) or using a table, the development of policy and legal drivers to interprofessional collaboration in your area of practice interest, over the past twenty-five years. Keep your notes, diagram or table as you will return to this later in the chapter.

COMMENT

This is a useful exercise from a range of perspectives. It will take some time, but will develop your understanding of how these drivers and the context of current practice have emerged. It is also a good way of practising using the literature in an integrated manner, drawing out the key elements that you need from a range of sources, which is exactly the skill you need as you write academic essays and papers. A similar exercise has been undertaken by the Social Care Institute for Excellence and the result is accessible through their 'resources and publications' area of their website (full details of this are given at the end of this chapter). The result of working through this activity yourself, though, will be that you have a diagram relevant to your practice that will act as a resource, a revision tool and a quick reminder for you in the future. Many people, myself included, find pictorial, diagrammatic representations very helpful to reinforce their learning. However, it is important to remember that what you have produced here is, as stated, a quick reminder tool, a diagram – it cannot be a substitute for critical, analytical discussion, text and debate; it is more like a list.

Your list is likely to demonstrate that over recent years, there has been 'increasing support' politically 'for the premise that collaborative practice will improve the quality of service delivery' (Barrett et al. 2005: 11). Whilst Glasby and Littlechild (2004) do consider developments before the 1980s, they give more of their text over to the last twenty-five years. Similarly, Whittington (2003a) considers the national policy context largely from the late 1980s. Of specific note, though, is the later emphasis over approximately fifteen years and first seen in the 1990s, by a Labour government on the importance of interprofessional working within a modernisation agenda.

Whilst this complex range of policy initiatives universally steers practice towards interprofessional collaborative approaches, the underlying policy goals in respect of coordinated services are arguably less clear. It is suggested that policies are informed by the following aspirations: 'achievement of greater efficiency in the use of resources'; 'clarification of roles and responsibilities'; 'improved standards of service delivery'; and 'the delivery of comprehensive, holistic services' (Biggs 1997: 192). In order to achieve such aspirations and overcome the perceived barriers to partnerships working, a range of approaches and strategies, or 'carrots' and 'sticks', can be identified. Petch (2008) identifies three key drivers that underpin these strategies and, by implication, the legislation and policy through which they are commonly implemented. These drivers are detailed in Figure 2.2.

Types of strategies	How collaboration will be achieved
Cooperative strategies	Through mutual agreements
Incentive strategies	Through some form of inducement, often financial, for example greater resource allocation
Authoritative strategies	Through mandates, instructions, commands and use of authority

Figure 2.2 Types of strategy

Source: Petch 2008: 7

By kind permission of Dunedin Academic Press, Edinburgh

Activity 2.3

As a way of summarising and revising your learning from this chapter so far, consider the typology outlined above and find examples of policy and/or legislation within which you can identify evidence of each of these strategies. You are encouraged to look beyond the examples given here, using, for example, the resources outlined at the end of this chapter. Aim to be specific about why you feel that driver ('carrot' or 'stick') is evident and then reflect upon how those drivers might influence interprofessional collaborative practice. A proforma table is given below, although you may need to rewrite the table onto a larger piece of paper!

Types of strategies	How collaboration will be achieved	Examples of policy and legislation that show evidence of incorporating this strategy	How might the underpinning strategy influence interprofessional collaborative practice?
Cooperative strategies	Through mutual agreements		
Incentive strategies	Through some form of inducement, often financial, for example greater resource allocation		
Authoritative strategies	Through mandates, instructions, commands and use of authority		

COMMENT

You may find that it is useful to return to this activity later in your studies through this book in order to be able to fill in more of the blank areas on the table and give some more depth to your reflections on how those drivers might influence interprofessional collaborative practice. Indeed, it may be useful to keep the table accessible, so that as you study, you can add to the table and build it into a useful reference and revision source. This is also an interesting activity to work on with other students or in a practice team, as there are no right or wrong answers, but attempting to categorise policies and legislation and reflecting on how they may influence practice can stimulate some very interesting debate.

Here are some possible examples that will help you to get started but, as stated above, these ideas are all up for debate, critique and challenge. It is in reality very difficult to separate different strategies in this way. However, an example of a 'cooperative strategy' might be the Framework for the Assessment of Children in Need (DoH 2000*b*), for whilst this builds upon a statutory requirement in the Children Act 1989, it sets in place a process that requires cooperation and mutual agreements between agencies, professionals, children, their parents and carers. You may also have considered different 'codes of practice', or 'practice guidelines' or even maybe the National Service Frameworks under this category. Incentive strategies, both those that offer inducement and those that do the reverse by putting in place penalties, are discussed towards the end of the next section of the chapter. Examples of incentive strategies might include the Community Care (Delayed Discharges) Act 2003, which 'introduced a system of reimbursement by social services to the NHS where a delayed discharge is caused solely by the failure of the social services authority to provide timely assessment and/or social care services' (Henwood 2004: 4). Depending on your perspective, of course, this approach might be considered as a penalising strategy rather than an incentivising one. Finally, turning to Authoritative strategies, I would suggest that there are many, usually given the status of statute. Braye and Preston-Shoot (2010) offer a useful discussion of the law in relation to 'partnership between professionals' in the seventh chapter of their book. Here, they helpfully clarify where working together in particular ways is a 'duty' or a 'power'/'permission'.

Despite the almost overwhelming number and powerful impact of national policies and legislation, they are not the only influences on the context of collaborative social work practice. There are also complex social and economic factors at play. In the following section, you will further your understanding of how these factors are also significant determinants of the context of interprofessional collaboration in social work practice.

THE SOCIAL AND ECONOMIC CONTEXT

As you study this final section of the chapter, which explores the social and economic drivers for change, it is important to be mindful of the reality of interprofessional practice being driven and developed through a continuous interaction between a multifaceted array of factors, none of which occur in isolation. Social and economic pressures can be seen to be energising the agenda for change and influencing the context of interprofessional practice. Such imperatives are also embedded in policy, legislation and politically driven agendas. Indeed, the political ideology espoused by New Labour recognised the interrelated nature of social and economic issues (Anning et al. 2010). These factors and the dynamic relationships between them compound to make the study of interprofessional collaboration in social work rich and interesting.

Society has arguably developed greater expectations of its welfare services, with those receiving care services having more control, being perceived as 'consumers' and 'customers' and very often being required through different means to pay for the services that they receive (Loxley 1997). As a result, there are changing demands, tensions and expectations on professionals, their organisations and services. Furthermore, there are demographic changes taking place across adults and children, a significant example being the increasing number of older people in the population acknowledged as those most likely to have the greatest levels of need for welfare services (Loxley 1997).

> Demography means an increasing number of people are living longer, but with more complex conditions such as dementia and chronic illnesses. By 2022, 20% of the English population will be over 65. By 2027, the number of over 85 year-olds will have increased by 60%. People want, and have a right to expect, services with dignity and respect at their heart. (DoH 2007: 1)

Alongside this, public inquiries into deaths and abuse where services have failed to protect vulnerable people have fuelled concerns about the effectiveness of joint-working practices across the 'helping professions'. Similarly, Serious Case Reviews (also known as 'Part 8 reviews'), undertaken when abuse and neglect are known or suspected to be factors when a child dies or is seriously harmed (DCSF 2010), have highlighted lessons to learn about the ways in which professionals and agencies work together to safeguard such individuals. Whilst such reviews are less well-established in services for vulnerable adults, they are deemed to be good practice. These reviews set out to establish how joint working practices can be improved and are intended to have their main impact at the local level (Reder and Duncan 2004: 98).

There have been inquiries and Serious Case Reviews across the full spectrum of welfare services, including children living at home, mental health services in the community, homecare support and residential care provision (for older people, people with learning difficulties and people who are disabled). Speaking particularly about 'interprofessional communication in child protection', Corby states that:

> Since the first of the modern-day inquiries into child abuse deaths, that of Maria Colwell (DHSS 1974), to that of Victoria Climbié (Laming 2003), one of the key problems associated with safeguarding children has been seen to be inadequate communication and co-operation between the various professionals involved. (Corby et al. 2009: 65)

Similarly, in a study that examined all available reports into the deaths of children from non-accidental violence or neglect published in Britain between 1973 and 1989, a total of thirty-five reports (Reder et al. 1993) found that 40 per cent reported an error in communication that had serious repercussions on the case because it was not detected:

> If one feature of the thirty-five inquiries stands out above all others, it is … that inter-agency communication was flawed. Report after report highlights how crucially relevant information was not passed on to new workers or agencies and that information was not shared amongst concurrently involved professionals. (Reder et al. 1993: 60)

More recently, the deaths of eight-year-old Victoria Climbié in 2000, seventeen-month-old Baby P(eter) in 2007 and seven-year-old Kyra Ishaq in 2008 became highly publicised, with the subsequent reviews and inquiries being significantly influential in the landscape of collaborative practice. The Laming Inquiry (2003) into the death of Victoria Climbié, the later 'progress report' (Laming 2009), and the Serious Case Review into the death of Kyra Ishaq (Radford 2010), all drew attention to concerns about interprofessional collaborative practice.

The first of these, the Laming Inquiry (2003), was a particularly 'public' inquiry, having a website with oral evidence being available verbatim which was updated on a daily basis – 'the inquiry was therefore a global event' (Parton 2004: 83). The inquiry (Laming 2003) exposed a complete breakdown in the multiagency child protection system, with social services, health, police and other organisations failing to work together effectively to protect Victoria:

> In his opening statement to the Inquiry, Neil Garnham QC listed no fewer than 12 key occasions when the relevant services had the opportunity to successfully intervene in the life of Victoria. As evidence to the Inquiry unfolded, several other opportunities emerged. (Laming 2003: 3, paragraph 1.18)

And,

> The support and protection of children cannot be achieved by a single agency … Every service has to play its part. All staff must have placed upon them the clear expectation that their primary responsibility is to the child and his or her family. (Laming 2003: 361, paragraphs 17.92 and 17.93)

Baby P(eter) died in 2007. His mother, her partner and his brother were all convicted of causing or allowing the death of a child. Peter was subject to a child protection plan, and he and his family had extensive contact with different agencies. This contact is detailed across six phases of activity in the Serious Case Review, which summarises agency and interagency involvement with this family (Haringey Safeguarding Children Board 2009). The summary of the Serious Case Review addresses a need to 'improve inter-agency communication', the following extract giving a stark example of how failings in communication can result in such tragedies:

Nothing illustrates the agencies' failure to communicate effectively more than Ms A's attendance at the Mellow Parenting programme. This health-led programme offered an intensive day long experience of social learning and support to parents with relationship difficulties with their children. The social workers who commissioned the programme saw Mellow Parenting as an important current arrangement in protecting Peter and the other child on the register, and also for the longer term in helping Ms A to be a more thoughtful parent. The social workers and the programme providers had different expectations of each because they were not clarified, and Peter was left for long periods on the programme days with somebody unknown. There was no arrangement to inform the social worker if Ms A did not attend, and crucially no alert if, when she did attend, Peter did not accompany her. Ms A attended 9 of the 13 sessions with the other child but Peter only accompanied them on 4 of those sessions. Nobody knew who was looking after him on those days when he did not attend. (Haringey Safeguarding Children Board 2009: 19, paragraph 4.2.1)

As discussed earlier in the chapter, following political and public concern at the death of Baby P(eter), Lord Laming was asked to produce a progress report about the current state of safeguarding nationally. In this report, Laming stated that:

It is evident that the challenges of working across organisational boundaries continue to pose barriers in practice and that co-operative efforts are often the first to suffer when services and individuals are under pressure. Examples of poor practice ... include child protection conferences where not all the services involved in a child's life are present or able to give a view; or where one professional disagrees with a decision and their view is not explored in more detail; and repeated examples of professionals not receiving feedback on referrals. (Laming 2009: paragraph 4.3)

The Serious Case Review into the death of Kyra Ishaq (Radford 2010) also highlights concerns about failures in interprofessional working. In particular, ignorance and assumptions made about the roles and constraints of other professionals, and opportunities for knowledge and information-sharing being delayed or not recognized. The synopsis of the review concludes that: had there been better assessments and effective inter-agency communication over a period of time it [Kyra's death] could have been prevented. (Radford 2010: 13)

An example from the vulnerable adults' sphere of practice is a Serious Case Review carried out by a Safeguarding Adults Board following an incident where a mother took her own life and that of her eighteen-year-old daughter who had learning difficulties. Their deaths were linked to persistent anti-social behaviour and bullying. The review noted significant deficiencies in partnership working, insufficient sharing of information and a need for a 'more rounded assessment of the complex range of pressures on this family' (Leicester, Leicestershire and Rutland Safeguarding Adults Board 2008: paragraph 3.13). Another example is the Serious Case Review into the death of Steven Hoskin, a man with learning difficulties who was brutally murdered (Flynn 2007). This review concluded that 'with better inter-agency working, Steven Hoskin would have been spared the destructive impacts of unrestrained physical, financial and emotional abuse in his own home' (Flynn 2007: 20–1).

Similarly, in mental health services, inquiries have received media attention and stimulated public debate, influencing national and local policies (Stanley and Manthorpe 2001). In their examination of the findings of a series of mental health inquiry reports published during the 1990s, Stanley and Manthorpe (2001) identified communication at individual and agency levels as being an area of weakness in all the reports. One example cited is the inquiry that followed the death of Jonathan Zito, murdered by Christopher Clunis in 1992 (Ritchie et al. 1994). Clunis was acknowledged to have lived a transient lifestyle, frequently moving across boroughs in London and visiting the West Indies. The inquiry noted concerns about information sharing, not only across professional and agency boundaries, but also across these geographical borders (Ritchie et al. 1994).

'The media clearly play a key role in magnifying the profile of some inquiries' (Stanley and Manthorpe 2004: 6) and yet the media are engaged in a two-way interaction, for whilst the media are highly influential, their content and approach is shaped by the current social climate and input from a range of external commentators. Thus, inquiries and the media have a dynamic relationship, with inquiries becoming one of the more dominant vehicles through which services are scrutinised (Stanley and Manthorpe 2004).

Reflective practice question 2.2

Consider your own area of practice interest and experience – then locate one major national inquiry that has influenced service and professional changes in that area of practice. Read the whole inquiry if you have time; if not, locate the summary document and read this, being sure to focus on the recommendations.

- Consider the inquiry recommendations that relate particularly to interprofessional collaborative practice and make a note of these. What exactly are they telling you?
- Reflect on how these inquiry recommendations provide knowledge for your practice. How will you apply this knowledge to your own practice?
- Were you aware of these prior to reading this book and to reading the inquiry?
- Do they suggest areas in which you need to further develop your practice?

COMMENT

It is suggested that 'inquiry reports in health and social care have been issuing in a seemingly continuous stream since the early 1990s in the UK' (Stanley and Manthorpe 2004: 1) and yet these inquiries receive very different levels of public attention and social reaction (2004: 4). Many public inquiries do not 'hit the headlines' and those that do are selectively reported; in other words, only particular aspects are drawn out and the media may report these aspects in highly subjective ways. Yet, some of these reviews can be seen to have led to widespread changes in how services are organised, the response to Laming (2003) through the Every Child Matters agenda and The Children Act 2004 being a particular example. However, there is a view that such individual inquiries are only ever partial and therefore provide an inadequate basis for large-scale reform (Masson 2006). For all of these reasons, you, and practitioners more generally, should never rely on secondary reporting of public inquiries, but should always read the important source documents and reflect upon how the findings and recommendations might influence your practice and/or your service:

> A careful reading of the original reports … identifies issues relevant to social work practice that may not have grabbed headline attention but nevertheless offer valuable learning points for practitioners, managers, students, and policy makers. (Stanley and Manthorpe 2001: 78)

Furthermore, teams of practitioners can develop their joint practices by sharing their reflections on the outcomes of inquiries, particularly where either good or concerning collaborative working practices are identified. I would recommend that you share your notes and reflections from the above activity with other students and with your colleagues in practice when you have that opportunity.

At the start of this section of the chapter, the social and economic influences on practice were acknowledged as interconnected. So far, however, the section has focused on the first of these, so the discussion now moves on to explore how economic considerations are also a significant feature influencing the context of collaborative social work practice. At the start of this discussion, it is important to note that there are fundamental differences in how services are funded and that these differences may have consequences for how the services then work together. Some services, for example in the voluntary or private sector, may be contracted for and commissioned, or purchased, by other agencies. The health service is funded through central government finance arrangements and has always been coined as 'free at the point of use'; that being said, of course, prescriptions, dentists, opticians and some other health services are charged for, even if the charge is considered to be a 'contribution' rather than reflecting the full cost. Social services, whether commissioned or provided by local authorities, are charged for through 'means-tested' mechanisms. These differences need to be considered and sensitively negotiated to ensure that they do not result in barriers to collaborative practice.

Earlier in the chapter, you explored Petch's (2008) typology of key drivers that underpin strategy, legislation and policy that sets out to remove barriers to partnership working. 'Incentive strategies' offering, for example, additional resources, were one example of a strategic approach, with parallel 'penalties' in initiatives such as the Community Care (Delayed Discharges) Act 2003. Further to this, Biggs (1997: 195) makes the link between 'financial clout' and issues of professional power, within the increasingly managerialist and quality-driven environment of health and social care, referring, for example, to 'changing external demands', 'contracting out' and 'customer requirements' (Biggs 1997: 195). As we have seen, there is an argument that collaborative working is driven by a desire to save money and reduce budgets: 'the words "efficient" and "effective" appear again and again in all the documents alongside the idea of rationalisation and of overcoming duplication which is assumed to be wasteful and therefore inefficient' (Loxley 1997: 15). However, there is also evidence that the government has invested heavily in the facilitation of integrated working practice. For example, as cited in Petch (2008: 19), a £647 million 'Partnership Grant' was made available under the 1997 Social Services Modernisation Fund to 'foster partnerships between health and social services in promoting independence'. Indeed, section 31 of the 1999 Health Act, which was replaced by section 75 of the NHS Act 2006, promotes collaborative working by removing a range of legal and financial barriers to joint working. Thus, for example, 'lead commissioning', 'integrated service provision' and 'pooled budgets' were encouraged and enabled as part of the modernisation process. These processes became known, together, as 'flexibilities'.

Activity 2.4

I have just introduced three concepts that may be new to you, or you may be aware of them from your practice experience and previous learning. Using the literature and your own previous knowledge, write a few sentences to explain the meaning of each of these terms:

- Lead commissioning.
- Integrated service provision.
- Pooled budgets.

These concepts were first introduced in 1999 and have been consolidated and updated in the 2006 legislation. How far, in your view, can such strategic, economic initiatives enable collaborative working practices?

COMMENT

Each of these concepts was introduced to improve service delivery through joint working across agencies. 'Lead commissioning' refers to a process whereby one authority (usually the health or local authority) can delegate responsibility for the commissioning (purchasing) process to the other partner, regardless of the type of service being purchased. This usually takes place within a framework of clear agreements, funding arrangements and partnership boards or meetings.

'Integrated service provision' refers to services that are delivered from one organisation and brought together from elements of others. Sometimes, in practice, this is about elements of one service being transferred into another, but it commonly results in what is recognised as a 'one-stop shop' type provision. The integrated care pilots, cited earlier in the chapter, provide different examples of how such integrated provision might be achieved in practice (DoH 2009c).

'Pooled budgets' are exactly what they sound like! This refers to where each of the partners put funds into one joint fund, or pool, which has been designated as the budget for a specific joint service. Petch (2008) cites Glendinning et al. (2004), who undertook a research evaluation in respect of the effectiveness of these flexibilities. Their findings demonstrate that despite the possibilities opened up, issues related to incompatible information technology systems, information sharing concerns and resource constraints continued to 'plague' collaborative endeavours. Hudson et al. (2002) undertook a national evaluation of these 'flexibilities' for the National Primary Care Research and Development Centre. Again, findings from this research indicate that implementation had not been straightforward, although there were a number of benefits identified. You may find it useful to access the executive summary of this research report, freely downloadable from the Internet, which includes references to a range of barriers and drivers to collaborative and integrated working practices (Hudson et al. 2002).

THE CHANGING EXPERIENCES OF SERVICE USERS AND CARERS

This final section of the chapter is only brief as the changing experiences of service users and carers within the context of the collaborative environment of practice is a theme that you will return to throughout this book, but more importantly it forms the focus of Chapter 4. However, it is relevant here, in a chapter about the context of interprofessional social work practice, to be mindful of the place of service users and carers as partners in the collaborative enterprise.

First, it is important to be mindful that the experiences, needs and perspectives of service users and their carers are often very different (Mathews and Crawford 2011). However, for both users and carers, the context of the care and support environment is again one characterised by change. Indeed, these changes, particularly the ones related to the status and role of service users and carers, are pertinent as factors that have, and continue to, push forward interprofessional collaborative working. In other words, the changing perception and prominence of users has been a fundamental influence on the current context of collaboration in social work practice. There are clear links here to the political context of practice as discussed earlier in the chapter. You may recall that 'third way' politics, as espoused by New Labour, is characterised by a commitment to public participation. 'The movement for consumer rights and empowerment of service users and carers' (Whittington 2003a: 18) alongside the 'rise of consumerism', increasingly effective participation and changes in the balance of power between service users and professionals may both impact and be impacted upon by interprofessional collaborative working (Øvretveit 1997b: 79). There is a general consensus among health and social care professionals that integrated care, with its emphasis on effective collaborative practice, can improve services for users; equally, where collaboration is ineffective, there can be 'tragic consequences' for users (Barrett et al. 2005: 13). Writing from a service-user perspective, Barton (2003) acknowledges that changes have and are taking place, but argues that progress is slow. She states that the rhetoric of collaborative working practices is 'meaningless unless accompanied by cultural change in society as a whole and the social care workforce in particular' (2003: 105). These debates and the issues they raise are explored throughout Chapter 4 of this book.

To summarise your learning from this section of the chapter, work through this final activity.

Activity 2.5

Earlier in the chapter, you were asked to attempt to represent diagrammatically the development of policy and legislative drivers relevant to your area of practice interest over the past twenty-five years. Now go back to your diagram (or table) and add in the social and economic drivers that you now know about that have emerged over that time.

COMMENT

I apologise if your diagram just became very messy! You may want to rewrite or redraw it. You should now have included, for example, some of the most influential public inquiries relevant to your area of practice, and, if you did not include them before, strategies that are underpinned by economic imperatives. In whatever way your diagram or table is developing, it would be useful to keep this as a reference to add to and to develop as you work through this book; it could serve as a very helpful reminder and a tool for reflection and revision.

CONCLUSION

This chapter, as one of three context-setting chapters in this first part of the book, has explored the background that shapes the contemporary interprofessional collaborative environment in which social work practice takes place. Through an overview of the historical, political, legal, policy, social and economic influences, the chapter has shown how a powerful case for collaborative working has developed. In summary:

- There is a political drive for effective, efficient and economic services that is evident throughout the current legislative and policy landscape.
- There is political and professional aspiration to overcome perceived fragmentation caused by recurrent reorganisations and to manage change in the wider system.
- There have been numerous public inquiries where failures of interagency and interprofessional cooperation, coordination and communication are publicly blamed for deaths or harm to individuals.
- The experience and position of service users and informal carers, supported by the values of empowerment and the movement for consumer rights, has developed and changed, and demand and expectation have risen.

Across these wider influences, there is also a clear recognition by practitioners them-selves that providing services involves working with other professionals and agencies. This is supported by an increasing range and depth of empirical research and evidence that demonstrates the gains of working together and the harmful effects of not working together. Examples of this growing knowledge base for practice are provided throughout the chapters in this book. As part of that knowledge base, in the following chapter you will have the opportunity to explore the ways in which we make sense of collaborative practice, in particular considering some examples of theoretical perspectives and research that have provided models and frameworks for the complex collaborative environment.

FURTHER READING

Glendinning, C., Powell, M. and Rummery, K. (eds) (2002) *Partnerships, New Labour and the governance of welfare* (Bristol: Policy Press).

You will find this edited collection of chapters useful as you explore the political and policy context of collaborative practice. A range of debates is explored across the chapters, including consideration of partnerships across the statutory, private and voluntary sectors. Whilst this text is not exclusively about social work practice, it draws heavily from the context of health and social services to critically examine the collaborative discourse.

Petch, A. (2008) *Health and social care: Establishing a joint future?* (Edinburgh: Dunedin Academic Press Ltd).

This small research-based book is part of a series of texts that focus on exploring the Scottish perspective and will therefore be of particular interest if you practise in Scotland. That being said, the whole of Chapter 2 explores the United Kingdom context for partnership working.

Quinney, A. (2006) *Collaborative social work practice* (Exeter: Learning Matters).

This book is part of the Learning Matters 'Transforming Social Work Practice' series. The first chapter of the book considers the question, 'What is collaborative practice in social work?' exploring, for example, 'policy milestones' and the 'modernisation agenda'.

INTERNET RESOURCES

Social Care Institute for Excellence (SCIE) – http://www.scie.org.uk

The Social Care Institute for Excellence (SCIE) was established by the government in 2001 to improve social care services for adults and children in the United Kingdom. It offers a wealth of resources and publications that are usually free and downloadable. You are encouraged to explore the whole site, but particularly the 'Resources and Publications' pages which will take you to e-learning resources about interprofessional and interagency collaboration.

3

UNDERSTANDING AND EVALUATING CONTEMPORARY COLLABORATIVE PRACTICE

Chapter summary

When you have worked through this chapter, you will be able to:

- Discuss how theory can support your understanding of organisational and professional working practices.
- Evaluate some specific theories and models that can support your understanding of interprofessional collaborative practice, in particular:

  - Systems theory.
  - Social exchange theory and social network analysis.
  - The concept of 'Communities of Practice'.
  - Activity theory.

- Explain some of the drivers and barriers to effective interprofessional collaborative practice.
- Identify some examples of research that further our understanding of the drivers and barriers to effective collaborative practice.

INTRODUCTION

In the previous chapter, you considered a range of factors that shape the context of collaborative social work practice. Having set the context, this chapter further develops your understanding by exploring how theory, frameworks and models enable you to explain, critique and evaluate collaborative and integrated working practices. It is important to emphasise at this point that the chapter focuses on ways to explain and understand interprofessional collaborative practice. Hence, the theories and models are considered from this perspective and not from the viewpoint of their relevance to social work practice with individuals. This is a noteworthy distinction that you should be mindful of as you study this chapter.

This chapter explores how systems theory, social exchange theory, social network analysis, Communities of Practice and activity theory can be drawn upon to aid your understanding of collaboration in social work practice. As well as providing an overview of these theories, the chapter highlights how research has provided models for effective practice, and frameworks that explain the barriers, drivers, tensions and contradictions for interprofessional practice. Later chapters in Part 2 of this book will draw on the theories, models and frameworks explored here for theoretical underpinning and to give you more examples of these concepts as they apply to practice. The chapter starts by reminding you about what theory is and the different ways it may assist in understanding and analysis.

UNDERSTANDING THEORY

In this first section of the chapter, you will have the opportunity to further your understanding about theory and theoretical frameworks. Essentially, for many readers, this will serve as a reminder or revision from previous learning. However, given that this chapter focuses on using theory, it seems appropriate that you should be confident about what theory is before progressing. Furthermore, as stated in the introduction, this chapter invites you to consider how theory is helpful in understanding organisational and professional working practices, rather than direct work with individual people and their carers, so essentially you are being asked to explore the use of theory at a different level.

If you have studied theory before, I hope that your earlier studies of theory for social work practice have given you confidence in critiquing and analysing theoretical approaches. However, for some students, the mere mention of theory and frameworks in the introduction makes them wary and anxious; for other students, they feel that studying theory may be boring and irrelevant. Hopefully, you have not started reading this chapter with any of those perceptions, but if you have then perhaps this early section will help to dispel those thoughts. According to Howe:

> The best way to get into a theoretical way of thinking about what you do and how you do it is to ask the question 'why?' People who are curious and want to know what's going on tend to be interested in ideas, theories and explanations. (Howe 2009: 7)

Activity 3.1

Think about your own understanding of the term 'theory' at this time. Without referring to the texts, make a list of words that might describe what theory is, then try to 'work up' a definition of theory that encompasses your ideas.

COMMENT

If you have studied theory before, I hope that this activity will have 'jogged' your memory of your earlier learning. In the broadest use of the term, we all construct and make reference to theories in our daily lives, although we are unlikely to call our beliefs and ideas, 'theory'. Theories usually start from a premise, supposition or assumption which is then investigated or researched. The premise, or hypothesis, would commonly make a causal link between two phenomena which may, for example, be incidents, behaviours or events; in other words, surmising that if a certain phenomenon occurs then it can be predicted that another phenomenon (or other phenomena) will follow or result. There are many different theories which arise from different perspectives and may lead to different explanations or ways of understanding. Loxley (1997: 72) states that: 'theory is an explanation independent of the phenomenon being studied, based on principles which are coherent, general and transferable, and of continuing applicability'.

In his seminal theory text, Howe (1987: 12) defines the purposes of theory thus: 'proposing order and pointing out relationships, theories enable their users to do four important things as they set about their particular bit of the world:

- To describe
- To explain
- To predict ... and
- To control and bring about.'

Reflective practice question 3.1

Reflect on Howe's definition of theory, then working through each bullet point above, make some notes on how you might use theories both to further your learning about interprofessional collaborative practice as you study this book, and to support your development in professional social work practice.

COMMENT

The definition given by Howe (1987) and referred to above is a generic definition of what theory is and its purpose. So, this approach applies to theory very broadly rather than more specifically in terms of how it can support our understanding and evaluation of interprofessional practice. My aim here is to help you to develop a more 'theoretical way of thinking' by demonstrating the relevance and value of theories as 'very practical things to have under your belt and in your head' (Howe 2009: 2). Thus, theory can assist understanding and analysis of interprofessional collaborative working practices by enabling you:

- **To describe** what happens when different professions, different disciplines and different organisations work together to meet the needs of communities and individuals. Theory can help you to describe the behaviours that you see and experience, and it may help you to describe and understand more clearly why interprofessional collaborative working is complex and not straightforward.
- **To explain** why there are strengths and challenges in working collaboratively. Theory can give you a way of explaining how different arrangements for working together have come about and how they are effective, or sometimes less effective, in meeting the needs of communities and individuals. Theory can help you to explain service users' and carers' experiences of interprofessional collaboration.
- **To predict** the potential benefits and challenges of working in particular ways. Theory may help you to predict some of the implications that collaborative working could have for individual practice, for the experience of service users and carers, and for further development of collaborative working arrangements.
- **To control and bring about** change, not only in your own professional working practices, but also in the collaborative practices of the teams, departments and agencies within which you work. By using theory to assist reflection on practice, you may be able to 'control and bring about change' through recognition of the skills and knowledge that you need to develop in order to practise more effectively within the collaborative working environment.

Whilst theories may achieve some or all of these things, models and frameworks are often the practical interpretation or representation of theory and, as such, provide the more descriptive, illustrative and potentially practice-orientated approach. As we move on now to explore briefly some particular examples of theories and models that help to examine collaborative practice, you should remain mindful of Howe's (1987) four verbs as you can draw on these to evaluate the effectiveness of each approach.

USING SYSTEMS THEORY TO UNDERSTAND INTERPROFESSIONAL COLLABORATIVE PRACTICE

Systems theory has made an important contribution to social work theory and it is being proposed here as one example of a theoretical approach that can help our understanding and evaluation of collaborative working practices. Before examining the main principles of systems theory, work through the following activity which will guide you to identify your own informal and formal networks and systems, their interconnections, boundaries and the purposes they might have.

Activity 3.2

- Think about the people you meet and interact with every day, in your personal life, through your studies and, if you are in work, then in your work setting too. Make a list of these contacts.
- Go back through your list and group these contacts according to the purpose or function of the interaction you have with them, for example personal support, workplace support.
- You could also try and represent this diagrammatically, showing the boundaries, interrelationships and connections between the different contacts.

COMMENT

You are likely to have listed family, friends and acquaintances, other students, work colleagues (if you are currently employed), managers, team leaders, university lecturers, senior managers in the work setting and colleagues in other jobs or agencies with whom you have contact in regard to work. Your starting point could be to refer back to the activity you undertook in Chapter 1 (Activity 1.1), although the lists are not necessarily the same. One thing is for sure – your list could be very long! However, it is usual to be able to group these into different systems or networks and to be able to 'map' these so that you can begin to visualise and understand further the boundaries, connections and interrelationships between them. This is fundamentally how systems theory helps us to explain and describe interprofessional collaboration. Loxley (1997: 36) states that systems theory contributes 'key ideas about structures and processes to a framework for understanding collaboration'. Systems theory has, however, been criticised for overly focusing on the 'whole' and for not taking account of individuals within the systems (Payne 2005). Referring to the work of Pincus and Minahan (1973, cited in Payne 2005: 145), Payne identifies three kinds of helping system:

- Informal or natural systems, such as family, friends or fellow workers;
- Formal systems, such as community groups or trade unions;
- Social systems, such as hospitals or schools.

You may be able to group your list using this typology. You should keep your notes from this activity as you will be asked to return to them in the next section of learning in the chapter, where you will consider more specifically the types of relationships that you develop with others to progress collaborative practice.

Payne (2005: 144) provides a useful summary of the main concepts or principles of systems theory, which has been underpinning aspects of social work practice since the 1970s:

- Systems are entities with boundaries within which physical and mental energy are exchanged internally more than they are across the boundary;
- Closed systems have no interchange across the boundary, as in a closed vacuum flask.

Open systems occur where energy crosses the boundary which is permeable, like a teabag in a cup of hot water which lets water in and tea out but keeps the tea leaves inside (Payne 2005: 144).

Concepts on processing in systems, the way systems work and how we may change them (Grief and Lynch 1983, cited in Payne 2005: 114) are as follows:

- Input – Energy being fed into the system across the boundary
- Throughput – How the energy is used within the system
- Output – Effects on the environment of energy passed out through the boundary of a system
- Feedback loops – Information and energy passed to the system caused by its outputs affecting the environment which tell it the results of its output
- Entropy – Systems use their own energy to keep going, which means that unless they receive inputs from outside the boundary, they run down and die.

Activity 3.3

In order to explore the use of systems theory as an approach to understanding interprofessional and interagency practice, read through the extract from Payne (2005) above again, but this time as you read, replace the word 'systems' with 'agencies'. Then read it a second time and replace the word 'systems' with 'professional disciplines':

- How relevant does Payne's summary seem to you now?
- Can you find examples from your own practice experience that are explained by systems theory as outlined in Payne's summary?

COMMENT

This activity has given you a brief introduction to the core principles of systems theory and I am aware that as you transposed the replacement words, the sentences may have lost grammatical accuracy. However, I hope that through the activity you have become more aware of how systems theory can explain what goes on within and across agencies and professional disciplines as the 'helping professions' aim to work collaboratively across boundaries. Thus, an agency or a professional discipline can be seen as a system. It is important to be aware, however, that the system of interprofessional collaborative practice may be very large and complex, going beyond and across services for particular service-user groups. For example, the *Think Family* initiative, that you read about in Chapter 2, provides the following examples of collaborative practice across various systems of service provision:

A housing officer might identify a parent's language difficulties and refer them to English for Speakers of Other Languages (ESOL) training; or a probation officer might identify signs that an ex-offender has gone back to an abusive relationship and offer the family domestic violence support services.

... an alcohol treatment service might combine treatment with parenting classes, while supervised play is provided for the children. Or a family learning programme builds the parent's literacy skills and encourages involvement in their children's learning. (Social Exclusion Task Force 2008: 7)

The ways in which these different systems work, the extent of 'closedness' or open-ness will depend on, amongst other things, its legal duties to work cooperatively with others, its attitude to collaborative working and how far it needs other agencies or disciplines to meet its objectives. More open systems are likely to be more flexible and able to adapt to change (Reder et al. 1993), although systems which are too open can potentially impede collaborative practice, as much as those that are too closed. It is evident, therefore, that the notion of 'boundaries' and the way in which organisations and professionals work within and across those boundaries are sig-nificant factors in understanding the system and the processes of working across organisations. This is reflective of the inquiry that followed the death of Jonathan Zito, murdered by Christopher Clunis in 1992 (Ritchie et al. 1994) that you read about in the previous chapter, within which it was seen that Clunis moved in and out of many systems, with concerns about working practices across boundaries high-lighted. O'Sullivan considers agency boundary issues as he explores decision-making in social work and states that:

Whether interagency and interprofessional collaboration actually happens in practice can hinge around how frontline practitioners manage boundaries between the agencies and professions ... Given the nature of the situations frontline practitioners deal with, there is a tendency for agencies, professions and individual workers to endeavour to maintain a boundary around what they regard as their territory, resulting in points of tension. (O'Sullivan 2011: 35–6)

Your understanding of systems theory may be helped by the following two examples of models that provide an interpretation of, and are underpinned by, this approach. The first is Whittington's (2003a) Model of Collaboration; the second example is an approach to service development and practice called 'A Whole Systems Approach'.

Whittington (2003a) developed a 'Model of Collaboration', which, with its sys-tems theory basis, illustrates the interrelationships between participants in inter-professional practice. Much like Howe's approach described earlier in the chapter, Whittington's model sets out to:

- 'lend order' and 'to assist ... the practice and analysis of collaboration by providing a framework' and to
- provide 'a baseline for identifying and reviewing' and to
- 'describe the parties and systems as they actively engage in collaboration'. (Whittington 2003b: 39)

The model has two stages, which are shown in Figure 3.1 below. The first stage effectively sets out or identifies the main systems or participants in collaborative practice, with the second stage developing this to include description of the interface and relationship between them. This model is not hierarchical, but represents the central-ity of service users and carers. Hence, you can see that Whittington's model does all of the things that are given as the stated purpose of theory, but very specifically it does these things to assist understanding and analysis of the interrelationships between professionals and organisations in practice.

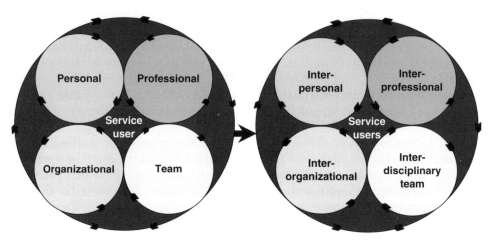

Figure 3.1   Whittington's model

Source: Whittington, 'A model of collaboration', in Weinstein et al. 2003b: 41, 46

Reproduced by permission of Jessica Kingsley Publishers

Activity 3.4

Consider Whittington's (2003b) Model of Collaboration and how this might be applied to your own experience and knowledge of collaborative and integrated working practice:

- Think of a particular example from your practice learning or a case study you have used in your course work.
- Work through Whittington's two stages, using a blank sheet to replicate the spheres in the model. First stage: fill in the spheres with the key participants. Second stage: consider the spheres of interaction and fill in the diagram with some key words explaining how you think those interactions take place.

COMMENT

This was not a straightforward activity and you may have found yourself needing several sheets of paper to map the various spheres of interaction. That in itself highlights the complexity of these issues! At the end of his chapter, Whittington (2003b: 56–7) helpfully gives us some clear summarising key points as he states that the model offers a strategy for service development which:

- Puts service users and carers at the centre.
- Through interpersonal trust establishes common visions whilst leaving sufficient flexibility in roles and structures to allow creative development.
- Develops interprofessional shared responsibility that guides and supports service users throughout.
- Stresses the importance of integrated care through interdisciplinary teams and interorganisational partnerships.

Finally, according to Whittington (2003b: 57), this is achieved by participatory collaboration 'across the shifting boundaries of professions and organisations, and in the spaces between'. This model is replicated in the whole system approach that you will read about next.

The NHS Modernisation Agency (2004: 14) offers a definition of the whole system 'as comprising of service users and their carers, the individual teams delivering care, the community of organisations providing integrated care to its population and the environmental context set by policy, regulation and social-economic factors'. Furthermore, in guidance on the Care Programme Approach (CPA) for mental health, it is stated that the 'whole system approach to care planning and delivery should aim to promote and co-ordinate care, and support activity across the individual's life domains and circumstances' (DoH 2008: 27). A memorable metaphor offered by Hudson (2006) is that of a heap of separate parts of a bicycle, being relatively ineffective as disconnected components and yet when put together to make the whole vehicle, have the potential to be an effective mode of transport. In this way, Hudson (2006: 8) stresses the importance of the relationship between the parts and the concept that: 'systems are seen as more than the sum of the parts – an outcome that has been termed the "emergent properties"'. However, as you have seen, systems theory itself does provide us with a theoretical model that allows us to 'break this down' further and consider practice that takes place within and across the subsystems of this whole system.

Before moving on to consider another theoretical approach to understanding collaboration and integration, consider this example of how a systems approach can impact upon practice.

The 'knock-on' effects of making a decision in one part of the system

Some of the staff on the hospital ward are unclear of the criteria and process for referring patients to social services. They are busy and have little time to discuss this with the social services team to clarify the issues. This results in frequent inappropriate and incomplete referrals which overburden both the ward staff and the social workers in the care management team who are required to respond to each referral. Consequentially, there are delays in seeing other users that in turn lead to delayed discharges from the hospital. Furthermore, this could impact upon elective admissions and emergency patients experiencing long delays, whilst at the same time social services lose credibility and money, and it could result in a very poor outcome for service users.

With a bit of planning, it could be like this: the hospital ward manager decides their staff will invest time getting a clear understanding of the referral criteria to social services; this frees up the social workers' time as there are far less inappropriate referrals. All of this means that people are not delayed, everyone feels a lot happier with the service they either give or receive, there are financial savings and it helps all the organisations concerned to meet their targets.

Source: NHS Modernisation Agency 2004: 15

COMMENT

This example may seem fairly simplistic, but it is useful as an example to show how systems theory can help to explain collaborative working. In this example, some of the key elements of systems theory are apparent, as explained by Loxley:

> The key elements from General Systems Theory relevant to an understanding of collaboration are those of interaction and interdependence, the emphasis on the management of processes, the recognition of equi-finiality (that is the achievement of the same goals from different possible starting points) … . (Loxley 1997: 35)

Systems theory is also often implicated in wider studies of organisations, being encompassed within the collective term of organisational theory. Organisational theory arises from a range of theoretical perspectives but is commonly linked to a sociological background. As well as attempting to explain organisations from a systems perspective, organisational theory includes theories and approaches that analyse bureaucracy, management, structures and hierarchies in organisations. Organisational theory fully acknowledges that organisations themselves do not think, act or make decisions; rather, it is the behaviours and interrelationships between the people within organisations that are of interest (Crowther and Green 2004).

As a final activity for this section, consolidate your learning by considering how a systems approach applies to your own practice experience.

Reflective practice question 3.2

Having developed your understanding of systems theory and how it can aid understanding and analysis of interprofessional collaboration in practice, reflect on your own experiences of practice, if you have them, or the systems that support your studies, and answer the following questions:

(Continued)

(Continued)

- Why do you want to work across systems? (What can it achieve?)
- What and who is included in your definition of the system in which you work?
- What and who is not included in your definition of the system in which you work?
- How, from your perspective, does the system you work or study in and the systems you work across, impact upon the experiences of service users and carers?

In the next section of this chapter, two theories are examined that help to explain aspects of collaborative practice in a way that does not conflict with systems theory: social exchange theory and network analysis.

USING SOCIAL EXCHANGE THEORY AND SOCIAL NETWORK ANALYSIS TO UNDERSTAND INTERPROFESSIONAL COLLABORATIVE PRACTICE

In this section of the chapter, the focus is on theories that help to understand the specific nature of working relationships within interprofessional practice. Social exchange theory is commonly attributed to the work of Emerson (1976), although it now has a theoretical tradition in social psychology, sociology and anthropology. There are many similarities between social exchange theory and social network analysis, with both approaches explaining social structures as made up of social relations between individuals linked into networks. The subtle differences between the two theories relate more to level and purpose than to key principles. Both theories stress the exchange aspect of interrelationships and attempt to examine the patterning of people's interactions. Network analysis, however, suggests a particular research methodology, with its focus on the wider networks of connected exchange relations and opportunities.

Although the theories emanate from a broader hypothesis about human interactions and the subjective nature of human relationships, Loxley (1997) explores social exchange theory in the context of collaboration in health and welfare. With regard to the relationships that are developed as a response to the need for collaborative working, social exchange theory and network analysis suggest that they are based upon an appraisal of the rewards, or benefits, and the 'costs'. In other words, there is a link to motivation and what it is that may drive or hinder motivation to collaborate. These approaches suggest that all relationships are put under a form of subjective scrutiny or negotiation by the parties involved, who then decide whether it is in their interests to maintain and strengthen the relationship. It is suggested, therefore, that large-scale collaborative ventures can be understood by giving attention to the individual, more local social situations and interactions.

Consequently, social exchange theory suggests that: 'there is some element of self-interest in all instances of social exchange, and the incurring of obligation or indebtedness' (Loxley 1997: 36). Social relations are established and sustained through reciprocity and mutual gratification. Thus, in the context of collaborative social work practice, professionals establish and maintain effective joint-working relationships on the basis of their expectation or subjective calculation that the interaction will be mutually advantageous. Caution is raised, though, with regard to power within professional relationships, with perceptions of professional superiority being seen as damaging to the collaborative process (Barrett and Keeping 2005). Potentially, the process of effective working together may be perceived as a threat to dominant professions and agencies that may fear losing their power or control (Loxley 1997) and because of this, they may not effectively enter the 'social exchange'. Issues of power, professional identity and culture are discussed in more depth later in this book, in Chapter 6. Furthermore, Chapter 7 considers the influences that organisational cultures may have on effective collaborative working.

Activity 3.5

Refer back to Activity 3.2 which you completed earlier on in the chapter, within which you made a list of, and grouped, your day-to-day contacts:

- Now separate out your list of contacts, identifying those who work for other agencies or other disciplines. Identify the main activities which bring you into routine contact with each of them. You may find it helpful to draw up a simple two-column table, heading the first column 'Activities' and the second column 'Contacts'. Can you see any patterns in the type of relationship or contact that you have with these colleagues?

COMMENT

Whilst it may not resemble your chart, here is an example table, with the first rows completed:

Activities	Contacts
Facilitating a service user to make contact with an advocacy group when you are unable to provide them with a needed service	Contacts in voluntary sector organisations and user-led groups
Enabling a service user to be rehoused outside your own local authority to an area near their support networks by liaising with a country-wide housing association	Contacts in a range of housing associations and with Local Authority Housing Officers

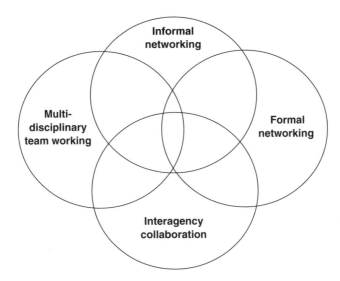

Figure 3.2   Forms of collaborative relationship

Your table will give useful examples of the potential types of relationships that social workers may develop with others, as identified by Pincus and Minahan (1973). These are:

- Collaborative – where there is a shared purpose.
- Bargaining – where an agreement needs to be reached.
- Conflictual – where purposes are in opposition.

It would be interesting to look back now at the table you developed in response to Activity 3.5. Using the typology from Pincus and Minahan (1973) above, work through your table to identify the different types of relationships you are engaged in.

These relationships occur within different forms of networking or exchange. Figure 3.2 illustrates four forms or ways that interagency and interprofessional cooperation take place as part of day-to-day practice; this is also discussed in Chapter 7 where you will explore different organisational approaches to collaboration. Each mode of interaction is discussed separately here, however the diagram demonstrates the overlapping, interconnected and concurrent nature of these activities.

- **Informal networking** – as you will have seen in completing the activities of this chapter, informal networking is something you are likely to be involved in as a routine and normal part of your daily work, with colleagues, service users and carers.
- **Formal networking** – this refers to the contacts and negotiations that take place as part of social work processes and procedures, through referral, planning, intervention and evaluation, for example.
- **Interagency collaboration** – this is where collaborative working is created at a formal organisational level when two or more agencies agree to work together to share information or to plan jointly or deliver

services. The most formalised interagency collaborations are likely to be integrated services; you will learn more about integrated services in Chapter 7 of this book.
- **Multiagency and multidisciplinary teams** – a large amount of interprofessional working is now organised through and within multidisciplinary teams. You will have the opportunity to learn more about collaborative teamworking in Chapter 6 of this book.

The terms 'collaborative', 'bargaining', 'negotiation' and the different 'forms' or ways of organising collaborative work, all give some clues to the reason, function or purpose of the interaction or relationship that is the focus of the collaborative venture. Social exchange theory and social network analysis can be seen to describe partnership working in a way that focuses on perceived purposes or benefits from the collaborative 'exchange'. Some of the terminology used in explaining these theoretical positions is similar to those used when you consider markets, market forces, economic exchanges, buying and selling and so forth. I am thinking of words like 'negotiation', 'bargaining', 'transaction' and 'cost'. The concepts are thus framed as though the collaborative venture were an impersonal economic exchange, and indeed there are similarities in how these things are perceived. Emerson (1976: 336) states that 'the exchange approach in sociology might be described ... as the economic analysis of non-economic social situations'. However, there are fundamental differences and Loxley (1997) draws these out, in particular raising the importance of mutual commitment, personal trust and obligation and the development of longer-term, mutually beneficial collaborative relationships.

Activity 3.6

- Having explored social exchange theory, make some notes about your own views on the theory and its ability to help develop understanding and analysis of the interrelationships between professionals and organisations in practice.
- Are there any significant issues that have not been covered in your view?
- How applicable and relevant is this theory to your knowledge, and if you have it, experience of collaborative working practices?

COMMENT

In the discussion above, you may have wondered about the omission of the impact of these approaches on the interaction or exchange with service users and carers. Loxley (1997) does address this, albeit briefly, however the main issue is that social exchange theory does not, in my view, adequately explain where the benefit or success of the exchange may be for a 'third party'. In other words, surely it is the case that many successful collaborative arrangements are entered into in order to secure effective outcomes and changes for service users and carers, with potentially less, or at least implicit and less tangible, direct benefits for the professionals involved?

This leads me to consider issues of professional power and equity in exchange networks. Social exchange theory and social network analysis may be effective in explaining some of the perceived barriers to collaborative working, such as issues of funding and professional inequalities. Whilst the complexity of power and cultures in professions is considered further in Chapter 6 of this book, it is relevant to note here how power differences could lead to one or another party not perceiving benefit and from the self-interest viewpoint, not seeing a reason to participate. This explanation logically begs the question of how service users might experience and participate in collaborative and integrated working practices. If social exchange theory is seen to be helpful in explaining such practice, and we acknowledge that issues of power difference between the participants may hinder the development of trust and the progression of social exchange, then the consequence would seem to suggest that collaborative working practices do not facilitate meaningful participation. However, this issue remains 'up for debate' and is considered further in Chapter 4.

USING THE CONCEPT OF 'COMMUNITIES OF PRACTICE' TO UNDERSTAND INTERPROFESSIONAL COLLABORATIVE PRACTICE

Having examined systems theory, social exchange theory and social network analysis, it seems logical also to look at the concept of 'Communities of Practice', as all of these theories take a similar focus on the social interactions that are inherent within collaborative practice. Stemming from social learning theory, 'Communities of Practice' focus on identity (in this case professional identity), creativity and knowledge developed through social participation (Anning et al. 2010). Of particular interest is the way in which the notions of practice and community are brought together. Wenger (1998) proposes three ways in which practice provides coherence to a community, and these are illustrated in Figure 3.3.

Wenger (1998) also stresses the importance of identity as integral and inseparable from issues of practice, community and meaning. This may, of course, relate both to individual and collective identity and 'brings to the fore the issues of non-participation as well as participation ... exclusion as well as inclusion' (Wenger 1998: 145).

You may be wondering how these ideas help us to understand and evaluate interprofessional practice. I would argue that the concepts that underpin Communities of Practice can help us to understand what we mean by a professional identity as a social worker and how this might influence the ways in which we work with other professionals. In Chapters 5 and 6 of this book, you will consider this further.

Communities of Practice provided one of the underpinning theoretical frameworks for research undertaken by Anning et al. (2010) into the delivery of public and voluntary sector services by multiagency teamwork. The authors explain that multiprofessional working involves coming together to 'achieve a cultural consensus and a shared discourse' and that this is not the result of 'static agreement' but is likely to be 'a process' (Anning et al. 2010: 83). This research also drew on a second theoretical framework, that of activity theory, which is outlined in the following section.

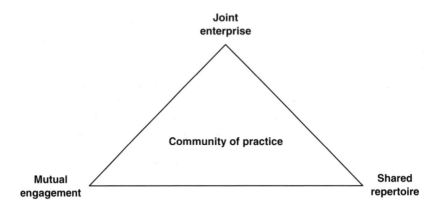

Figure 3.3   Communities of practice

Source: Wenger 1998: 73

USING ACTIVITY THEORY TO UNDERSTAND INTERPROFESSIONAL COLLABORATIVE PRACTICE

Activity theory, also known as cultural historical activity theory (CHAT), as mentioned, is used as a tool to inform research, particularly research concerned with professional learning within multiagency settings (Leadbetter et al. 2007) and interprofessional practice (Anning et al. 2010; Daniels et al. 2009). It is descriptive rather than prescriptive, in that it does not suggest a solution, but describes processes. Activity theory tells us that the behaviour and approaches of professionals in practice cannot be understood without examining the social, cultural, historical and institutional context in which they practise. This model can be seen to encompass perspectives from other approaches – for example, similar to Communities of Practice, activity theory, whilst it enables an understanding of the behaviours of individuals, starts from a focus on joint activity, practice and the processes of change and development (Engeström 1999).

Figure 3.4 illustrates the way in which activity theory conceptualises the relationship between a range of interdependent elements operating within an activity system, which may be the agency, organisation or team. These are all seen as important aspects that need to be considered when multiagency working is being examined (Leadbetter et al. 2007). Some of the terminology used is complex, but essentially there are six factors which are seen to mediate, or influence, activity. These are described below:

- the overall 'object' of the collective activity system;
- the 'subject', person or group of individuals who are engaged in the activity;
- the 'community' or people and social relations in the system;
- the 'division of labour' which directs the balance of roles and responsibilities;
- the 'tools and artefacts' which form the resources and means to support the activity; and
- the 'rules' which are the conventions, policies and requirements that are supported, accepted or imposed within the activity system. (Engeström 1999)

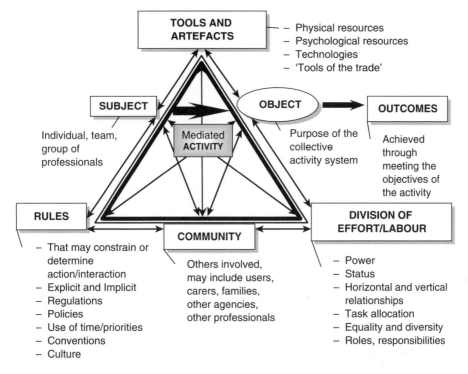

Figure 3.4   Activity theory

Source: Developed from the work of Engeström (1987), cited in Engeström 2001: 133–56

Activity theory can therefore help to further understanding of the consistencies, contradictions and tensions that may occur in interprofessional practice, these being shown as arrows in Figure 3.4, where the interrelated elements are connected in the activity system. Importantly, activity theory proposes that 'conflict is inevitable as tasks are redefined, reassigned and redistributed within changing organizations and teams in the world of work' (Engeström 2001, cited in Anning et al. 2010: 12).

DRIVERS AND BARRIERS TO EFFECTIVE COLLABORATIVE WORKING

As you worked through this chapter, you have been exploring how theory has provided knowledge and models that can influence practice, and within this a number of research studies have been referred to. To draw this chapter to a conclusion, this final section presents two examples of research in a little more detail in order to show how such studies have improved our understanding of some of the drivers or enablers and, conversely, challenges or barriers, that impact on the effectiveness of collaborative working. There are potentially many factors which may be seen to facilitate or hinder organisational, team and individual collaborative working – furthermore, there will be a complex interaction and range of variables between these factors – so it is not possible to detail them all in this chapter. For that reason, it is recommended that you access further reading and research that will expand your knowledge of the key issues. This discussion is also carried forward into the later chapters of this book where you will consider organisational cultures and service users' experiences of collaborative services. Additionally, you have already explored some potential influences on collaborative practice in Chapter 2, such as policy, legislation and social and economic drivers, so it is not my intention to restate these here, but you may find it useful to look back at these and consider how they facilitate or hinder collaborative practice.

The two examples of contemporary research into collaborative working practices, summarised here, offer a good overview of many of the key issues: one relates to services with children, their families and carers; and the second relates to services with adults, their families and carers.

A NATIONAL GOVERNMENT EVALUATION OF EARLY PILOTING OF THE COMMON ASSESSMENT FRAMEWORK AND LEAD PROFESSIONAL WORKING

Research on the national government evaluation of early piloting of the Common Assessment Framework (CAF) and lead professional (LP) working was published in the journal *Child Abuse Review* in an article titled, 'What appears to be helping or hindering practitioners in implementing the common assessment framework and lead professional working?' (Brandon et al. 2006). The CAF and LP working are part of a government strategy in England and Wales for early intervention and more integrated services for children and families. This research was a national government evaluation that set out to study the early pilots operationalising CAF and LP working in twelve areas in England. The findings suggest that there were a number of interrelated factors, which appeared either to help or to hinder the process of implementing these collaborative practices.

Brandon et al. (2006) explain that where there was enthusiasm for the work and a clear structure, which was understood and internalised by practitioners, CAF and LP were seen to be promoting better multiagency working, helping agencies to come together much faster and enabling a more rigorous follow-through of services. Conversely, however, hindrances included there being no local 'track record' of successful multiagency working, which seemed in turn to generate professional mistrust and anxiety. Anxiety was also caused by fears about change and a lack of confidence in new skills. For many practitioners, aspects of this work were at that time new and the emotional impact of change needed to be acknowledged through support and training. It is considered that the task of local implementation would have been easier if there had been firmer national guidance about CAF and LP roles and processes available at that time (Brandon et al. 2006).

SUMMARY OF FINDINGS

Factors that helped implementation	Factors that hindered implementation
Enthusiasm at 'grass roots' and managerial level	Lack of agency 'join up' and conflicts of interest
Perceived benefits for families	Lack of professional trust
History and practice of good multiagency working (including previous CAF/LP working)	Mismatch between the 'vision' and the practice
Learning from others	Confusion and muddle about processes
Existing IT system	Skill and confidence gaps
Clear structure for CAF/LP process	Lack of support
Good training, support and supervision	Anxiety about increased workload and new ways of working

A MATRIX OF DRIVERS AND BARRIERS TO INTEGRATED WORKING

A study on the drivers and barriers to integrated working was commissioned by the Scottish Executive in 2002 (Stewart et al. 2003). It sought to identify the barriers and drivers to integrated working based on an overview of collaborative health and social care projects throughout Scotland (over 200 of them) and on a detailed examination of nine case studies. A matrix highlighting the barriers and drivers at three levels was produced. The results were published in an article in the *Journal of Interprofessional Care* (Stewart et al. 2003). The full matrix is also reproduced as an appendix to Petch (2008), within which one of the original article authors summarises the lessons to learn from this research as:

- All stakeholders need to be involved at the earliest possible stage;
- A shared vision for meeting an agreed need is required in order for progress to be made;
- Individual agency and senior management support needs to be visible;
- Dedicated resources to support change management or development are crucial to moving forward any shared agenda;
- Roles and responsibilities require to be agreed by all stakeholders and need to be clear and unambiguous;
- Joint financial arrangements, pooled or otherwise, should be clear;
- Practical issues are important and can promote ownership and team building; the following issues should be clear in order to reduce the possibility of conflict and loss of focus: location, job description, terms and conditions, workload, appropriate professional supervision;
- Ongoing support to the staff involved on the ground is important to maintain momentum, including joint training. (Petch 2008: 39)

SUMMARY OF FINDINGS

	Drivers	**Barriers**
National policy frameworks	Joined-up strategic Realistic	Piecemeal Contradictory 'Projectitis'
Local planning context	Cycles mesh Owned at all levels	Not needs-led Issues seen in isolation
Operational factors • Relations between partners • Organisational culture • Change management • Enabling staff • Professional behaviour • Attitudes • Outcomes	Centred on user need Willing to take risks 'We have nothing to lose' 'Can do' culture	Lack of trust Defensive Disown common purpose Covers own back Staff expendable Winners and losers

Reflective practice question 3.3

Examine the summaries of the two research examples above whilst also reflecting on the theoretical perspectives you have learned about in this chapter.

- Are there aspects of these research findings that surprise you? If so, why?
- Can you see aspects of the research findings that might be explained by theory? If so, which theory and how?
- In what ways might these research findings provide learning to inform your practice?

COMMENT

It has only been possible in this chapter to give you a summary of these research examples. Given the breadth and depth of these research studies, you are encouraged to read the full reports and reflect on their implications for practice. Even from the summary detail you have here, though, there may be many aspects of their findings that surprise you. I think it is of interest that although the exact wording may differ, there are many common threads across the projects, including for example the need for strategies, policies and initiatives to be aligned, articulated as being 'joined up', 'meshed' and 'shared'. The recurrence of the importance of trust and the professional culture, with a background or history of successful joint working might be explained by the principles of social exchange theory; whilst systems theory would help to describe the emergence of the emphasis on 'clarity of roles and responsibilities', and the significance of a 'shared vision with mutual goals'. The concept of Communities of Practice can also be identified within the notions of 'learning from others' and a 'can do' culture.

CONCLUSION

In this chapter, you have examined theoretical frameworks, models and research that assist understanding and analysis of the interrelationships in collaborative practice. You have also been encouraged to reflect upon how these approaches might have implications for your practice and professional development. To achieve this, the chapter initially discussed the broad concept of theory, before exploring the examples of systems theory, social exchange theory, social network analysis, Communities of Practice and activity theory. There are, of course, others that you may wish to explore – these were only chosen as examples to look at within the space confines of this text. Having set this theoretical context, we then examined some examples of research that have highlighted a range of potential drivers and barriers to effective collaborative working.

In summary, this chapter has taken elements of your learning from earlier chapters and furthered your knowledge through consideration of theoretical frameworks and their contribution to promoting understanding about interprofessional collaboration. Throughout the chapter, there have been examples of collaborative practice along with an emphasis on critique and reflection. You should now continue your study into Part 2 of the book, where you will encounter more examples of how the theories, models and frameworks apply to collaborative social work practice. Chapter 4 highlights a key theme that runs throughout the book: understanding service users' and carers' experiences of collaborative and integrated organisational and professional practices.

FURTHER READING

Glasby, J. and Dickinson, H. (2008) *Partnership working in health and social care* (Bristol: Policy Press).

This very small paperback book is surprisingly packed with information about working across boundaries. Of particular interest and relevance to your study of theoretical approaches to understanding collaboration is Chapter 4, titled 'Useful frameworks and concepts'. With a focus on outcomes, the authors present a number of models, including Benson's (1975) framework for understanding whole systems working (cited in Glasby and Dickinson 2008: 81).

Leathard, A. (ed.) (2003) *Interprofessional collaboration from policy to practice in health and social care* (Hove: BrunnerRoutledge).

Chapter 7 of this edited book, 'Models for interprofessional collaboration', pp. 93–119, is particularly useful in that it details a range of models and approaches using helpful diagrams to support your understanding of interprofessional practice.

Weinstein, J., Whittington, C. and Leiba, T. (eds) (2003) *Collaboration in social work practice* (London: Jessica Kingsley Publishers).

To support your study of theories and models for collaborative practice, I particularly recommend that you read Chapter 2 of this edited book, 'Collaboration and partnership in context', pp. 13–38. Here, Whittington develops the model of collaboration outlined earlier in this chapter.

INTERNET RESOURCES

The Integrated Care Network (ICN) – http://www.dhcarenetworks.org.uk/icn/

The Integrated Care Network (ICN) Web pages provide a range of freely downloadable resources. The ICN provides information and support for organisations and seeks to improve the quality of provisions to service users, patients and carers by integrating the planning and delivery of services. The ICN facilitates communication between agencies and government so that policy and practice inform each other.

PART 2

PROFESSIONAL PRACTICE IN THE COLLABORATIVE ENVIRONMENT

4

WORKING WITH SERVICE USERS AND CARERS IN THE COLLABORATIVE ENVIRONMENT

Chapter summary

When you have worked through this chapter, you will be able to:

- Discuss the changing relationships with service users and carers.
- Describe the impact of power on relationships with service users and carers.
- Use theory to support your understanding of relationships with service users and carers.
- Reflect on how service users and carers might experience the collaborative environment.
- Discuss the two 'P's of Partnership and Participation.
- Explore the personalisation agenda and its influence on partnerships and participation.

INTRODUCTION

As you study this first chapter of the second part of this book, you will draw on your learning about the context of interprofessional collaboration from earlier chapters by directly addressing the implications for social work practice. In particular, the focus in Chapter 4 is the position and experience of service users and carers in the collaborative environment. In Chapter 2, for example, you developed your understanding of the changing context of collaborative practice by exploring some of the political, social, economic and policy drivers that are moving forward the agenda for collaborative working. Arguably, the national agenda for interprofessional practice has never been stronger. One of the driving factors, as mentioned briefly in Chapter 2, is the promotion of the rights and empowerment of service users and carers, together with their changing experience, status and role (Whittington 2003a). Additionally, findings from inquiries have highlighted the importance of the service user and carer 'voice' in effective practice, as seen in the conclusions from the inquiry into the death of Denis Finnegan (Robinson 2006). Denis Finnegan was a retired banker, aged 50 years, who was stabbed to death by John Barrett on 2 September 2004 as he cycled through Richmond Park. John Barrett experienced psychotic symptoms and was receiving care from mental health services. He lived with a long-term partner, who had serious concerns about his actual and potential violence, yet the inquiry concluded that the team did not communicate effectively with John Barrett's partner. Perhaps these drivers are in part responsible for the often taken-for-granted view that effective collaborative practice will always result in improved experiences and outcomes for those who use services (Barrett et al. 2005). In this chapter, however, you will be encouraged to reflect upon this assumption to consider whether collaborative working environments are always the most effective practice in providing the outcomes service users and carers strive for. Furthermore, following on from your learning in Chapter 3, you will consider how theoretical explanations might aid an understanding of the service user's position in the collaborative landscape.

Finally, as you read this chapter, you need to remain mindful that 'not all of those who use health and social services identify themselves strongly as "service-users", it being a term that is "stigmatised and … devaluing"' (Brown and Barrett 2008: 43). Also, as outlined in Chapter 2, service users and their carers may have very different and potentially opposing experiences, needs and perspectives (Mathews and Crawford 2011) of collaborative practice.

CHANGING RELATIONSHIPS WITH SERVICE USERS AND CARERS

Together with the drive towards collaborative practice, evident within national policy and legal frameworks, there has been a growing emphasis on meaningful participation of the public, including service users and carers, in the development and enhancement of all public services. Daly and Davis (2002: 97) refer to this as 'partnership and participatory decision making'. In England, one such example has been the growth of Local Involvement Networks (LINks). Local Involvement Networks have been established to give people a stronger voice in how their health and social care services are delivered. They are organised and managed by local people, groups and communities. According to the NHS National Centre for Involvement (2008), LINks find out what people like and dislike about local services, monitor the care they provide and use their powers to hold services to account. A similar initiative in Scotland has been the Patient Focus and Public Involvement strategy (more information on this is available from NHS Education for Scotland at http://www.nes.scot.nhs.uk).

Alongside this, for social work practice, the concepts of participation, choice and the importance of users and carers being able to inform and influence services have become gradually more embedded into professional practice at all levels. Consequently, there have been changes in the relationships between professionals and service users, coupled with an increase in service-user power within those relationships (Øvretveit 1997*b*); the significance of power and empowerment are considered more specifically later in the chapter. The impact of these changes goes beyond influencing individual relationships, also affecting 'strategic and operational aspects of social care provision' (Brown and Barrett 2008: 43). Whilst the mechanisms, processes and effectiveness of various approaches that aim to enable the meaningful engagement of those who use social work services may be debated, it is unlikely that many would dispute the fundamental values and objectives that underpin these developments.

Activity 4.1

As you have read, relationships between professionals and service users have changed and arguably continue to develop and change. Look back at your notes from Chapter 2 of this book and think about other aspects of your social work studies, then write down your thoughts about why these changes are taking place and what the trigger factors for change might be. Consider, too, whether there are different perspectives or debates about the factors that you regard as influential in these changes.

COMMENT

Øvretveit (1997*b*: 81) suggests that there are two sources for these changes: first, the rise of consumerism and people's expectations; and second, the influence of professional values and philosophies. These two aspects of change are explored in more detail below.

'People have been influenced by the rise of consumerism in the 1980s and expect more of health and social services' (Øvretveit 1997*b*: 81). Accordingly, those people who may have previously been seen as less likely to have their 'voice' heard, being disadvantaged, marginalised and often socially excluded, for instance many of those who use social work services, have been influenced and helped by consumerism and rights-based movements. As a result of some groups of service users being dissatisfied with services and the way they were provided (Glasby and Littlechild 2006), users have increasingly become more likely to demand a greater say in their own care and in what is provided for them (Øvretveit 1997*b*). Hunter and Ritchie (2007) link the notion of consumerism to market models, which you read about in Chapter 2, although the connection is not straightforward as service users do not in reality operate as customers in a free market (SCIE 2007: 36). Whilst acknowledging the limitations of consumerism in the context of social care, the underpinning ethos of 'service to customers' indicates a shift of power that provides:

> a useful way to challenge the traditional service delivery model, where professional and resource allocation power are aligned on one side, with professionals responsible for defining the problems as well as prescribing, authorising and implementing the solution. (Hunter and Ritchie 2007: 14)

Developments in the status of the social work profession have made our values and philosophies more explicit. For example, professional registration and regulatory mechanisms, the degree requirements, post-qualifying education and the professional codes of practice all stand testament to the growing influence of professionalism on practice. The extracts from the General Social Care Council (GSCC) Codes of Practice for social care workers (2002) that follow illustrate how aspects of participation and partnership are embedded in the standards for social care practice:

1.3   Supporting service users' rights to control their lives and make informed choices about the services they receive;

6.5   Working openly and co-operatively with colleagues and treating them with respect;

6.7   Recognising and respecting the roles and expertise of workers from other agencies and working in partnership with them; and

6.8   Undertaking relevant training to maintain and improve your knowledge and skills and contributing to the learning and development of others.

This was followed in 2008 by a statement on the roles and tasks of social workers, which included the expectation that social workers 'work in partnership with people to find the solutions and achieve the outcomes they want, and to collaborate with other agencies and disciplines to ensure support is delivered in a coordinated way' (GSCC 2008: 6–7). According to Trevillion:

> The quest for effective ways of operating across professional boundaries is entirely consistent with the search for other forms of good partnership practice, such as service-user involvement. It is also fully in line with values such as choice and empowerment. (2007: 941)

However, Øvretveit (1997b) suggests that practitioners may, at times, find themselves working with people in ways which are divergent from those learnt about during their professional education and which may even be contrary to their values. Such concerns have resulted in challenges to management approaches that are seen to constrain potentials for user empowerment. Indeed, Seden (2008) suggests that the values and ethics of social work practice and the sensitivities of work with vulnerable and disadvantaged people mean that further innovation and change in service structures and delivery may be necessary if meaningful participation is to be realised. Similarly, Brown and Barrett (2008: 47) state that 'organisations cannot "do" participation without changing their own attitudes and structures'. Taking this argument further and wider, Barton (2003), writing from a service-user perspective, acknowledges that changes have and are taking place, but argues that progress is slow. She states that the rhetoric of collaborative working practices is 'meaningless unless accompanied by cultural change in society as a whole and the social care workforce in particular' (Barton 2003: 105). Despite these reservations, it is evident that changing expectations, increasing professional recognition, organisational and structural developments may be altering the balance of power between service users and professionals (Øvretveit 1997b). The issues of power and, alongside it, empowerment, are major factors to consider as you develop your understanding of the service user and carer experience of interprofessional, collaborative practice.

UNDERSTANDING THE IMPACT OF POWER ON RELATIONSHIPS WITH SERVICE USERS AND CARERS

If we accept Øvretveit's (1997b: 81) view that 'professional power derives from the professional's position in an organisation and from exclusive access to knowledge', then it is evident that both of these 'power-enhancers' may be fundamentally changed by collaborative practice with service users, carers and interprofessional working. Beresford and Trevillion (1995) emphasise the importance of trust and sharing in the collaborative relationship with service users, which is particularly vital if we are to prevent users and carers from feeling disempowered when engaged with a whole range of powerful professionals. It is true to say that the agenda for participation is usually set and managed by the professionals involved. It can therefore be difficult for service users to experience this on an equal basis, or to have confidence that their involvement will effect any change. At the same time, social workers face a particularly high number of expectations and priorities that potentially compete with the drive for user participation; examples include organisational change, deluges of policy initiatives and budgetary constraints, as you have seen in Chapter 2.

Minhas, writing from a service-user perspective, describes how he perceives the collaborative practice environment:

> Meetings will be held, e-mails exchanged, minutes circulated, documents sent out for consultation, faxes sent and received, working parties attended, and the telephone never stops ringing – in the midst of all this you might find ten minutes to talk with the client! (Minhas 2009: 261–2)

If you have experience of working in a social work practice setting, does Minhas's statement above reflect your experiences of practice? It is crucial to consider how such a demanding practice environment might impact on users' experiences of services, particularly where a range of professionals or agencies are involved.

One mechanism that is often considered to offer users some power and control over the relationship with professionals and services is access to a procedure for a complaint. Local authorities are legally required to have such procedures (Children Act 1989, and National Health Service and Community Care Act 1990), yet it is argued that 'they provide limited post-hoc redress rather than proactive avenues for empowering services users' (Braye and Preston-Shoot 2010: 27). If the value of complaints procedures in relation to opportunities for empowerment is generally doubted in this way, then the effectiveness of such mechanisms is likely to be even more uncertain where multiagency or interprofessional practice is in question. This is because service users may simply be unsure who or which agency to complain to, partly because they may not be clear about the different affiliations of the professionals they come into contact with. Similarly, where services, practitioners and agencies are working effectively together, perhaps providing integrated services, the user may feel disempowered by the sheer strength of professional numbers and cohesion. In some areas of practice, advocacy services have been developed in an attempt to redress this imbalance by facilitating and supporting users in making challenges to services. Significantly, this again raises the ever-present need to be aware of and proactive in addressing power inequalities, but also the importance of service users being supported to gain appropriate knowledge and understanding about the processes, procedures and professionals they are working with.

Activity 4.2

Identify a social work support service in your local area, preferably one that is either an integrated service or that explicitly participates in multiagency work in the area. A Children's Trust or Mental Health trust might be a useful example. Then imagine you are a user of their services who wants to make a complaint or challenge a decision. Try to find the information you would need to carry this through:

- Who would you need to contact? Is there one point of contact, or do you need to know which part of the service or professional area your issues relate to?
- Is there an information leaflet?
- Is the information available in different formats, including different languages, electronically and in hard copy?
- Overall, how accessible is the information and knowledge that you need?
- Is there information available about advocacy services to assist complainants?

If you have the opportunity to work with other students or practitioners on this activity you may find it helpful.

COMMENT

The quotation 'knowledge is power' is commonly attributed to Sir Francis Bacon (1561–1626). Today, it is recognised that service users and carers access information about services and about their own needs from a range of sources – commonly, this does not include practitioners. This increased access to knowledge may be another contributor to the changing relationship between professionals and service users. However, whilst the information acquired may often be more suited to the person's needs at the time, and be easier to understand, it may not necessarily be more accurate (Øvretveit 1997b). Thus, service users and carers are not only experts on their own experience, but are potentially becoming broadly more knowledgeable about particular needs and service provision. Beresford (2005: 2) states that 'user knowledge' is that which is 'based on direct experience – on what people know from living through it – from being on the receiving end of policy and services ... .' In essence, the knowledge, understanding and perspectives that arise from those experiences will include opinions, views on priorities and perceptions on the realities of 'what works well' and 'what works less well' for those whose lives are changed by their involvement with a range of professionals. Therefore, the 'choices and values' of those who use services may differ from, and potentially sometimes conflict with, the choices and values of those who provide those services (Newman et al. 2005: 120).

Mary is a student social worker. She is working in a Local Authority Children's Rights and Participation Team as part of her final practice learning opportunity. A social worker, working with 14-year-old Kyle, has contacted the team. The referral is allocated to Mary. Kyle currently lives in a small local authority residential home. He has been there for three weeks, having previously lived with foster carers. The social worker is planning a review meeting to include everyone involved in supporting and caring for Kyle. Kyle has refused to attend the meeting, which concerns his social worker. Kyle tells Mary that he knows that his Mum might be there, with one or more of his teachers, as well as staff from the residential home and the Youth Offending Team and his social worker. He says that he hates to see his Mum get upset, but also that some of these people do not like him, whilst others do not really know him, and anyway he feels they all get together and decide whatever they want, regardless. Whilst he would like to tell them what he thinks, he says 'that will only get me into more trouble'. Mary begins to work with Kyle, first explaining that his social worker and the staff in the home will also be supporting his Mum if she comes to the meeting. Mary suggests some ways in which Kyle could be supported to put forward his views.

- Mary suggests that she could attend the meeting with him to support and help him to speak out during the meeting – Kyle says, 'I am not going to the meeting even if you are there, it won't make any difference, there will be at least five or six of "them" and I already know what they think of me.'
- Mary explains that Kyle will have an opportunity to write his views on the review form before the meeting, and she could help him think through what he wanted to record – Kyle says, 'I can't write very well, my spelling and handwriting is really bad, that's one of the reasons the teachers don't like me, they are always getting at me about it, so I'm not writing on any forms.'
- Mary suggests that, as the meeting is being held in the residential home, she could ask Kyle's social worker to talk to Kyle before the meeting to get his views, then to come out of the meeting before any decisions are made at the end, to tell Kyle about the discussion and get his views on any proposals before they are finalised – Kyle is ambivalent about this and simply says, 'You can if you like, but I still don't think it'll make any difference.'
- Mary then suggests that she could help Kyle to make an audio or video recording giving his views and that this could be played to the meeting. Mary explains that this would be a bit like some of the reality television programmes' 'diary room' sessions – Kyle finds this idea quite appealing; he likes using technology and thinks he could express his thoughts verbally quite well in this way. Kyle says, 'That would be good, they would have to sit and listen to me wouldn't they? It might not make any difference, but at least they'll have to listen to me.'

CASE STUDY

It appears from the case study that Kyle's experience of working with a range of professionals is that his choices, values and perceptions are in conflict with theirs and that they are collectively very powerful. Thus, whilst the professionals are working together with the aim of supporting Kyle effectively, he does not feel able to participate or contribute. There is a danger that social workers become engrossed in the complex dynamics of interprofessional working and, as a consequence, the views and choices of service users become secondary or peripheral (Minhas 2009). Barton (2003), a disabled person and service user herself, recounts some disabled people's experiences of using collaborative services:

> 'Seamless services' – a solution to many of the barriers faced by disabled service users, but more often I hear the words 'bureaucracy', 'fragmentation', 'isolation' and 'frustration'. For most of us reality falls a long way short of an approach that is holistic, seamless and person-centred. (Barton 2003: 103)

You may agree that some of the words Barton (2003) uses portray significantly negative experiences. However, further within her text, Barton helpfully puts this into the context of societal change, developing her thinking perhaps from the social model of disability. Therefore, Barton appears to suggest that the complexities of interagency and interprofessional service provision represent yet another disabling barrier to be negotiated and overcome. This is really quite an indictment of services and professional practice. It is worrying, in fact, that there are few positive comments to be found in Barton's descriptions of disabled people's experiences, although she does make suggestions about how practice can be improved from her perspective. These are reflected in Figure 4.1.

USING THEORY TO UNDERSTAND RELATIONSHIPS WITH SERVICE USERS AND CARERS

As shown in Chapter 3, theory can help you to understand collaborative practices. In this next section of the chapter, you will explore how social exchange theory and systems theory can further your understanding of the service-user experience of the collaborative environment.

Reflective practice question 4.1

Reflect back to the discussion in Chapter 3 about social exchange theory (you may find it useful to go back to that section briefly at this point).

- In what ways might social exchange theory help you to understand the interrelationship between yourself as the professional and the service users you work with in the complex collaborative environment?

From	To
Service providers are in control.	Service users are in control.
Services are fragmented and separated by rigid boundaries.	Services work together in a person-centred approach.
Health and local government service providers have separate budgets and provide separate services.	Health and local government service providers have pooled budgets and work together.
Separate services produce their own information. This is fragmented and difficult to find.	There is a single access point for information.
Information leaflets use jargon and complicated sentence constructions. They are produced in one format only.	Information is produced using plain English in appropriate formats.
Service providers determine support needs and solutions.	Service users determine support needs and solutions.
Teams work in a single discipline.	Teams are multidisciplinary.
Workers have skills in one service.	Workers are multi-skilled and work across services.

Figure 4.1   The direction of change

Source: Barton 2003: 116

Reproduced with kind permission of Jessica Kingsley Publishers

COMMENT

It is first important to acknowledge that social exchange theory can be drawn upon to assist your understanding of all of the interrelationships that occur within inter-professional collaborative practice, not only those that happen between the many professionals. As seen in the previous chapter, social exchange theory suggests that such relationships are based upon an evaluation of the benefits and the 'price' or loss inherent in the 'transaction'. If you understand your relationship with the service user in this way, you gain a different perspective on the importance of ensuring 'trust', openness and honesty across all professional relationships. However, Loxley (1997: 17) states that there is a need for both parties in the relationship to be 'competent to engage in social exchange', going on to explain that competence relates to issues of power and an understanding of how to participate. Thus, relationships and networks between professionals, between professionals and service users, and within user groups can be oppressive and sometimes exclusive as relationships are reinforced through familiarity, history, experience of success and commonality of interest. Even at a more formal, strategic level, Daly and Davis (2002: 97), in their study of wider partnerships between local authorities and the public, raise concerns about 'representativeness, social inclusion, accountability and utility' of such partnerships. Social exchange theory therefore offers insight into the dynamics of the professional interaction with service users and the added complexity that may arise through collaborative practice. The theory highlights the importance of building trust whilst recognising how inequalities of power and 'competence' can severely impede effective professional relationships with service users.

Reflective practice question 4.2

Reflect back to the discussion in Chapter 3 about systems theory (as before, you may find it useful to go back to that section briefly at this point).

- In what ways might systems theory help you to understand the service user's experience of interprofessional collaborative practice?

COMMENT

The systems theory explanation of the landscape of practice, discussed in Chapter 3, with many different processes, systems and connections between them, makes the complexity of the professional environment starkly evident. The NHS Modernisation Agency (2004) likens this to the London Underground, suggesting that the system is made up of many different processes, such as the process for buying a ticket and locating the different Underground lines. Everything needs to work together as a system for things to run smoothly and one problem in one part may impact across the whole system.

If you are not familiar with the London Tube map, you can view it at the Transport for London website (http://www.tfl.gov.uk/). The map itself is complicated, being made up of many different colours, names and places, yet maps of this type are much simpler than the landscapes they portray (Beckett 2006). The same could be argued for interprofessional collaborative practice, in that our attempts to 'map' this for service users, by providing, for example, information leaflets, websites or verbal explanations, often do not fully depict the reality that users experience when negotiating collaborative services. It is little wonder then that, as Barton (2003) described earlier, for service users and carers, the system alone can present as a disabling barrier.

EXPLORING THE SERVICE-USER EXPERIENCE

Consider the service-user experience from the following case study.

Amelia, aged 83, lived alone in a bungalow. Despite having severe osteoarthritis since she was 55 years old, Amelia had been independent, with minimal support from her daughter, who lived nearby, and some adaptations to her home. However, after several falls and a brief hospital admission, Amelia's health deteriorated. On discharge from hospital, Amelia's daughter noticed that Amelia was often irritable, disorientated and low-spirited. Following assessments by occupational therapists, a district nurse, social worker and general practitioner (GP), Amelia's medication was revised to reflect her changing needs and Amelia reluctantly agreed to accept some short-term homecare visits to support her whilst her daughter was at work and to continue the assessment whilst the new medication took effect. However, despite general agreement from all concerned on Amelia's needs and how they could be met, problems arose between the services when it came to providing for these needs.

It was agreed that the homecare service would help Amelia with some personal care tasks and preparing meals and would ensure that her medication was taken. The revised prescription included an anti-depressant which the GP anticipated would have the effect of changing Amelia's outlook and improve her eating and sleeping patterns, the disruption of which may have led to the disorientation and confusion she experienced. However, it was necessary for the tablets to be taken regularly as they would not make any difference until several days of regular dosages were taken.

It soon became apparent that Amelia was not taking her medication. Through the use of a 'dosette box', it was clear to the homecare team that tablets were not being taken. Locally agreed joint-working and homecare service policies were unequivocal that homecare staff could not administer medication, but could only prompt and encourage, indeed they were not even to put the tablets out for the user. It was Amelia's daughter who filled the 'dosette box' at the beginning of the week; her daughter was also concerned that the tablets often remained in the box, untaken. Amelia herself was unperturbed by this, but was generally very unhappy, constantly tearful and not sleeping or eating regularly. When notified, the social worker contacted the GP and district nurse requesting regular nursing visits or a change to more slow-acting medication, to reduce the dosage frequency. The GP explained that there were no other suitable alternative prescriptions and that, in his view, Amelia was capable of administering her own medication – she just needed prompting and reminding. The homecare service staff disagreed. In their opinion, Amelia needed someone to put the tablets into her hand and guide them towards her mouth – a task they were not permitted to undertake.

Whilst professional role demarcations were a hindrance in this situation, the disagreements really centred on assessments of Amelia's abilities, but either way, Amelia and her family were 'in the middle', and Amelia's health continued to deteriorate. The relationship between the different workers also deteriorated as they could not reach agreement. Amelia's daughter was frustrated and angry, but also felt very guilty as she sensed that she was the only person who could resolve this and believed it was her duty as a daughter to do so. Thus, Amelia's daughter resigned from her job, resulting in a massive reduction in her family's income, so that she could provide the regular support her mother needed, particularly with regard to her medication. Amelia's health improved significantly over a matter of a few weeks, but then she became aware of the decisions her daughter had made, which subsequently reduced her self-esteem and made her feel like a burden to her family.

This seemingly simplistic case study raises so many questions and debates! It provides a useful example, from an adult services perspective, for you to reflect on your learning across all of this book, particularly this chapter, as it raises, for example, issues of professional identity, clarity of roles and responsibilities, and significantly here, the experience of the service user and carer.

Activity 4.3

Consider Amelia and her daughter's experiences of collaborative provision of services. Write down your thoughts in response to the following questions:

- How might Amelia have felt during this time? How would you describe her experience of collaboration in practice?
- Does this situation in any way mirror your knowledge and experience of practice? Have you worked with service users or carers who may have similar experiences to Amelia?
- What could have been done differently? Are there processes, practices, procedures and ways of working which would ensure that Amelia's experience was different?

COMMENT

There is little doubt that Amelia may have found this experience demoralising and potentially very difficult to understand. How could Amelia or her daughter have any knowledge of the issues that underpin the tensions here and how could they possibly begin to challenge this? You may have been able to think of similar circumstances from your own practice, although the service setting and issues may be very different – sadly, these kinds of debates are still common. There are, however, policy and procedural initiatives that set out to address the issues, such as the Single Assessment Process (DoH 2001*b*) and, more recently, the drive towards Individual Budgets (DoH 2007). However, Minhas (2009: 262) argues that often the managerial, bureaucratic policies are unhelpful and that 'it is quite feasible for a partnership to demonstrate how successful it is "on paper", yet fail to deliver on these crucial values'. Indeed, in this case study, the professionals were referring to confirmed local agreements, but these did not offer a resolution. Minhas (2009) goes on to suggest that the most important consideration is the approach taken to working with users and carers in jointly delivering services. Crawford and Walker (2008) explore the complexities of partnership and participation for older people through the example of the Single Assessment Process (SAP) (DoH 2001*b*). Crucially, Crawford and Walker assert that:

> The potential for confusion, duplication, fragmentation and error is easy to see [i]t is important … that you develop not only an appreciation of the possible difficulties inherent in partnership working, but also develop the skills and understanding to overcome these issues in your own practice … each profession and agency has a significant contribution to make to the whole integrated approach, but … this whole system approach will only be effective if it is organised and centred around the older person. (Crawford and Walker 2008: 158)

The literature cited above (Minhas 2009; Crawford and Walker 2008) uses the terms 'partnership' and 'partnership working'. I first introduced and discussed the concept of partnership with you in Chapter 1 of this book. Now, in the following section of this chapter, you will examine the concept of partnership further, in particular working in partnership with service users and how this approach aligns with participatory practice.

THE TWO 'P's: PARTNERSHIP AND PARTICIPATION

The title of this chapter, 'Working with service users and carers in the collaborative environment', could equally have been 'Partnerships with service users and carers in the collaborative environment'. Partnerships are relationships and in this context they 'have multiple and sometimes contradictory dimensions that need to be recognised as part of a critical and reflective understanding' (Whittington 2003a: 32). Building on your learning about how such relationships have changed, and issues of power and empowerment within collaborative social work practice, in this next section of the chapter you will consider what this all means for participation, drawing on the particular example of personalisation and self-directed support in practice.

Activity 4.4

Think about people that you interact with across different aspects of your life. How many of these would you consider to be your 'partners'? How many of these interactions, in your view, constitute a relationship you would think of as a 'partnership'?

Reflect on your thoughts on the above and then make some brief notes to answer the following questions:

- What does being a partner mean to you?

  … in your everyday life?
  … in your professional life?

- Who do you consider to be your partners and why?

COMMENT

You may have thought of a partner in your personal life or maybe a business partner, or perhaps you thought of other students that you have worked with on projects or presentations as partners in that endeavour. Did you think of other professionals that you have worked alongside, perhaps on practice placement, as your 'partners' or did you think of service users as your 'partners'? O'Sullivan (2011) suggests that partnership involves decisions being jointly made between the partners with agreement being reached. Therefore, the concept of partnership is likely to relate to many people that you interact with on a daily basis. If, then, partnership describes a form of relationship, in this case between the user or carer and professionals, it is important to examine the variety of ways in which such relationships may be shaped.

Arnstein (1969) suggests that 'partnership' is one level in a hierarchy of levels of participation. Arnstein's 'Ladder of Participation' was developed many years ago in the context of town planning and community participation (1969). Despite the potential contextual constraints, this typology and the article in which it first appeared have much to say about social inequalities and power in society. The ideas have been developed by Hart (1992), with a particular focus on children's participation in an international context.

It is likely that you will find that Figure 4.2 provides a self-explanatory illustration of Arnstein's ideas, although perhaps some of the words used are unfamiliar. In summary, this typology (and Hart's 1992 development of it) is about the redistribution of power with relationships that are experienced at the higher rungs of the ladder being more likely to be characterised by the user having increasing power in decision-making processes.

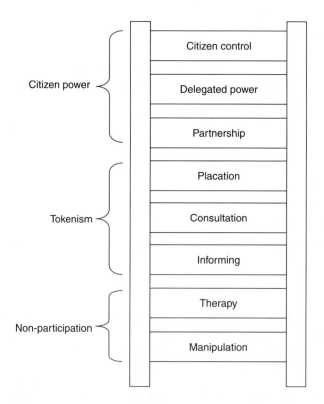

Figure 4.2   Arnstein's Ladder of Participation

Source: Arnstein 1969: 216–24

Starting at the bottom rungs, *manipulation* and *therapy* are both seen as non-participatory, with the relationship being very one-sided and professionals taking control and making decisions without the involvement of the user. The next three levels, *informing, consultation* and *placation*, whilst clearly offering more control, do so in a tokenistic and meaningless way. At this level, users may be provided with information, they may be asked for their opinions or a small number of key activists may be included in forums and committees, but the reality is that the power to make decisions remains firmly with the professionals. These approaches are commonly recognised as being contrived to meet a requirement for user participation, or colloquially, to 'tick a box' and demonstrate some form of involvement; whereas, the upper three rungs of the ladder begin to evidence a shift in power towards the user.

Partnership is described by Arnstein (1969) as a relationship where decision-making responsibilities are shared and distributed through negotiation. *Delegated power* takes this further in that users have the overall balance of power in their favour: they are able to make the decisions. The uppermost level of this model is *citizen control*, where users command, manage and direct the whole process. At this level, users have no concerns about having their voices heard by the more powerful, as the users are the most powerful in the relationship.

Arnstein uses the term 'citizen' throughout her work, but if you replace this with the term 'service user', or 'carer' if that is applicable, then you can see that the model translates to collaborative social work practice today. Whilst not originally conceived to reflect practice at the level of working with individuals, this is potentially a powerful model from which to reflect upon, critique and analyse practice and the ways in which we think about power and control. Of course, it is not without problems, as a model or typology, in that it is 'one-dimensional', offering arguably a simplistic view of relationships in what is now a very complex and multifaceted practice environment. Furthermore, it provides a mode of description, a way of categorising relationships with service users in practice, but does not actually provide guidance about how to move those relationships higher up the ladder. That being said, any model of this type can be useful as a catalyst for dialogue, stimulating debate. You may find it very interesting to take this model to your colleagues in practice if you are currently practising or to your next practice learning experience if you are in full-time study. Then ask colleagues, particularly professionals from across different disciplines, where on the ladder they perceive their relationships with service users would currently be placed and why.

Reflective practice question 4.3

Reflect back on the case study of Amelia, or if you prefer, reflect on work you have undertaken in practice. Use the case study or your experiences in practice to consider the following questions:

- At which of these levels did you feel participation took place? Why do you think that this is the case?
- What difference does the complex collaborative environment make to the service user's experience of the relationship?

COMMENT

It is perhaps the last part of the question that is particularly pertinent to the issues raised throughout this chapter. There is no doubt that participation in the collaborative environment holds more complexity than simply finding your way around the Tube map (as discussed earlier). You need to understand fully the map, the relationships, dynamics and issues if you are going to be in control. Thus, there is a need for information, advocacy and advice (O'Sullivan 2011). Furthermore, as discussed throughout this chapter, the user–professional relationship is fraught with potential power inequalities which may be compounded when a range of professionals and agencies are involved. There may also be differing views from across the agencies or professionals about what participation means, how it can be made possible, how it is resourced and when it has been achieved. Thus, it is important that the service user, carers and professionals develop clarity and agreement about the purposes of their joint work, what is possible and the outcomes being sought. There are acknowledged limits on the level of participation in practice (O'Sullivan 2011), such as where a user is a danger to themselves or others, or where the user is a very young child or does not have the necessary mental capacity. For example, Anning et al. (2010: 123) found from their evaluation of multi-professional teamwork in integrated children's services that 'accessing the views of young people and children was difficult. Professionals cited difficulties with ensuring representation and "authentic" participation'. However, even being mindful of these constraints, professionals should always seek possibilities to enhance user participation. The importance of this is highlighted in the Serious Case Review into the death of Kyra Ishaq in which it was found that:

> The lack of any prescribed opportunities for children to formally express their views, or to actively participate within the assessment or decision making process of home education, or to have any independent access to external processes, represents a direct contradiction to the aspirations of safeguarding and human rights and guidance. Given the tragic outcomes identified with this review, it also represents a major safeguarding flaw. (Radford 2010: 8)

Additionally, in the government's guidance, *Working together to safeguard children: A guide to inter-agency working to safeguard and promote the welfare of children*:

> Lord Laming reiterated the importance of frontline professionals getting to know children as individual people and, as a matter of routine, considering how their situation feels to them. Ofsted's evaluation of 50 Serious Case Reviews conducted between 1 April 2007 and 31 March 2008 highlighted 'the failure of all professionals to see the situation from the child's perspective and experience; to see and speak to the children; to listen to what they said, to observe how they were and to take serious account of their views in supporting their needs as probably the single most consistent failure in safeguarding work with children'. (DCSF 2010: 32–3)

Hunter and Ritchie (2007: 11) use the term 'co-production' to describe partnership 'between people who use services and people who provide them'. This is partnership working at an individual level, in everyday practice, bringing service users and practitioners together in a collaborative, productive partnership. Co-production is set out as a philosophy that is particularly relevant to the development of personalisation in social care (Hunter and Ritchie 2007). The following section of this chapter explores how the personalisation agenda impacts on social work with service users and carers in the collaborative environment.

THE PERSONALISATION AGENDA

Personalisation, sometimes also known as 'self-directed support', in social care, whilst not a wholly new concept, is developing and emerging as a very different way of working with individuals who need support and care services. It is important to note that this paradigm shift in approach is not only happening in work with adult service users, but the concepts can be found across all services including those for children, their families and carers and health services. Indeed, Leadbetter (2004) suggests that personalisation offers a new organising principle for services as an alternative or even a challenge to current hierarchical approaches and 'new public management', which you read about in Chapter 2. This is, however, a contested development that can equally be interpreted as 'allowing the market to dominate the supply of care services, misrepresenting the interests of carers and people who use services, while deprofessionalising qualified practitioners' (Cree 2009: 33). However, in the context of this chapter, I cannot set out all that you need to know about personalisation, so would recommend that you source additional reading, particularly from organisations such as the Social Care Institute for Excellence (http://www.scie.org.uk), who provide straightforward guides for practice (for specific references, see Further Reading at the end of this chapter).

In your previous studies or practice experience, you may have come across 'Direct Payments', 'Individual Budgets' and 'person-centred care'. These are all examples of approaches to personalisation. These developments are taking place across all four countries of the United Kingdom, albeit at different speeds and in different ways. If you are interested in practice in Wales and Northern Ireland, for example, you will find up-to-date information on the Web pages of a partnership organisation called 'In Control' (available at http://www.in-control.org.uk). In Scotland, the Scottish Executive has published *National guidance on self-directed support* (2007), also accessible online (http://www.scotland.gov.uk). You can read more about these initiatives on the Department of Health website, on the pages dedicated to 'Personalisation' (http://www.dh.gov.uk/en/SocialCare/Socialcarereform/Personalisation). The concept of 'personalisation' is described on these Web pages as meaning 'that people are able to live their own lives as they wish; confident that services are of high quality, are safe and promote their own individual needs for independence, well-being, and dignity' (http://www.dh.gov.uk). Other authors have been more explicit about the importance of interprofessional collaboration in personalisation:

> Personalisation involves thinking about individuals in a more holistic way than hitherto – an approach that is not constrained by traditional organisational and professional boundaries. (Hudson and Henwood 2009: 80)

and

> Personalisation means finding new collaborative ways of working and developing local partnerships, which produce a range of services for people to choose from and opportunities for social inclusion. (Carr 2008: 4)

Carr (2008: 4) also refers to the need for a 'total system response' to ensure people have equal access to the appropriate range of services. The 'total system' mentioned here can be interpreted as synonymous with 'whole system approaches' that you read about in the previous chapter of this book. The DoH (2007: 2) is unequivocal that 'the relationship between health, social care and wider community services will be integral to the creation of a truly personalised care system', and that 'services across transport, leisure, education, health, housing, community safety and the criminal justice system and access to information and advice are vital to ensuring people's independence and overall quality of life' (DoH 2009*d*: 14–15).

Thus, the principles of personalisation in social care embrace meaningful participation, whilst, on the other hand, also offering an opportunity to enhance partnerships with service users. As a way of moving the relationship to the top of Arnstein's (1969) ladder that you learnt about earlier:

> Personalisation through participation makes the connection between the individual and the collective by allowing users a more direct, informed and creative say in rewriting the script by which the service they use is designed, planned, delivered and evaluated. (Leadbetter 2004: 57)

Figure 4.3 is developed from Leadbetter's work (2004) and illustrates seven components of practice that enable 'personalisation through participation' and thereby change the role and status of service users working with a range of professionals and organisations.

Figure 4.3 shows not only the changing experiences of service users with regard to their position in the collaborative relationship, but also illustrates on the left-hand side some of the significant changes needed from services, and practitioners working within them, to reach the goal of co-production. However, moving in this direction is far from straightforward, as research undertaken for the Social Care Institute for Excellence into the benefits of user participation noted:

> Differing priorities and unequal power relationships between service users and professionals were a key barrier … This was seen as impacting on the individual situation of service users, particularly in relation to direct payments, and wider developments and change. (SCIE 2007: 75)

The activity and reading that follow aim to encourage you to think more about the skills and attributes you might need to ensure you avoid such barriers in practice, and work effectively in the complex and changing collaborative environment.

Intimate consultation: Where social workers work with service users to help them identify needs, preferences and aspirations through processes like assessment, review and preriod of working together

Advocacy: Social workers having a continuing relationship with service users, advocating for the user and supporting them through the systems, rather than the user experiencing a myriad of disconnected relationships with professionals

Partnership provision: Services working together to assemble solutions personalised to individual need

Expanded choice: Ensuring service provision is user-led with the service user having power to decide how their needs might be met

Funding: Should be 'attached' to the individual user, with the user being able to make the decisions about how they use the funding to meet their needs, with the support and advice of the social worker

Co-production: Service users and practitioners working in partnership with users having power and responsibility to become actively participant in the delivery of services

Enhanced voice: Where users are supported to explore a range of choices they can express their views and preferences, thus enabling the user to articulate their views more easily

Figure 4.3   Partnership and participation in the personalisation agenda

Source: Developed from Leadbetter 2004: 57–60

Activity 4.5

The following extracts are taken from a report commissioned by the Department of Health as a contribution to the discussion about the development of the social care workforce so that practitioners can meet the needs of the personalisation agenda:

- Read through the extracts and make notes on any points that strike you as particularly interesting, surprising or noteworthy.

Extract from Hudson and Henwood (2009: iii):

14. Different professions and organisations need to relate to one another at all levels, from front line to middle and senior management and at system-wide levels. Questions of partnership and

(Continued)

(Continued)

inter-professional working have tended not to be explored in relation to personalisation, but these issues are highly pertinent. The management of change, and the significance of 'boundary spanners', are issues that are recognised as significant in transformational change. The workforce implications are less in evidence, not least because these roles depend on various personal attributes rather than simply knowledge-based skills.

15. The personalisation imperative requires consideration of the whole system, how its parts interact and – crucially – how it can secure major cultural change and transfer of power from professionals and providers towards people who use services and their carers. The accompanying workforce strategy needs to be correspondingly broadly defined and targeted across.

Extract from Hudson and Henwood (2009: 80):

6.2 There is a long tradition of attempts to get professionals from kindred backgrounds to work together (though this report is not the place to scrutinise the literature) but the debates on interprofessionalism and personalisation tend to proceed along parallel tracks. The position of interprofessional working in the context of personalisation is unclear, especially if the only income stream to constitute an 'individual budget' (IB) comes from adult social care. Where this is the situation, there is the problem of discontinuity in culture, structure and process, with different agencies supporting the same people in different (and sometimes incompatible) ways. Individuals leaving adult social care for 'continuing health care' support from the NHS, for example, are likely to experience significant reductions in their degree of choice, flexibility and control. If, on the other hand, there is a radical joining-up of a range of income streams to form an IB 'single pot' then it is reasonable to expect professionals to work together more closely than in the past to deliver integrated and personalised support.

COMMENT

It is firstly important to be mindful that here you have only some very short extracts from the full report and as such there is a risk of taking these extracts out of the context of the whole document from which they originate. Thus, you are encouraged to source the full report or at least the executive summary in order to supplement your learning. Furthermore, you should also remain cognisant of the intention of the report, in that issues of interprofessional and collaborative practice were not part of the purpose or fundamental scope of this work. It is therefore all the more interesting and noteworthy that whilst this report was commissioned to explore issues in relation to the social care workforce, it identifies clear concerns about interprofessional working in the context of personalisation.

I was surprised, however, that there is not more emphasis on the importance of partnership or 'co-production' with service users, for whilst in point 15, cultural change and power transfer between worker and user is prominent, the rest of the extracts give little attention to this. This may, of course, be the result of the focus of the study being on workforce development issues and hence on exploring the issues from a more organisational perspective. I would, however, argue that most noteworthy here is the recognition that working collaboratively to achieve personalisation requires 'personal attributes rather than simply knowledge-based skills' (Hudson and Henwood 2009: iii).

As a totally new way of working, a new approach, a new philosophy to underpin practice, it is clear that personalisation will require different skills, knowledge, values and culture in practice, not only in social work, but across the interprofessional sphere. For example, as a social worker you and other professionals that you work with are likely to need to hone the skills that will enable you to take more of an advisory and sometimes advocating role. Commonly, the social work task will be a brokering task, one that empowers and guides service users to identify resolutions and ways to change their circumstances, themselves. Chapter 8 of this book is specifically dedicated to considering how your individual practice in the collaborative environment can be enhanced and developed. As such, it will address notions of personal attributes, knowledge-based practice, skills and values. Finally, did you notice that these extracts again make mention of the 'system' and of 'boundary' issues? Thus, here is another link to systems theory and your learning from Chapter 3. The idea of 'boundary spanners' (Kessler and Bach 2007, cited in Hudson and Henwood 2009) as practitioners who work across the boundaries of organisations, disciplines and/or user groups, mirrors the notion of 'champions' to support involvement and change, identified in the SCIE user participation research (2007) referred to earlier. These concepts are further drawn upon in Chapter 7, where you will consider professional practice in the collaborative organisation.

As stated earlier, one example of personalisation is 'Individual Budgets', which have been piloted in thirteen English local authorities, as a new way of providing personalised support for older people, disabled adults and adults with mental ill health. The underpinning ethos of Individual Budgets is that they will give more choice and empower users to take control and make decisions about the care that they receive. Professionals, in particular social workers, are required to take on the role of advocate and to support brokerage processes. Individual Budgets are a development from 'personal budgets' and 'direct payments', in that they go beyond the allocation of funding to users after assessment, by including a range of funding streams beyond social care. Thus by drawing on, for example, Access to Work funding (which is to support disabled people in the workplace), community equipment services (equipment and wheelchair services in England) and Supporting People monies (which support vulnerable people by providing a stable environment enabling greater independence), flexibility to meet the user's priorities and desired outcomes and collaborative practice are being embedded in the process.

The national evaluation of the Individual Budgets pilot programme was carried out by the Individual Budgets Evaluation Network (IBSEN 2008). These reports are available to download online, with shorter executive summaries making the overall findings easily accessible. You are encouraged to read these research reports to further your learning about personalisation and the experience of service users and carers in this new landscape of collaboration. Here is an extract from the IBSEN summary report:

- Broadly, the evaluation found that people in receipt of Individual Budgets felt in control over their daily lives. However, within this broad finding, there were acknowledged differences between different groups of service users;
- Mental health service users reported significantly higher quality of life;
- Physically disabled adults reported receiving higher quality care and were more satisfied with the help they received;
- People with learning disabilities were more likely to feel they had control over their daily lives;
- Older people reported lower psychological well-being with Individual Budgets, perhaps because they felt the processes of planning and managing their own support were burdens. (IBSEN 2008: 2)

The main report notes that 'the changes involved in implementing Individual Budgets were reported to have generated new imperatives for collaborative engagement', with one research respondent stating that: It makes buy-in more important, the idea that we do have to be working together as partners ... You can't do it as an individual organisation' (IBSEN 2008: 224).

From the perspective of practitioners, however, whilst collaboration, flexibility and choice were to be expected, there is acknowledgement of some challenges. The research report notes that barriers included incompatible eligibility criteria; legal restrictions on how resources could be used; and poor engagement between central and local government agencies (IBSEN 2008). Crucially, however, this section of the chapter has shown how the concepts of participation, partnership and personalisation are inextricably linked into a dynamic relationship, with it arguably being very difficult genuinely to implement one without the other two.

CONCLUSION

Brown and White (2006: 10) state that 'it is apparent from reviewing the literature on partnership working and integrating services ... that the majority of studies focus on the process of integrated working rather than the outcomes achieved from such working'. In this chapter, however, the outcomes and the experiences of service users and carers have been the focus. You have explored the changing relationships that professionals have with service users by examining issues of power in those relationships and opportunities for empowerment. Drawing on your learning from Chapter 3, you have also considered how theory might aid your understanding of the dynamics of these relationships. To illustrate the particular significance of participation and partnership working with service users, you examined the contemporary example of developments towards personalisation. Throughout the discussion, the chapter has challenged the assumption that collaborative practice is always most effective for service users by considering their experiences from the literature and a case study example.

Having studied this chapter, if you were asked to summarise the main points in just a few words, what words would you choose? For me, the main points to take forward from this chapter are that not only must the service user be at the centre of collaborative practice, but they must also be the focus of it. Furthermore, the different sections and examples all indicate the importance of empowerment and addressing imbalances of power when working with service users. This may be particularly challenging when you are also working with a range of colleagues from different disciplines. Fittingly, the last words of the chapter go to Minhas, a service user and practitioner:

> you cannot underestimate the importance of engaging with whatever client group you work with – in a spirit of truth, honesty, justice, care and respect. (Minhas 2009: 262)

FURTHER READING

Minhas, A. (2009) 'On the receiving end: Reflections from a service user', in R. Carnwell and J. Buchanan (eds), *Effective practice in health, social care and criminal justice: A partnership approach*, 2nd edn (Berkshire: Open University Press), pp. 251–62.

This chapter in an edited book provides an interesting and very personal and reflective account of using services. Amir Minhas is an Asian man who is physically disabled and uses a wheelchair. He is also a probation officer, so offers his views from different perspectives. Whilst in his chapter he does not always focus directly on issues related to collaborative practice, the insights and experiences he shares are powerful and valuable.

Carr, S. (2008) *Personalisation: A rough guide* (London: Social Care Institute for Excellence).

This is another SCIE publication, but is a small, short book offering easily accessible information about personalisation. The book explains what key terms mean and briefly sets out the background to current developments. Section 3 of the book is particularly useful in addressing the question of what personalisation means for various stakeholders, including user-led organisations and social workers. There are a number of practice examples within the text and some helpful additional sources and links at the end of the text. The author of this guide has also produced some e-learning resources about personalisation, which are freely available from the SCIE website (http://www.scie.org.uk).
    Furthermore, you may also be interested in two research briefings from SCIE:

Carr, S. (2009) 'The implementation of individual budget schemes in adult social care', Research Briefing 20; and
Needham, C. (2009) 'Co-production: An emerging evidence base for adult social care transformation', Research Briefing 31.

Social Care Institute for Excellence (SCIE) (2007) *Developing social care: Service users driving culture change*, Knowledge Review 17 (London: SCIE, available at http://www.scie.org.uk/publications/knowledgereviews/kr17.pdf).

Freely downloadable from the Internet, this SCIE guide was collaboratively developed by three organisations: *Shaping our lives, National Centre for Independent Living and University of Leeds Centre for Disability Studies*. This is essentially a report on research that explored the literature and practice around service-user participation and the extent to which it has brought improvements to social work and social care. You will find the report useful in supporting your learning in relation to this chapter, but more than this you will find it useful throughout your studies as this is primary research that should be influential as part of the knowledge base for professional practice.

If you are particularly interested in working with children in the collaborative environment, the following two sources will be useful and both are freely downloadable from the Internet:

Hart, R. (1992) *Children's participation: From tokenism to citizenship*, Innocenti Essay No. 4 (Florence: UNICEF International Child Development Center, available at http://www. unicef-irc.org/cgi-bin/unicef/download_insert.sql?ProductID=100).

Kirby, P., Lanyon, C., Cronin, K. and Sinclair, R. (2003) *Building a culture of participation: Involving children and young people in policy, service planning, delivery and evaluation* (Nottingham: Department for Education and Skills, available at http://publications.education. gov.uk/eOrderingDownload/DfES-0827-2003.pdf.pdf).

INTERNET RESOURCES

Department of Health, Care Networks – http://www.dhcarenetworks.org.uk/Personalisation

The Web pages of the Personalisation Network are within the DH Care Networks site. DH Care Networks, as part of the Department of Health, lead on the Putting People First (DoH 2007) agenda – in particular, integration and whole system reform, housing with care, assistive technology and partnership working. The Personalisation Network pages offer a wealth of resources related to change in the Adult Social Care system, including guidance and case study examples.

5

IMPLICATIONS OF COLLABORATIVE WORKING PRACTICES FOR THE INDIVIDUAL PRACTITIONER

Chapter summary

When you have worked through this chapter, you will be able to:

- Describe a range of ideas about 'being professional'.
- Reflect on your professional identity as a social worker working interprofessionally.
- Identify your skills and knowledge for interprofessional working.
- Discuss Common Assessment Frameworks as specific practice examples of interprofessional collaboration in relation to children and young people, and adults.

INTRODUCTION

The General Social Care Council (GSCC) *Codes of practice for social care workers* (2002) set clear standards that include:

- 'Working openly and co-operatively with colleagues and treating them with respect' (6.5) and
- 'Recognising and respecting the roles and expertise of workers from other agencies and working in partnership with them' (6.7).

The GSCC codes of practice underpin all aspects of social work practice in the United Kingdom. As such, they can be seen to help define individual professional identity and the concept of social work as a profession. In this chapter, you will explore your professional identity, particularly considering what this means as you develop as an interprofessional practitioner. Then in Chapter 6, you will further your understanding by exploring professionalism as a wider concept, in particular considering some of the tensions of professionalism, such as issues of power and boundaries. Within this, you will learn more about the identity of social work as a whole profession and the contribution it makes to interprofessional teamworking. Thus, this chapter and the following chapter develop the focus on professionalism and professional identity at two different levels. Both chapters draw on the theories introduced in earlier chapters, particularly on social exchange theory and the concept of Communities of Practice to explore the complexities of working with others in a meaningful, effective way.

YOUR PROFESSIONAL IDENTITY AS AN INTERPROFESSIONAL SOCIAL WORKER

In the introduction to this chapter and elsewhere in this book, I frequently use the terms 'profession' and 'professional', referring, for example, to the profession of social work and professional practice. Indeed, the whole of this book is about 'inter-*professional*' social work. To work effectively and confidently with other professionals, you first need to understand your own professional identity as a social worker. The starting point for this is to consider what the term 'professional' means and implies. With more clarity about the key aspects of professionalism, you can consider how those aspects are related to your perceptions of yourself as a social worker.

Reflective practice question 5.1

What does being professional mean to you? Think about yourself, in the context of your studies and any practice opportunities that you have experienced. Make some notes in response to the following questions:

- Do you consider yourself to be a 'professional'? Why or why not? What is it about yourself or your practice that either warrants, or does not warrant, describing in this way?
- What do you understand by the term 'professional'? Can you write a definition of this term?
- In the light of your notes so far, what do you understand by 'professional identity'?

COMMENT

The concepts of 'professional' and 'professionalism' are politically charged and have been the subject of many sociological studies and texts. These are complex, dynamic, multidimensional and potentially problematic notions. The *Cambridge dictionary online* suggests that the term 'professional' can be defined in a number of ways as it relates to:

- work that needs special training or education;
- having the qualities that you connect with trained and skilled people, such as effectiveness, skill, organisation and seriousness of manner;
- someone who does a job that people usually do as a hobby (such as the professional golfer);
- the type of job that is respected because it involves a high level of education and training. (http://dictionary. cambridge.org)

This definition demonstrates that the concept of being professional is not straightforward, being socially constructed and varying according to context. For example, it potentially has different implications when used in the context of sport. 'Professionalism', or 'being professional', is often reflected within a frame of esteem and dignity as it holds connotations of 'service', status and standards. It may be that you connected being 'professional' with a status conferred by recognised professional bodies, such as the General Social Care Council (GSCC), who also require commitment to codes of conduct or codes of ethics, that in turn influence professional behaviours. Consequently, 'professionalism' can be related to a concern for ethics, principles and having an explicit shared set of values. As reflected in the definition above, 'being a professional' also implies that you are part of a recognised group of people who have successfully undergone prescribed training and education and maintain continuing professional development, which is itself influenced by the values, ethics and principles of the profession. Hammick et al. (2009: 19) offer the following definition:

A profession acts collectively to restrict access to rewards (e.g. remuneration or social status) through establishing criteria by which others, non-members, are excluded. They lay claim to specialist knowledge and this underpins the services they offer; they exercise control of their knowledge and thus autonomy over their area of work. Each profession has a unique culture, influenced by its own values and beliefs. Through the education and training practices of a profession, its members are socialized into the professional culture and, in this way, practitioners from a particular profession adopt certain attitudes and conduct their practice in certain ways.

The latter part of this quotation relates to the development of a professional identity. We build our identity by 'negotiating meanings of our experience of membership in social communities' (Wenger 1998: 145). In other words, the development of professional identity occurs through an interaction between yourself, as the individual, and your social environment, that is to say your education, practice, colleagues and networks. Professional identity can also be associated with the need for recognition of professional contribution, status, validity and uniqueness; it has also been associated with self-interest, power and authority: complex issues, which are addressed in the next chapter of this book.

Activity 5.1

Imagine you are out with a group of friends, none of whom have any experience of social work either as students, practitioners or service users. One of them asks you what you do and, after you reply, they follow this up by asking, 'But what is social work?'

• How would you answer?

COMMENT

It is possibly more likely that people would ask about the sort of activities or tasks that social workers undertake, but in order to answer that question you need to have some clarity in your mind about how you might define the social work profession as a whole entity. The title strap line for a Department of Health leaflet promoting social work and social work careers is 'Social Work. It's all about people. It's that simple and that complicated' (DoH 2009*a*). It is, indeed, complicated, for even the International Federation of Social Workers (IFSW) states that 'social work in the 21st century is dynamic and evolving, and therefore no definition should be regarded as exhaustive' (http://www.ifsw.org). The IFSW redeveloped their definition of social work in 2000 to read as follows:

> The social work profession promotes social change, problem solving in human relationships and the empowerment and liberation of people to enhance well-being. Utilising theories of human behaviour and social systems, social work intervenes at the points where people interact with their environments. Principles of human rights and social justice are fundamental to social work. (IFSW 2000)

Within this definition, the earlier notion of social work being 'all about people' is clearly embedded. However, it is argued that social work attempts to balance two possibly competing functions: working to empower and support individuals, whilst also working for and within the particular structural contexts that, in themselves, may constrain and influence people's lives (Horner 2009). Hugman (2009) argues that questions about whether social work's focus is on the 'micro' or the 'macro' continue to be debated and are testament to the contested nature of the profession. However, Hugman goes on to argue that social work is developing a broad, flexible identity that enables practice, across different international contexts, to be understood (Hugman 2009).

The different aspects of professionalism you read about earlier in this section of the chapter will of course apply not only to social work, but to other professionals that you work with. Having furthered your understanding about how social work is defined and what 'professional' means, it is pertinent to consider how these concepts might relate to being 'interprofessional'.

Reflective practice question 5.2

What does being interprofessional mean to you? This opportunity for reflection follows Reflective practice question 5.1 from earlier in the chapter. In the light of your notes so far, how would you now describe your 'professional identity'?

Re-read the chapter so far and write down the key factors that are associated with professionalism and social work. With these in mind, reflect on your own practice, both in the context of your studies and any practice opportunities you have experienced. Make some notes in response to the following questions:

- Do you consider yourself to be 'interprofessional'? Why or why not? What is it about yourself or your practice that either warrants, or does not warrant, describing in this way?
- Make a list of the attributes and behaviours that you feel you demonstrate in your practice, that make you 'interprofessional'.

COMMENT

I believe that many of the identified attributes and characteristics of *professionalism* and *social work* are necessary for effective *interprofessional* practice – for example, a commitment to 'service', agreed standards and principles, codes of conduct and ethics, explicit values and attitudes, a specialist knowledge base, shared professional learning and an understanding and recognition of the specific disciplinary contribution. Additionally, for effective collaboration, partners need to recognise and nurture the mutual benefits of working together. Within this there are specific qualities and abilities that individual practitioners, like you, can bring to effective collaboration. Barrett and Keeping (2005) give particular emphasis to the importance of 'knowledge of professional roles' (pp. 18–19) and 'trust and mutual respect' (pp. 21–2). Hammick et al. (2009) add to this, highlighting the necessity to be a skilful communicator and being able to recognise who in the interprofessional team is best placed to meet the particular needs of the service user. You will learn more about the interpersonal communication skills necessary for effective collaborative work later in this chapter.

Significantly, it is argued that of all these qualities that make up the interprofessional practitioner, having a shared set of values is most essential (Davis and Sims 2003). According to Eby and Gallagher (2008: 114–15), professional values are the 'beliefs, ideas and assumptions' that are 'learnt and internalised through professional education'. Different professions will therefore hold to different professional values, in the same way that they will draw upon different forms of knowledge, codes of practice and ethics. The relationship between these distinct professional characteristics is, however, dynamic. In other words, one aspect will influence another and may move and change over time. For example, the models we choose to use for practice processes, such as assessment and intervention, are influenced not only by our knowledge base, but also by our professional values. Your attitudes and behaviours as you go about your practice are, in part, determined by your values, beliefs and ideals. Whilst each profession will hold to its own professional value base, there are core values or common values which can underpin effective interprofessional collaboration, leading to enhanced practice and new ways of thinking about joint practice:

> Attitude is drawn from values. It is argued that a collaborative culture which knowledge, skills and structures would reflect depends on an essential set of values which makes possible both enrichment from diversity and the reconciliation of difference. (Loxley 1997: 89)

Reflective practice question 5.3

Your professional values are the aspects, behaviours and ways of working that you believe to be valuable or of worth. Reflect on your own values, with particular regard to working with others. Note down some bullet points that reveal your reflections and ideas about what might be the core values for interprofessional collaborative working.

COMMENT

Hammick et al. (2009: 23) suggest that the core values for interprofessional work include having:

- Respect for everyone in the collaborative team;
- Confidence in what you know and what you don't know, and in what others know;
- A willingness to engage with others rather than take a detached view of proceedings;
- A caring disposition towards your colleagues;
- An approachable attitude and showing a willingness to share what you know as a means to the best possible outcome for the user of your service.

Loxley (1997), however, is unequivocal that collaboration cannot succeed without trust and sharing. As such, Loxley identifies these as being core values that impact on all aspects of collaborative practice. As you read earlier, Barrett and Keeping (2005: 21–2) also stressed the importance of 'trust and mutual respect'. You will recall from your reading of Chapter 3 of this book, that the notion of trust is fundamental to a social exchange theory of interprofessional relationships. Furthermore, through an understanding of the social exchange, it is evident that trust implies a two-way responsibility with mutual expectations (Loxley 1997). You may also have considered the importance of understanding each other's roles, responsibilities, values and knowledge base, as ignorance of these can have a significant impact on communication and the social exchange and therefore negatively influence the effectiveness of collaborative working.

Similarly, you may also have considered shared accountability to be a core value. As a social worker, you will hold multiple accountabilities. You are accountable to the service users you work with, to the General Social Care Council through the codes of practice, to your manager and employer, to your colleagues and to the other professionals with whom you practise. Crucial within this is the way in which accountability is understood in the context of enhanced service-user participation and partnership (Davis and Sims 2003). Accountability is linked to the ideas of trust and respect, discussed above, but more than this, it also requires integrity, openness, self-awareness and a clear sense of responsibility. Within organisations, interprofessional working environments can make the lines of accountability difficult to distinguish and work to. Anning et al. (2010: 104) give the following example:

> We have seen, in some teams a worker might be seconded from an agency that retains responsibility for their service conditions, be line managed by the team manager of the multi-professional team and perhaps receive supervision from a third party. Joined-up, multi-professional teams therefore often have complex lines of accountability.

It is important, therefore, that in your practice, you ensure you understand how accountability is managed and exactly to whom you are accountable. Anning et al. (2010) stress the significance of supervision as a process for facilitating and supporting accountability. In the next two sections of the chapter, you will learn about the knowledge, skills and mechanisms that support some particular aspects of practice. The next section considers, for example, the broad areas of interprofessional communication and the use of supervision to support your development as a reflective practitioner. The final section of the chapter then explores some more specific practice examples.

SKILLS AND KNOWLEDGE FOR INTERPROFESSIONAL SOCIAL WORK

So far in this chapter, you have furthered your understanding of your professional identity as a social worker and, crucially, as an interprofessional social worker. This required awareness of a range of what I called 'qualities and abilities' that contribute to effective collaborative practice. These qualities or characteristics are underpinned by certain skills, some of which have already been discussed. By way of revision and further reflection, consider the following question.

Reflective practice question 5.4

In Reflective practice question 5.3, you made notes about the core values for interprofessional collaborative working. In a similar way, this question asks you to think about the skills and knowledge that you might need to develop as an interprofessional social worker.

(Continued)

(Continued)

- Reflect on your own skills, with particular regard to working with others. Note down some bullet points that reveal your reflections and ideas about the skills that you bring to practice and what types of skill might be necessary to facilitate effective interprofessional collaborative working. You could start by re-reading earlier sections of this chapter.

COMMENT

You can think of a skill as being an ability, expertise, aptitude or competence in doing something, that is often acquired through training, learning and practice. Many of the skills that facilitate effective interprofessional practice are known as 'soft skills', which means they are intangible and hard to measure – sometimes also colloquially termed 'people skills'. Another term you may come across which is related to the concept of 'soft skills' is 'emotional intelligence'. Butler (2007) explains that the emotionally intelligent practitioner is aware of and understands the impact of their own and others' emotions and how they influence the effectiveness of relationships in practice.

Many of the skills that you will need to develop for social work practice will also support and enhance your collaborative working. Some of these skills are personal skills, abilities that you perfect that come from within yourself and influence all aspects of your interprofessional practice, for example a heightened and reflective sense of self-awareness, problem-solving skills and critical thinking skills. Other skills, whilst still being developed from within yourself, more directly influence your interpersonal relationships with others, such as person-centred and holistic practice skills and communication skills. You need to have awareness of the implications for how you and those you work with give information and receive or understand that information. Figure 5.1 illustrates this range of skills for interprofessional practice.

You could argue that all of the above skills influence, or make a difference to, the ways in which you communicate and that, potentially, enhanced and advanced communication skills are paramount to effective interprofessional work. For this reason, your learning in this chapter will now focus on issues of communication in interprofessional social work.

There are three core issues related to communication that recur in different guises in the literature and research about the factors that facilitate or hinder interprofessional working: information sharing across boundaries, confidentiality, and working with information and communication technologies (ICT). You will develop your understanding about each of these issues as you work through this part of the chapter.

O'Sullivan (2011) suggests that one of the benefits of collaborative practice is that it enables comprehensive information sharing. However, as you have seen in Chapter 2, inquiry reports across a range of services (mental health, child care, adult protection) continue to highlight 'the lack of shared information between agencies as a reason why children have not been protected and adults at risk have been involved in tragedies' (O'Sullivan 2011: 72). With regard to sharing confidential information between agencies, Petch (2008: 74) states that there is a need for agreed protocols as:

This can often be cited as a barrier to progressing partnership working without consulting with individual users and carers who may be only too happy for such information to be shared; indeed they may assume that the information provided to one professional is shared with others.

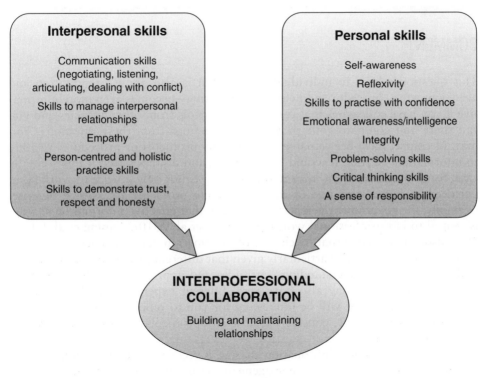

Figure 5.1   Skills for interprofessional social work

Activity 5.2

For this activity, you need to make contact with an organisation that provides social work services – this may be where you have undertaken a practice learning opportunity, it may be your previous employer or your current employer. As part of your developing practice, investigate whether this agency has information sharing

(Continued)

(Continued)

protocols for interprofessional and interagency working. If they exist, then obtain a copy of them and consider the following questions:

- How easy were the protocols to access? Do you think that they are widely known about and referred to by practitioners?
- How do the protocols enable or hinder effective joint working practices?
- Which agencies have come together to agree this protocol?

COMMENT

This question relates to individual practice but is also about organisation and agency practice, procedure and culture. The activity becomes even more informative if you have colleagues that can access protocols from other agencies and you can share and compare your thoughts and findings from these questions. You may, of course, have been unable to locate any protocols or procedures relating to information sharing. It would be surprising and disappointing if this were the case, for as you have seen, information sharing is not only crucial to working in partnership, but is also one of the areas where problems are known to arise. Certainly, the government perspective has been that effective information sharing is central to interprofessional working (Anning et al. 2010). Anning et al. (2010: 107) also acknowledge that 'exchange of information across agencies and disciplines is no easy matter', particularly given that different professions and agencies will have different understandings, attitudes and approaches to the concept of confidentiality. They may also have very different experiences and histories of sharing information. It will be interesting for you to reflect on your research in response to Activity 5.2, considering how any protocols you examined address these complex issues.

Whilst effective timely information sharing is recognised as being fundamental to early intervention and risk management across all services (Radford 2010), concerns and uncertainties related to confidentiality may result in key information not being communicated. You are under legal and ethical obligations to maintain confidentiality, with certain exceptions. It is, therefore, vital that with appropriate support, you are able to differentiate between information that is confidential and that which is not. In particular, being aware that where you have any cause to believe that an individual may be suffering, or may be at risk of suffering significant harm, it may be possible to justify sharing information without that person's consent. Whilst information sharing requires professional judgement, there is a range of legislation and policy guidance addressing the issues. Although not an exhaustive list, here are some examples (in reverse chronological order) that are particularly relevant to interprofessional social work practice:

- *Working together to safeguard children* (DCSF 2010).
- *Information sharing: Guidance for practitioners and managers* (DCSF 2008*a*), explored in further detail in this section of the chapter.
- Confidentiality and Disclosure of Health Information Toolkit (British Medical Association 2008, available at http://www.bma.org.uk).
- Mental Capacity Act 2005 and Code of Practice (2007).
- National Health Service Act (2006).
- Children Act (2004).
- Health and Social Care Act (2001).
- Multi-Agency Public Protection Arrangements (MAPPA) (2001, available at http://www.probation.homeoffice.gov.uk).
- *No secrets: Guidance on developing and implementing multi-agency policies and procedures to protect vulnerable adults from abuse* (DoH 2000*c*).
- Freedom of Information Act (2000).
- Regulatory and Investigatory Powers Act (2000).
- Data Protection Act (1998).
- Human Rights Act (1998).
- Crime and Disorder Act (1998).
- *Report on the review of patient-identifiable information* (Report of the Caldicott Committee) (DoH 1997*b*).
- Access to Health Records Act (1990).

For more information about some of the legislation listed here, you can freely download the DCSF (2009*a*) guidance titled *Information sharing: Further guidance on legal issues* from http://www.ecm.gov.uk/informationsharing.

These documents provide support and guidance for effective information sharing practice, helping practitioners to tread the difficult balance between ensuring service users' and carers' personal information is secure and safe, whilst also ensuring that individuals are safeguarded and afforded necessary early invention from appropriate services. Further to this list of national statute and policy, there are, of course, likely to be local agency protocols and guidance, as you discovered when you undertook Activity 5.2.

In 2008, the Department for Children, Schools and Families published guidance on information sharing (DCSF 2008*a*). This cross-governmental guidance has been endorsed and welcomed by a wide range of national agencies. It complements the General Social Care Council codes of practice for social care workers (GSCC 2002) and is structured around 'seven golden rules for information sharing' (DCSF 2008*a*: 11). These are reproduced here:

Seven golden rules for information sharing:

1. **Remember that the Data Protection Act is not a barrier to sharing information** but provides a framework to ensure that personal information about living persons is shared appropriately.
2. **Be open and honest** with the person (and/or their family where appropriate) from the outset about why, what, how and with whom information will, or could be shared, and seek their agreement, unless it is unsafe or inappropriate to do so.

3. **Seek advice** if you are in any doubt, without disclosing the identity of the person where possible.
4. **Share with consent where appropriate** and, where possible, respect the wishes of those who do not consent to share confidential information. You may still share information without consent if, in your judgement, that lack of consent can be overridden in the public interest. You will need to base your judgement on the facts of the case.
5. **Consider safety and well-being:** Base your information sharing decisions on considerations of the safety and well-being of the person and others who may be affected by their actions.
6. **Necessary, proportionate, relevant, accurate, timely and secure:** Ensure that the information you share is necessary for the purpose for which you are sharing it, is shared only with those people who need to have it, is accurate and up-to-date, is shared in a timely fashion, and is shared securely.
7. **Keep a record** of your decision and the reasons for it – whether it is to share information or not. If you decide to share, then record what you have shared, with whom and for what purpose. (DCSF 2008a: 11)

Additionally, and perhaps not recognised within these 'golden rules', it is important that you remain mindful of the service users' and carers' situation within the collaborative environment. Service users are often themselves in a position to be the conduits for information sharing, but need to be fully aware of who is involved in their care, which agencies and disciplines they represent, what partnerships or multiagency arrangements are in place and what information is of use to them. In the final section of this chapter, you will consider some particular examples from practice related to interprofessional assessment processes, within which the service user is the hub and source of key information.

The issues raised by confidentiality and information sharing are very complex and interface with a number of other barriers and drivers to collaborative working practice, including, for example, the use of information and communication technologies (ICT). ICT has been recognised as having the potential to facilitate effective communication and information sharing, although where systems are absent or not compatible, ICT can pose a significant barrier (Petch 2008). Information systems are subject to frequent change, often related to ensuring that agencies can evidence achieving targets and government requirements; furthermore practitioners do not always have the level of training and proficiency necessary to ensure accurate data inputting (Anning et al. 2010). A particular example of an ICT initiative which set out to achieve a number of objectives including, as its name suggests, integration, is the electronic *Integrated Children's System* (ICS), which acknowledges that 'work with children in need requires skilled use of detailed and complex information' (available at http://www.dcsf.gov.uk/everychildmatters). According to the Department for Schools, Children and Families:

A key aim of ICS is to provide frontline staff and their managers with the necessary help, through information communication technology (ICT), to record, collate, analyse and output the information required. (http://www. dcsf.gov.uk/everychildmatters)

The Integrated Children's System does not exist in isolation from other initiatives as assessment, for example the Common Assessment Framework (CAF) is integral to the system. The ICS has, however, come under much criticism, on the one hand from official reports (DCSF 2009*c*; Laming 2009), and on the other hand from research-evaluating pilot sites in England and Wales (Shaw et al. 2009). Broadly, these reports highlight that the system is bureaucratic, overly time-consuming, inflexible, rigid and standardised, does not support professional judgement and distracts from a focus on children and young people. Shaw et al. (2009: 613) found that 'the evidence suggests substantial problems in accomplishing government policy aspirations'. In response to these reports, the government published a range of updates, guidance and funding proposals to support improvements and developments in ICS (these documents are available from http://www.dcsf.gov.uk/everychildmatters).

For you, as a developing interprofessional social worker, it is important to be open to embracing new technologies, whilst recognising the strengths and potential weaknesses of ICT. ICT is a tool that, developed and used appropriately, can support collaborative information sharing but is no substitute for professional judgement, interpersonal interaction and ethical practice.

In considering your practice in the interprofessional environment, particularly having highlighted the importance of professional judgement and ethical practice, this section of the chapter would not be complete without mention of how you gain support and develop in practice. In particular, the processes of professional supervision and your development as a reflective practitioner are key to providing the structure to guide your practice with others.

Activity 5.3

You may have experience of supervision and reflective practice, either from a practice learning opportunity or from direct employment in the social care sector. If you have not had these opportunities yet, then draw on your understanding of supervision and reflective practice from your studies to date to consider the following questions:

- How does professional supervision enable you to evaluate your own practice?
- How does reflective practice enable you to evaluate your own practice?
- How do these processes support your preparation and development for interprofessional social work practice?

COMMENT

Supervision will provide you with the opportunity to gain support and guidance in a setting that enables you to articulate your reflections. O'Sullivan (1999) distinguishes between professional supervision and managerial supervision. The latter is where supervision is used as 'a vehicle for management control of accountability and efficiency' (Lishman 2009: 65), whilst professional supervision 'helps social workers contain the contradictory demands, complexity and uncertainty of professional social work' (O'Sullivan 1999: 37).

Nazeera is a newly qualified social worker and has worked in an integrated Mental Health team for the past three months since graduating from university. At a recent case discussion, Nazeera felt that her assessment and views with regard to a particular service user were not taken into account by the team. Nazeera was upset, frustrated and later also became angry, as she believed her professional perspective was not being valued. She did not know why but wondered whether it was due to her lack of experience or the overt medical model that was often taken by the team.

At her next supervision session with her manager, Joanne, Nazeera described all of this and ended up in tears. Joanne had not been at the meeting, so she asked Nazeera a number of questions about what had been said, when, to whom and why. As Nazeera explained further, she thought more about the meeting and began to realise that perhaps there had been other ways she could have put forward her ideas. Joanne helped Nazeera to think through the most appropriate ways in which to present her assessment, to whom, when and how. Joanne also supported Nazeera when she attended a further case discussion, so that she could more formally present her assessment, views and ideas. Furthermore, Joanne arranged for Nazeera to participate in a short assertiveness course to give her more confidence to challenge appropriately in formal interprofessional settings.

As the example of Nazeera and Joanne illustrates, in the context of working collaboratively, supervision can enable you to evaluate your practice by discussing with your supervisor practice you have undertaken, how this was executed, what you achieved and your reflections on that practice. In a similar way, you can articulate your ideas and plans for further actions and how you might carry these out. Thus, through 'checking out', questioning and having to make your practice explicit, the processes of professional supervision and reflection can heighten your awareness of the standards, focus and effectiveness of your practice and facilitate change and development in your practice.

Canavan et al. (2009: 377), drawing on policy development work in Ireland, argue that reflective practice 'can help achieve the balance between policy and services blueprints and the realities of practice'. The concept of reflective practice stems from seminal work done by Donald Schön (1983) and has become central to social work practice and professional development. Reflection is effectively evaluation at a personal level, but evaluation that results in action, change and development of practice. Reflecting 'on action' means to ask yourself the following questions:

- How did I engage with that person?
- What did I do?
- Why did I do it? (Lishman 2009: 64)

These questions then need to be followed up by asking yourself, 'What would I do differently next time?' This is where changes to practice, learning and development are identified. The importance of professional development and reflection on interprofessional practice are further developed in the final chapter of this book, where you will have the opportunity to explore a range of ways in which you can enhance your individual practice in the collaborative environment.

In conclusion to this section of the chapter, rather than offer a lengthy textual summary, Figure 5.2 illustrates some of the key skills and processes that have been discussed as potential influences on your practice as an interprofessional social worker.

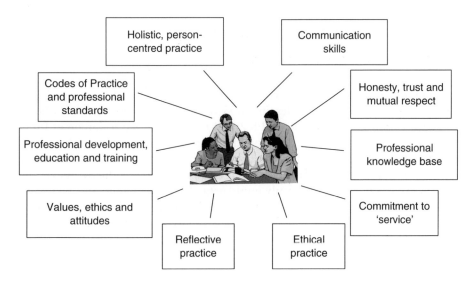

Figure 5.2   Key aspects of individual interprofessional practice

EXAMPLES OF INTERPROFESSIONAL COLLABORATION IN PRACTICE

As a way of consolidating your learning so far from this chapter, this final section draws on particular examples of collaborative processes, specifically assessment practice. Reporting on research in 2002, Hudson states that:

> In one locality alone, three approaches (to assessment) were identified: each profession separately assessed and provided information to the care manager; professions jointly visited; and professions visited separately but met to discuss their assessments. (Hudson 2002: 15)

To address some of these inconsistencies, the government has developed interprofessional shared assessment tools: the Common Assessment Framework (CAF) for children and young people progressing to pilots of the national electronic CAF (eCAF), and the Common Assessment Framework for Adults (CAFA). Each of these examples is briefly described here, with the support of case examples followed by consideration of the implications for interprofessional practice that have been illuminated through research findings. Whilst not explored in this chapter, you should note that in tandem with these developments, the concepts of 'Lead Professional Working' and the 'Team Around the Child' (TAC) are seen as key strands of effective collaborative work (CWDC 2009). You will find more information, guidance and factsheets about Lead Professional Working and the Team Around the Child on the Every Child Matters website (http://www.dcsf.gov.uk/everychildmatters/).

THE COMMON ASSESSMENT FRAMEWORK (CAF) FOR CHILDREN AND YOUNG PEOPLE

The Common Assessment Framework (CAF) for children and young people was introduced in England and Wales in 2003 as part of the Every Child Matters: Change for Children programme (DfES 2004) to promote better outcomes for children. It is a generic approach to support the assessment of children with additional needs and subsequent multidisciplinary and multiagency information sharing. Further to this, a national electronic CAF (eCAF) is being introduced. As yet, however, the CAF has not been uniformly implemented across England and Wales, being at various stages of piloting and implementation (Pithouse et al. 2009). The process of undertaking a CAF with a child and their family is envisaged as a three-stage process (DfES 2006), illustrated in Figure 5.3.

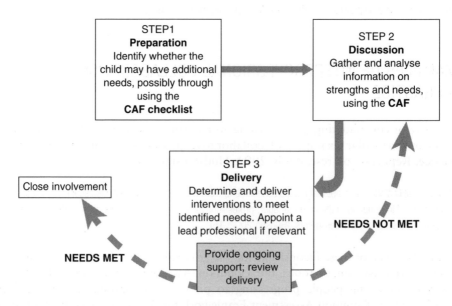

Figure 5.3   The three-stage Common Assessment Framework (CAF)

Source: DfES 2006: 13

Whilst acknowledging that it is not desirable to see this as a rigid process, Figure 5.3, taken from CAF guidance for practitioners (DfES 2006), illustrates the phases of undertaking a CAF. The first step, labelled 'Preparation', is seen to be the point where the practitioner would gather information about services the child or family may already receive. This would also include assessments that have previously been completed and details of professionals that may be working with the child. These professionals would be contacted to ensure work is not duplicated, that the most appropriate person takes forward the assessment and that ongoing or previous work is built upon. The second step in the process is 'Discussion' with the child, their family and carers. Crucially, this is not only about completing the assessment with them, but is also about ensuring that the information is appropriately recorded, with their permission. The guidance document offers further detail about this stage of the process, breaking it down into eight further substages (DfES 2006: 16–19). The next, or third, stage of the CAF process is termed 'Delivery' and relates to decisions about appropriate intervention. This is likely to involve a multiagency plan.

Whilst these stages are reflective of the recognised social work processes – assessment, planning and intervention (followed by review) – collaborative practice is overtly embedded throughout. In the following extract, Pithouse et al. (2009) describe how the CAF looks:

> The CAF in England ... is linked to a series of information and communication technologies (ICTs). First, the CAF is a Word document laid out as a series of boxes with pre-determined headings. There are also boxes for service users' comments, consents for sharing information and space for the parent's (but not the child's) signature. Second, in some areas (and eventually nationally), the CAF is completed online and stored in a local database. Some local systems include functions to complete the CAF jointly between professionals, to send as an electronic referral and to enable audit. (Pithouse et al. 2009: 600)

So there are many facets to the development and implementation of CAF, each having implications for practitioners working with children and their families and carers. First, it is a guide to a form of assessment that requires information to be sought about prescribed areas of the child and their life. The CAF aims to make it easier and quicker for practitioners to gain an overall view of the child and the services or professionals with whom they are already or have previously worked. Essentially then, for the child and their family, this should be a quicker, more streamlined, more efficient approach to interprofessional assessment. The CAF is also supported by the Team Around the Child, which brings together a small group of professionals to improve outcomes for a particular child (Cheminais 2009). From the description above, it is also clear that the CAF has an electronic element and thus requires access to ICT, confidence with using ICT and robust systems for ensuring that appropriate ethics of information sharing are embedded within electronic processes. This raises the debate discussed earlier in the chapter that practitioners tread a fine line between ethical use of personal information, whilst at the same time attempting to reduce duplication, work effectively across boundaries and ensure that children are safeguarded and can access early appropriate intervention.

CASE STUDY

CAF in practice – Anca

Anca is the middle child of three children in her family. She is nine years old. Anca's parents are Romanian and came to live in England when Anca was only two years old. Anca speaks English in school and with her friends, but Romanian is spoken at home. Her school teachers have noticed that Anca's behaviour has changed – she is usually very quiet, almost to the point of being withdrawn. Then occasionally, inappropriately and unpredictably, she will have loud outbursts, shouting at her friends and teachers. Teachers became particularly concerned when, during one of these outbursts, Anca angrily threw some schoolbooks against a wall and ran out of the classroom crying.

The school commenced a CAF, initially engaging with Anca and her parents through the home–school liaison service. A number of professionals became involved in the CAF and through the process of completing the assessment, it was established that Anca's parents had also become concerned about her behaviour and emotions. However, her parents were experiencing other problems in that her father had recently been made redundant, they were in significant arrears with their rent and her mother was suffering from acute homesickness for her home country and her family still living in Romania. The assessment resulted in a range of referrals, for example to Child and Adolescent Mental Health Services (CAMHS), a parent support group, welfare benefits and housing advice. It also enabled professionals to take a more holistic view of Anca's needs within the context of her whole family. Additionally, the school recognised that they needed to establish more creative ways of engaging with parents whose first language was not English, and so set about exploring different options that would enable more flexible, inclusive approaches to working with parents.

Research by Pithouse et al. (2009) in England and Wales found that in the realities of practice, the CAF is being implemented in a multitude of different ways. The authors refer to the 'CAF of policy' and the 'CAF of practice' (Pithouse et al. 2009: 599). Focusing on the 'CAF of practice', Gilligan and Manby (2008) undertook a qualitative evaluation of CAF processes in two areas of northern England over a six-month period. Drawing on the experiences of practitioners and service users, their research highlights the challenges of meaningfully involving children and their carers/parents in that 'practitioners have often found parental involvement a far from straight-forward process' (Gilligan and Manby 2008: 182). Additionally, research shows that there is a 'very low level of getting consent or the explicit views of children within the assessment process' (Pithouse et al. 2009: 605).

Research reports also indicate that as an interprofessional practitioner working with these processes, you would need to develop a wide range of skills and have access to supervision, guidance and support (Brandon et al. 2006; Gilligan and Manby 2008). Figure 5.4 summarises the findings of the national government evaluation of CAF in respect of factors that facilitate or constrain its implementation and consequently related collaborative practice.

THE COMMON ASSESSMENT FRAMEWORK FOR ADULTS (CAFA)

You may recall from your learning in Chapter 2, that following the White Paper *Our health, our care, our say* (DoH 2006), consultations and piloting of a Common

Factors that help implementation	Factors that hinder implementation
• Enthusiasm at grass-roots and managerial level	• Lack of agency join-up/conflicts of interest
• Perceived benefits for families	• Lack of professional trust
• History and practice of good multiagency working (including previous common assessment or Lead Professional Working (LP))	• Mismatch between the 'vision' and the practice
• Learning from others	• Confusion and muddle about processes
• Existing IT systems	• Skill/confidence gaps
• Clear structure for CAF/LP process	• Lack of support
• Good training, support and supervision	• Anxiety about increased workload
	• Anxiety about new ways of working

Figure 5.4   Factors that help or hinder the implementation of the Common Assessment Framework (CAF)

Source: Brandon et al. 2006: 401

Assessment for Adults (CAFA) have been taking place. As stated in that earlier chapter, there are many similarities between this development and the Common Assessment Framework for Children and Young People (DfES 2006), discussed in the previous section. The CAFA also builds on much of the work previously undertaken to implement the Single Assessment Process for older people (SAP) (DoH 2004), outlined in Chapter 2, and the Care Programme Approach (CPA) in mental health (DoH 2008). Thus, the CAFA removes the artificial boundary of 'older age', whilst also aiming to improve communications and information sharing across professionals and agencies through multidisciplinary assessment, planning and intervention.

It is also apparent that the process of the CAFA, its aims and objectives strongly align with the principles of the personalisation agenda discussed in Chapter 4. Personalisation is underpinned by a commitment to more holistic ways of working across professional boundaries (Hudson and Henwood 2009) and local partnerships that focus on the needs, wishes and feelings of service users. Thus, as the common assessment processes is piloted and implemented, it is likely to have a greater emphasis on self-assessment, person-centred planning, supported by coordinated local services and plans (DoH 2007). In their consultation on the proposals for the CAFA, the Department of Health suggests that the CAFA will establish the basis of a shared set of information, to include:

• Demographic information and contact details.
• Reason for referral/contact.

- Personalised information giving an holistic overview of the individual's physical, mental and social well-being, and environment factors.
- Specialist assessment outcomes.
- Care and support planning information made up of contributions from a range of professionals. (DoH 2009*b*)

CASE STUDY

CAF for Adults in practice – Jim

Jim worked as a farmhand all of his life and, despite retiring some four years ago, still lives in the old cottage belonging to the farm. Jim lives with his wife, Jessie. They have three grown-up children, all of whom have settled and have families and work many miles away from their parents. At 69, Jim was healthy and active, until having a sudden severe stroke whilst gardening last summer. Jim and Jessie live in an area where the Common Assessment Framework for Adults is being piloted, so prior to his discharge from hospital, a CAFA was commenced. The CAFA identified not only Jim's care, support and rehabilitation needs, but also the impact of those needs on Jessie's life.

Following pre-discharge home visits involving social workers, district nurses and occupational therapists, the CAFA was developed to include risk assessments and the contributions of each specialist. The CAFA system enabled timely information sharing and messaging between professionals at the crucial hospital discharge time. Jim and Jessie were given a named care coordinator as lead professional who would work with them and the other professionals to develop and manage his care and support plan. Whilst the pilot CAFA process in this area was underpinned by new technological solutions, for example enabling online self-assessment via a Web portal, Jim and Jessie had never used a computer and did not wish to have one. Thus, whilst the professionals could share agreed information through secure online systems, other methods of involving Jim and Jessie had to be found.

The technology, however, did allow for the person-centred, multidisciplinary assessment information to be captured and used to support the Resource Allocation System calculation (the calculation of available budget to meet assessed need). This meant that the care coordinator had accurate and clear information about how a personalised individual budget for Jim might be configured, so that the options could be explained and discussed with him.

The CAFA is at the early stages of piloting and implementation as part of an ongoing national evaluation. Importantly, the process cannot be seen in isolation, as it interfaces with other policy and legislative directives across health and social care, such as those related to eligibility criteria, charging for services, carers' assessments and data protection. The pilot sites share common goals to trial and evaluate innovative approaches to information sharing across professionals and organisations, however each area is working with a different range of partners across service users, health and the voluntary and private sectors. Much like the CAF for children, putting this into practice requires complex changes to processes and practicalities of assessment and care planning, professional development for staff related to skills and knowledge for collaborative practice, and the development of appropriate supporting technology.

> ## Activity 5.4
>
> The Common Assessment Framework is a relatively new approach and process for assessment with adults:
>
> - What might the strengths of the CAFA be?
> - What might the limitations of the CAFA be?
>
> From your reading of this book and particularly this chapter thus far, write down your thoughts on the above questions.

COMMENT

Given that there is limited literature on the implementation of the Common Assessment Framework for adults at this time, our knowledge has to be drawn from the experience of putting the Single Assessment Process (SAP) and the Care Programme Approach (CPA) into practice, and learning from evaluations of the CAF for children. Thus, for example, Brandon et al.'s (2006: 401) findings on factors that help or hinder implementation of CAF, shown earlier in Figure 5.4, are potentially transferable to the implementation of CAFA. Furthermore, recent guidance on the CPA in mental health considers the personalisation agenda, integrated care pathways and a whole systems approach (DoH 2008). In an evaluation of SAP pilots reported in 2006, Dickinson highlights three major factors that impacted on implementation:

- The process of implementing policy and change, including education, training, management, leadership, changing roles and ownership of the processes.
- Health and social care boundaries which had implications for working relationships, and trusting the assessments of others.
- Communication and sharing of assessments with particular regard for practical issues such as using paper-based versus technology-based systems. (Dickinson 2006)

A later evaluation of the implementation of a single shared assessment tool in Scotland not only raised concerns about unrealistic implementation timetables, but also suggested that the technicalities of the tool and process became key drivers with less attention given to issues of culture, professional development and staff time required to implement effective collaborative working (Eccles 2008). Furthermore, as discussed earlier in this chapter, concerns about meaningful participation of service users, the challenges of technology and the misuse of jargon are all potential difficulties to be mindful of. Yet, there seems little doubt that the overall concept offers a useful framework for interprofessional working, incorporating and building on existing practices, taking forward the personalisation agenda, with a focus on person-centred practice and co-production with service users.

CONCLUSION

Throughout this chapter, you have been furthering your understanding and awareness of your professional identity and your practice as an interprofessional social worker. As I write this conclusion, I am aware that much of the research and literature that has underpinned the discussion in this chapter may be perceived as offering a negative view of interprofessional practice, often highlighting challenges, things that can go wrong and things that are seemingly very difficult to overcome. However, the reality is that this knowledge is the foundation for enhancing practice, understanding, reflecting on and learning from experiences to improve outcomes for service users. Moreover, in this chapter, you have read about a number of strategies that will support your professional development and enhance your practice, including reflection, supervision, evaluation, education, training and reinforcement of professional identity and values. In Chapter 8 of this book, you will find more ideas and guidance to enable you to embed the skills of effective collaboration into all aspects of your professional practice. However, it is recommended that you continue your studies by moving on to Chapter 6 which builds on your learning from this chapter by examining the discipline and profession of social work and its specialist contribution to interprofessional practice.

FURTHER READING

Brandon, M., Howe, A., Dagley, V., Salter, C. and Warren, C. (2006) 'What appears to be helping or hindering practitioners in implementing the Common Assessment Framework and Lead Professional Working?' *Child Abuse Review*, 15(6): 396–413.

This journal article reports on a national evaluation of the early implementation of CAF and Lead Professional Working in twelve English pilot sites. The journal article summarises elements of the full research report which is over ninety pages long, but can be downloaded from the 'Publications' pages of the Department for Children, Schools and Families website (http://www.dcsf.gov.uk). If you are particularly interested in the CAF for adults, you are encouraged to read this article and reflect on how learning from the implementation of these processes with children and their families is helpful to practitioners and agencies implementing similar processes in work with adults.

Hammick, M., Freeth, D., Copperman, J. and Goodsman, D. (2009) *Being interprofessional* (Cambridge: Polity Press).

Many aspects of Hammick et al.'s text address issues that you have learnt about in this chapter. Aimed at students and practitioners from across the spectrum of health and social care professions, you will find the book offers helpful models and concepts that are relevant to all collaborative partners. The book starts by setting the context for interprofessionalism, before developing a focus on learning about, from and with one another. There is a chapter on information sharing (Chapter 9) and a number of tables, exercises and illustrations.

Horner, N. (2009) *What is social work? Context and perspectives*, 3rd edn (Exeter: Learning Matters).

You will find this text provides an accessible approach to helping you further your understanding about the fundamental basis of social work, what it is, how it is defined and how it has developed through history. Horner devotes individual chapters to specific aspects of practice, such as working with children, young people and families and social work with older people.

INTERNET RESOURCES

Every Child Matters, Department for Schools, Children and Families (DCSF), Information Sharing
 – http://www.dcsf.gov.uk/everychildmatters/strategy/deliveringservices1/informationsharing

Within the website section on 'Integrated working', the DCSF have located these informative pages on 'Information sharing'. Here you will find access to guidance, a DVD, factsheets and an information sharing quiz. Whilst this particular site and its materials are specifically related to Every Child Matters, the underlying issues and principles are transferable to all aspects of social work practice. Crucially, the site includes the freely downloadable resource *Information sharing: Guidance for practitioners and managers* (DCSF 2008a). Please note that as there are ongoing changes in governmental structures and the Internet sources that reflect them, references to the Department for Children, Schools and Families, and Every Child Matters websites may be sourced through the Department for Education at http://www.education.gov.uk.

6

THE CONTRIBUTION OF SOCIAL WORK TO THE COLLABORATIVE ENVIRONMENT

Chapter summary

When you have worked through this chapter, you will be able to:

- Consider the identity of social work as a profession.
- Reflect on the distinctive, unique contribution that social work makes to interprofessional collaborative practice.
- Debate competing views about the concepts of professionalism and professional identity, for example critiquing issues such as professional power, authority, boundaries, cultures and how they influence effective interprofessional practice.
- Discuss the challenges and opportunities of interprofessional social work.
- Identify the complexities of interprofessional teamworking.

INTRODUCTION

The focus of this book is partnership working with all stakeholders, service users, carers, across professional disciplines and agencies. However, the specific intention of this chapter is to consider the contribution of, and implications for, the profession of social work. Following on from the 'seeds sown' in Chapter 5, in this chapter you will develop your understanding about the significance of professional identity for the whole profession. Integral to this is an exploration of the problematic nature of professionalism in interprofessional practice. Professionalism is, on the one hand, associated with standards, recognition of professional contribution, validity and uniqueness, whilst on the other hand, it is associated with self-interest, power and authority.

This section of the chapter also considers the dangers of stereotyping and the challenges that changing approaches to practice may hold for social work's professional identity. With this understanding, you will have the opportunity to consider debates about what is distinctive about social work, as a profession and discipline, and how it contributes or adds to interprofessional practice. However, with the notion of a professional group being distinctive, having a specialism or some expertise, comes the risk that it may fail to recognise its interdependency on other professions and adopt behaviours that 'protect and promote its own perception, its own priorities, its own prescriptions as the whole story and to claim power and resources on that basis' (Loxley 1997: 49). These behaviours equate to 'professional protectionism', which is explored in this chapter through the specific examples of professional discourses, power, differing perspectives leading to diversity in models of working and professional values and ethics. Given all of these challenges, in the final section of the chapter you will have the opportunity to develop your understanding of how teams of diverse professionals can effectively work, learn and develop together.

THE IDENTITY OF SOCIAL WORK AS A PROFESSION

In Chapter 5, you considered the concepts of professional identity before exploring what this means for individual social workers in practice. The chapter referred briefly to the complex, dynamic, multidimensional and potentially problematic nature of the concepts of 'professional' and 'professionalism'. From this foundation, and to set the context for the debates that follow, you will start this chapter by considering the particular characteristics of social work as a role and profession. With an increased understanding of the identity of social work as a profession, you will be encouraged to reflect on the contribution of social work to the interprofessional, collaborative environment.

Professional identity could be seen to emerge from professional cultures, which are shaped by professional education, pervasive shared values, ethics, common rules and constraints, particular ideologies, knowledge bases and ways of understanding. Whilst such cultures may change over time, they are manifested in particular habitual ways of working that might be considered as professional norms. Within professions, there may also be subcultures that are evident within specific subgroups, for example mental health social workers or residential social workers.

In the UK, it could be argued that the professional identity of social work is, at least in part, defined by its professional bodies:

- The General Social Care Council for England – http://www.gscc.org.uk
- The Care Council for Wales – http://www.ccwales.org.uk

- Northern Ireland Social Care Council – http://www.niscc.info
- Scottish Social Services Council – http://www.sssc.uk.com

Since 2005, the title 'social worker' has been protected by law in England (Care Standards Act 2000), which means that only those who have achieved qualification through a recognised programme of study and are registered on the social care register can describe themselves as social workers. As well as being suitably qualified, in order to register, individuals must agree to abide by the Code of Practice for Social Care Workers (GSCC 2002). In your studies through Chapter 5, you read about the connection that was made between standards, codes of practice, values and ethics and notions of professionalism. Additionally, professionalism was seen to stem from our knowledge base – the theories, research and models that are embedded in our approach to practice.

These different aspects of social work are drawn together in a 'Statement of Social Work Roles and Tasks for the 21st Century' that takes account of the changing role of social work and aims to define its value (GSCC 2008). Despite Lymbery's (2006: 1123) caution that 'there has been a long debate about the nature of professions, alongside an equally lengthy dispute about whether or not social work can legitimately be characterized as one', the GSCC is clear that:

> Social work is an established professional discipline with a distinctive part to play in promoting and securing the wellbeing of children, adults, families and communities. (GSCC 2008: 4)

A further statement about the role of social work, but this time specifically about work with adults, was developed through a collaboration of the Department of Health, the Association of Directors of Adult Social Services, the British Association of Social Workers, Skills for Care and the Social Care Association. Their view is that:

> Social workers bring together knowledge, skills and values and put these into practice, according to the experiences, relationships and social circumstances of the people they work with. (DoH, ADASS, BASW, SfC and SCA 2010: 1)

The full statement, titled 'The Future of Social Work in Adult Services in England', was developed following a recommendation by the Social Work Task Force. The Task Force itself was set up in response to the death of Baby P(eter) and the progress report by Lord Laming (2009) (both are discussed in Chapter 2 of this book). Among a range of recommendations, the Task Force proposed further legitimisation and regulation of the profession through the concept of social workers being 'licensed to practice' (DCSF 2009c). This is underpinned by a proposal to develop a national career structure and an effective national framework for professional development, by strengthening and building on the social work qualifying degree.

Overall, these changes in the position and regulation of the discipline of social work can be seen as both a strength and a constraint for the profession. On the one hand, the profession has arguably achieved some equity – in terms of status, standards and education – with many of those professions with which it works, whilst on the other hand, the work of social workers is more regulated, measured, standardised and scrutinised than it has ever been – the latter point raising concerns about the scope for professional judgement and autonomy.

Furthermore, as we have seen in Chapter 4, the landscape of practice is changing, with consequent changes to the roles, knowledge, skills and attributes that the practitioner needs to acquire (Hudson and Henwood 2009). Whilst the recent statement about adult social work is clear that there is a key role for social work in the future of services (DoH, ADASS, BASW, SfC and SCA 2010), there remains a question as to whether changing approaches to services will lead to changing professional identities. In other words, as approaches to practice change, through increased emphasis on co-production, personalisation and interprofessional work in health and social care, our understanding of social work as a profession with a distinct identity may undergo change, too. New ways of working require 'new types of workers' and in 2003, the Department of Health established the 'New types of worker' (NToW) programme across social care, to encourage employers to be more proactive in developing a workforce that could meet the user-led, collaborative approach to services. These developments are taking place across all areas of service and are seen to complement drivers toward more integrated practice. There is no space or need to examine the developments of NToW further here, but if you are interested to know more, visit the Children's Workforce Development Council website (http://www.cwdcouncil.org.uk), or, for adult care services, the Skills for Care website (http://www.newtypesofworker.co.uk).

On writing the last few paragraphs about the changing status of the profession and the developing new ways of working, I realise the significance of the statement from the International Federation of Social Workers (IFSW), cited in the first section of Chapter 5, that indeed social work in the twenty-first century is undergoing transformation and that a static definition of social work is not possible or perhaps desirable.

Having established the complexity of social work as a profession, we can consider the contribution and place of social work in interprofessional practice. It has been suggested that the creation of multidisciplinary teams may represent a threat to the social work identity (Lymbery 2006). An example might be the establishment of a set of common core skills and knowledge for all practitioners working with children (http://www.cwdcouncil.org). Importantly, though, according to Whittington, we can achieve effective interprofessional collaboration if practitioners 'learn, negotiate and apply the following:

- What is common to the professions involved;
- The distinctive contribution of each profession;
- What may be complementary between them;
- What may be in tension or conflict between them; and
- How to work together.' (Whittington 2003b: 48–9)

Whittington (2003b) refers to this as a 'set of understandings'. The first four of these understandings are of interest at this point in the chapter, although you will have an opportunity to consider the last point in relation to teamworking later in the chapter.

Reflective practice question 6.1

Reflect on your experiences both within your studies and, if you have had them, during practice learning experiences.

- As a social worker, or a student social worker in practice, what do you consider to be your distinctive, unique contribution to interprofessional, collaborative practice?

It may help you to think about particular instances in practice, such as professional meetings, case discussions, joint assessments or other aspects of work shared across disciplines and/or agencies.

- What did or can your professional participation add to the process?

COMMENT

You may have thought about the importance of the social, holistic perspective that you could bring to discussions, or you may have been able to advocate for the service user or be the professional who empowered the user to have their voice heard in a particular situation. Perhaps you felt that there were certain skills or approaches that you brought to the 'table', or maybe you were able to offer a different way of working, a theoretical approach or intervention. Another important facet of social work is our value base, including anti-oppressive practice, person-centred work and our empowering approach. Many of these aspects of social work practice are highlighted by Lymbery (2006), who argues that the value of social work is in the entirety of these attributes, rather than in each one separately – this idea is captured in the phrase, 'The whole is worth more than the sum of the parts.' Further to this, the GSCC statement on social work tasks and roles, referred to earlier, states that social work is distinctive because of the combination of several features, which they group under the following headings:

- The characteristic situations of people who receive social work support or intervention;
- The functions for which social work skill and expertise are required;
- The types of outcomes social work enables people to achieve;
- The combination of knowledge, values and skills it possesses;
- The evidence base for social work practice;
- The methods and approaches it applies to assess, record and respond to people's rights and needs.
  (GSCC 2008: 10–11)

The more recent joint statement, related specifically to the roles and tasks of adult social work, reinforces the view that social work offers a distinct approach that:

provides an important contribution to multi-disciplinary teams, to support better outcomes. It also complements the contribution of other professions. Social workers in multi-disciplinary teams bring a perspective of the whole person, rather than just their symptoms or circumstances. Seeing the individual in the context of their family, friends and community, and reflecting their hopes and fears for their own future is where social work can bring an important contribution to the work of the team. (DoH, ADASS, BASW, SfC and SCA 2010: 2)

It appears, therefore, that a distinct professional identity may be important for effective interprofessional practice. Interestingly, Lymbery (2006), writing in the context of work with older people, suggests that the role of social work in interprofessional practice has yet to be defined, but he goes on to argue that there is a potential opportunity to develop a central role for social work. Perhaps the statement referred to above, on the role of social work in adult services, begins to seize that opportunity.

Therefore, it can be seen that as a profession, social work has specific and distinctive characteristics, knowledge base, roles and functions. However, for all professional disciplines that lay claim to discrete characteristics, there is the parallel risk of being stereotyped. Commonly based on unfounded generalisations, stereotypes are powerful images and ideas that promote very limited and inaccurate perceptions about certain groups of people, in this case groups of professionals:

Sixty-five years ago there was a stereotype of a social worker as a moralistic upper-middle-class older woman who carried a basket of food and had little understanding of the people she tried to help. The image is much more positive today, reflecting the improved professional nature of the training and services provided. (Zastrow 2009: 54)

Activity 6.1

Think about your own perceptions of other professional disciplines and roles. Work through the list below and write down three or four key things that you feel describe that profession or role. If you are good at drawing, you could also sketch how you think a typical professional in that role might look:

- Hospital nurses
- Community psychiatric nurses
- Midwives
- Health visitors
- School teachers
- Housing officers
- Volunteers
- General practitioners
- Police officers

(Continued)

(Continued)

- Consultant psychiatrists
- Youth offending officers
- Any other professional role/s that you have experience of working with

and finally ...

- Social workers!

COMMENT

You could argue, quite legitimately, that I am forcing you to make generalisations in this exercise. However, exploring your own perceptions of other professional disciplines in this way can often surface stereotypical views that you were previously unaware of. It should be noted, too, that such generalisations are not always negative, but are always oversimplified generalities.

Following research undertaken to explore undergraduate students' perceptions of different health and social care-related professionals, it was found that:

Students appear to have a more definite image or firmly held stereotypes of doctors, pharmacists, nurses, midwives and social workers as professional groups. There is also some indication from these profiles that doctors and pharmacists are seen as one subset of the HSC professions with distinguishing features such as high academic ability and being able to work independently. Midwives, nurses and social workers are another subset with distinguishing features such as high interpersonal skills and being a team player. (Hean et al. 2006: 178)

Hean et al. (2006: 179) conclude that the extent to which students hold stereotypical views of others 'may have crucial implications for future working relationships between professional groups'.

In many ways, this whole book is about working relationships between professional groups, but it is vital that you do not lose sight of the consequences of those relationships for the service users' experience. With regard to issues of professional identity and characteristics, service users may bring their own perceptions and stereotypical views, but importantly when people have support needs, they do not always attempt to define those needs as related to a specific disciplinary sphere. The following quotations are taken from a qualitative research study, published by the General Social Care Council that investigated the views of service users on a range of issues related to professional boundaries (Parker 2009). As part of this study, service users offered their perceptions of social workers working in mental health teams:

What is the role of a social worker in a mental health environment? I don't know. It's a hard question to answer because I don't know how they are trained. (Parker 2009: 7)

I don't know what social workers' therapeutic role is. What I found inappropriate was when a social worker comes to me and asks me – have I any side effects with my medication? I don't know what my side effects might be and as far as I'm aware social workers are not trained in medicines or their side effects. (Parker 2009: 7)

You need to clearly define the role of the social worker within these teams. For the service users. If it's not defined for service users, how can it be defined for the management? How can it be defined for the monitoring? (Parker 2009: 10)

I think it's really important when you first meet your social worker that you should be given clear guidelines on why they are there. Who their manager is, and what department they work for. (Parker 2009: 33)

Finally, for this section of the chapter, the following extracts from the two statements of social work roles and tasks referred to earlier, provide a summary of much of the discussion so far. These extracts appropriately lead into the next section of the chapter, where the tensions raised by professional power, cultures and professional boundaries are debated as they highlight the significance of the professional attributes for effective interprofessional collaboration.

Social work is good at building bridges with other disciplines and agencies, and helping overcome some of the barriers and gaps between different professions which can create difficulties for people with multiple or complex conditions using several services …

Social work should be clear and confident about the expertise it has developed, the distinctive contribution it makes and the features of its work particularly valued by people who use its services. It also has a responsibility to feed its knowledge, values and approaches into the work of joint teams to inform their culture and widen their frame of reference. Professionals working together in multi-disciplinary settings, in children's centres or community mental health teams, for instance, are likely to become familiar with one another's areas of expertise, and able to apply a common core of knowledge, whilst recognising when a particular professional's skills are required. (GSCC 2008: 17–18)

According to Shaping Our Lives National User Network:

People value a social work approach based on challenging the broader barriers they face; they place particular value on social work's social approach, the social work relationship and the personal qualities they associate with social work. These include warmth, respect, being non-judgmental, listening, treating people with equality, being trustworthy, open, honest and reliable and communicating well. People value the support that social workers offer as well as their ability to help them to access and deal with other services and agencies. (DoH, ADASS, BASW, SfC and SCA 2010: 2)

THE CHALLENGES AND OPPORTUNITIES OF INTERPROFESSIONAL SOCIAL WORK

In Chapter 5, I drew your attention to the problematic nature of the concepts of 'professional' and 'professionalism', being ideas that sociologists and organisational theorists have studied in depth. In this chapter, you have already considered how professional identity and stereotypical assumptions of others may impact on inter-professional practice (Hean et al. 2006) and have significant consequences for how users experience their interaction with services (Parker 2009). This section of the chapter takes these debates to more depth, analysing key aspects of the dimensions of professionalism that are particularly problematic from the perspective of inter-professional working: power, culture and boundaries.

Leiba and Weinstein (2003: 71) refer to the work of Hudson (2002) and West and Poulton (1997) when outlining some of the 'commonly found difficulties' in interprofessional collaboration, which include:

> status differentials, uni-professional education which socializes professionals into different language and different values; a lack of understanding about each other's roles; employment by different organizations with different cultures and in different locations; and a fear of 'dilution' and associated professional protectionism.
> (Leiba and Weinstein 2003: 71)

'Professional protectionism' refers to a concern to maintain not only what is 'special' or distinct about a profession and the skills and knowledge that it can bring, but also being unwilling to share and wanting to maintain professional power. The influential sociologist, Johnson (1972) describes how occupational specialisms have historically evolved to control entry and maintain standards in the professions, which effectively results in domination and exclusivity by denying knowledge and skills to others. Arguably, this elitism and protectionism is evident through the self-interested nature of much professional self-regulation. Yet, as the context of practice changes, the ability of professions to perpetuate this power and authority may be questioned, given the issues of managerialism, neoliberalism and bureaucracy discussed in previous chapters. The nature of professionalism can therefore be seen to be dynamic and changing. Thus, for example, professions such as social work and nursing might be seen to be still in the process of professionalisation, also coined 'the professional project' (Larson 1977), in that they continue to pursue, negotiate and explore ways in which further to establish, secure and maintain professional status, as such they may be treated as 'semiprofessions' (Etzioni 1969; Deverell and Sharma 2000).

Professions by their very nature are 'boundary setting practices' (Deverell and Sharma 2000), yet some practices can result in impermeable boundaries between professions and significant difficulties in interprofessional working. Professional identities and cultures, as you have seen, can present barriers and drivers to collaborative working. Wenger (1998: 145) explains how identity, in this instance identity as a whole profession, can raise issues of inclusion and exclusion, with individuals either being included as participants within the boundaries of that collective identity, or being outsiders, or sometimes being 'peripheral participants'.

In the same way, the use of language through professional discourses can facilitate interprofessional practice, creating common understanding and meaningful dialogue, or it can reinforce professional power, protectionism and boundaries resulting in practice that excludes. Truly effective collaboration and partnership can only be possible where all parties, including service users, can both understand and be understood; clear communications are fundamental to successful interprofessional, collaborative practice.

Reflective practice question 6.2

Reflect on your experiences of being in practice settings, perhaps on your practice learning opportunities and of working with others through your social work studies.

- Make a note of any examples you can think of where you felt that you were disadvantaged by not understanding some of the discussion or written communications. If you cannot think of examples from practice, you may have experiences in your private life where you have been confronted by complex professional jargon.
- Go back over your examples and reflect on why that may have been the case. What forms of language or terminology were being used that made it difficult for you to participate?
- How did you feel about this at the time?
- Did you do anything about it at the time? If so, what? Was it effective in enabling you to understand everything you needed in order to feel confident to participate fully?

Now think about your own behaviour and practice:

- Are you aware of any occasions when you have used jargon or acronyms or complex language that may have excluded others?
- If so, how did this happen? Were you aware of this at the time?
- How will you ensure when you are In practice, that you do not use language and terms that others cannot understand?

COMMENT

It is sometimes difficult to think of examples where you felt you were disadvantaged by not understanding some of the discussion or written communications as we often put these experiences to the 'back of our minds', possibly because they can make us feel uncomfortable at the time. Some possible examples might be taking part in an interprofessional meeting, or when first joining a new team where familiar protocols and tasks lead to the use of acronyms or familiar terms, or during your studies when working with a group who make reference to materials, theories or authors you have not yet read. Beyond work and studies, you may have experienced professional services where the language is not familiar to you, perhaps an electrician or computer technician explaining some work needed in your home or your general practitioner telling you why they are prescribing a particular medication for you.

It is likely that you found it difficult to understand because unfamiliar specialist terms or acronyms were frequently being used and were not being explained. In this position, you can feel very disadvantaged and excluded, sometimes to the point of frustration and anger, or you may have made a decision to disengage, to 'sit back' and not put in the effort to continue the dialogue. If you felt confident enough, you may have asked for an explanation, or even challenged the continued use of specialist terms, but often when this is integral to the conversation or discussion and continues throughout it, it is very difficult to engender change at this point. It is worth noting that even to raise such questions takes a good deal of confidence, as alongside it goes the risk of exposing a lack of knowledge and understanding which may further the feeling of being 'othered', being on the 'outside', excluded. If you were able to reflect on ways in which you may have used jargon or specialist language in your interactions with others, then you may be able to analyse how this happens and why.

We all use professional jargon at times and unfortunately are unaware of it because the terms and acronyms are so familiar that they become embedded in our everyday language, but sometimes there are more sinister underlying issues. Jargon and complex terminology can be used to portray expertise, special knowledge and hence power and control, effectively putting a distance between those 'in the know' and those who do not know. It is then, of course, as stated above, very difficult to challenge. Whilst the exercise and this discussion were related particularly to professionals working together, these issues are clearly paralleled in communications with service users and carers. Hence, it is very important that through reflective practice and self-critique, you maintain your awareness of the language you use and ensure that, in a non-patronising way, you always check that those with whom you work understand your verbal and written communications.

Stanley and Manthorpe (2001), in their exploration of mental health inquiries, highlight *The Case of Jason Mitchell* report (Blom-Cooper et al. 1996, cited in Stanley and Manthorpe 2001: 87) as being an inquiry that 'considered issues of status and professional territorialism explicitly when exploring failures of professional communication'. The report

> focused on the failure to pass on valuable information from the prison medical service to health and social services staff. This report also noted the failure of medical staff to recognize the validity of information concerning Jason Mitchell's homicidal fantasies which was collected by an unqualified and unsupervised occupational therapy technical instructor. (Stanley and Manthorpe 2001: 87)

Thus, you have seen how language and discourse can reinforce boundaries and difference with clear implications of power imbalance. Significantly 'power' and 'professional culture' are considered to be key inhibitors or enablers of collaborative practice (Barrett and Keeping 2005: 22–6). Similarly, O'Sullivan cautions that 'power is an important but problematic area when stakeholders meet together' (1999: 67) and moves on to state that 'the illegitimate use of power ... can be termed *oppression*' (p. 67, italics in the original). Indeed, in your reading of this chapter so far, you have seen how the misuse of power, through imposing stereotypical assumptions, professional protectionism and using language that excludes, results in disadvantage, disengagement and ultimately oppression.

Within his discussion of collaborative decision-making, O'Sullivan (1999) considers a number of dualisms or tensions, as illustrated in Figure 6.1.

Each of these opposing issues is further discussed in O'Sullivan (1999), so it is not my intention to duplicate that work here. Indeed, you may recognise having read about a number of these issues already in this chapter and in preceding chapters.

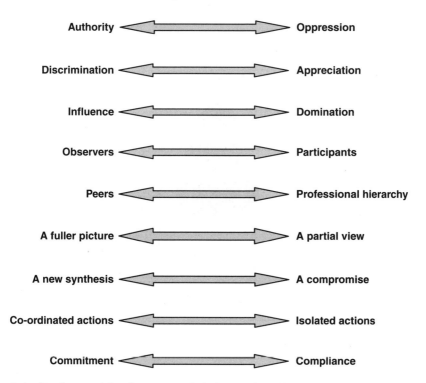

Figure 6.1   Dualisms arising from power imbalances in collaborative decision-making

Source: O'Sullivan 1999, pp. 67–74

Reproduced with permission of Palgrave Macmillan

Significantly though, O'Sullivan (1999: 77) reinforces the importance of fostering 'a climate of co-operation, collaboration and mutual support' through ensuring constructive engagement and appreciation of a common purpose: 'The healthy exchange of differing opinions in the context of endeavouring to achieve a consensus is different from individual stakeholders or factions being embroiled in personal feuds, in-fighting or win/lose arguments'.

Lymbery agrees that 'inter-professional rivalries do affect the quality of collaborative working that can be developed' (2006: 1121) with three main areas in which these rivalries are apparent:

- Professional identity and territory;
- Relative status and power of professions;
- Different patterns of discretion and accountability between professions. (Hudson 2002 cited in Lymbery 2006: 1121)

Additionally, divisions and tensions can arise as a result of professional groups using diverse ways of understanding, contrasting theories and differing models for practice.

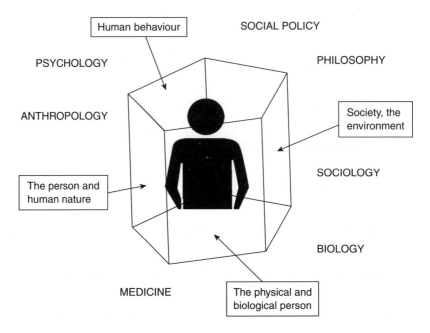

Figure 6.2   Differing perspectives and models for practice

As a result, each professional group may adopt different priorities and foci which can, across the professions, even appear contradictory. Effectively, this means that because the underpinning basis of the knowledge that informs their practice may be very different, the resultant practice, expertise and methods of working subsequently vary. The underpinning knowledge, theories and ways of understanding are developed from different disciplines or schools of thought. You can think of this as a number of different lenses through which a phenomenon is seen: different approaches or views of the work will affect your explanation, predictions and interventions. Figure 6.2 illustrates this.

In Figure 6.2, the central shape represents how different perspectives are gained when viewed from different angles, or, as explained above, different lenses giving different views. The diagram only represents some examples from a vast range of ways of understanding the needs and experiences of people in society. Very broadly speaking, sociology, philosophy and social policy focus on people within their society, the environment and the macro concepts and influences on people's lives, whilst biology, anthropology, medicine and psychology start from perspectives on human behaviour that consider the person and human nature. Some of these schools of thought concentrate more on the physical, biological being. Social work commonly draws its knowledge and theories mainly from sociology and psychology, often called a psychosocial approach. Importantly, these different approaches are not mutually exclusive and in practice people are likely to draw on a variation of knowledge and understanding. Additionally, it is recognised that these 'divisions are not static, but develop into specialisms and expertise in particular and specific knowledge and skills' (Loxley 1997: 49).

Earlier, I suggested that the different perspectives and approaches to practice can appear contradictory. Helpfully, though, Loxley (1997: 31) describes the range of approaches to practice as being on a continuum, which 'has implications for different models of intervention'. At one end of this continuum, Loxley places a biomedical model and, at the other, a psychosocial model (1997: 31). The more common labels of the 'medical model' and the 'social model' emerged from the disability movement and service-user groups. In short, the medical model of disability is seen to focus on the individual and their biological needs, with the aim of finding a cure through scientific means. At the other end of Loxley's (1997) continuum, the social model of disability centres on understanding the social and environmental factors that result in a range of barriers that individuals face. Social work places itself very firmly at the 'social model' end of this continuum. It is clear, though, that these two ways of understanding, the two lenses, have very specific knowledge bases that result in diverse ways of working. Furthermore, reminding you of the earlier part of this chapter, these different perspectives also result in distinct professional identities. However, as stated earlier, particularly for interprofessional collaborative working, 'in reality these different models of intervention are rarely discreet' (Loxley 1997: 31).

It is crucial to appreciate that to gain a holistic, full and in-depth appreciation of an individual's situation, all possible perspectives should be valued and brought together. The following extract from Hugman (2009) gives a useful, if amusing metaphor:

The Elephant

Let us imagine a group of people who are blind-folded and then asked to describe an elephant. One person notes that it is tall, thick and round like a tree trunk (she has hold of its leg); another that this animal is long, thin and moves in a manner like a snake (he has hold of its trunk); a third person notes that this animal is flat, leathery and very flexible so that it can flap (she is holding its ear). All perceive the elephant in very different ways; all are describing the same animal. However, while each of these insights tells us something about an elephant, only by standing back and considering the animal as a whole do the separate parts make sense so that we may appreciate the contribution they make to the holistic nature of this animal. (Hugman 2009: 1151)

This metaphor stresses the importance of valuing the knowledge that different perspectives can bring to understanding, for when looking at an elephant we are rarely aware of the specific details of each part of its anatomy. Similarly with interprofessional practice, without the expertise, knowledge and range of ways of understanding that different professionals contribute, our practice would be 'blindfolded' or severely limited.

As you have seen from earlier in this chapter and from your reading of Chapter 5, different professional groups are not only differentiated by their history as a profession, their knowledge bases and modes of working, but also by having different values, codes of practice or conduct and professional ethics. Professional ethics, which might be understood as behaviours and commitments, are drawn from core values (Davis and Sims 2003). Eby and Gallagher (2008: 119) set out a number of different ways in which we might approach and understand ethics in professional practice, but state that in health and social care ethics there are four basic principles:

- Respect for autonomy.
- Beneficence or doing good.
- Non-maleficence or avoiding harm.
- Justice.
  (Edge and Groves 1994; Banks 2001; Beauchamp and Childress 2001; all cited in Eby and Gallagher 2008)

Thus, whilst there may be variations in different disciplinary ethical statements and the codes of practice that arise from them, we can take comfort that at the highest level of generality, the most closely allied professions will hold to very similar professional ethics. However, it would be fair to argue that the last statement may be somewhat simplified and overly broad, because it does not take account of the whole range of professional groups that you may work with and hence the potential variation in approaches to ethics. Professional ethics is, in itself, a whole complex area of academic research and study. It is only possible here to draw your attention to the concept and to raise the issue that ethics embody the principles and 'rules' for good practice (Davis and Sims 2003) and, as such, are integral to effective interprofessional collaboration.

Activity 6.2

Thinking back to Hugman's (2009) elephant, what we might call the elephant of collaborative practice, make some notes on how you think this range of approaches to practice might manifest themselves within teams. In other words:

- How do different professionals, with potentially differing ways of working, values, ethics and ideals, practise together?
- Are there particular aspects or processes of practice that are influenced by these issues?
- How does the interprofessional team function, given these differences?

COMMENT

These are all 'big' questions with many possible answers. It would be interesting to take these questions with you when you are in practice and attempt to answer them in relation to the particular collaborations that you are part of. Questions like these were, in part, the focus of the research undertaken by Anning et al. (2010) and their findings shed some light on some of the possible answers. The case study summarises this aspect of Anning et al.'s (2010) research.

A research example

The research investigated multiprofessional teamwork in five integrated childcare teams in one city. One aspect of the research project explored how the different professionals constructed and gave meaning to their work together. It was found that each of the teams tended to hold a dominant model of explanation, but alongside this, there was also evidence of a secondary or complementary model of explanation in use. The researchers acknowledge, however, that these models were not always universally held across an entire team, with weaker and stronger versions of the prevalent model being drawn on by different team members and at different times. In the light of this, it is stated that: 'we should not imagine therefore that professional identities give rise to universally fixed or shared explanatory models' (Anning et al. 2010: 58). The particular aspects or processes of practice that were influenced by the different models included assessment, defining need, identifying predisposing factors and interpreting current problems being faced. Across the five teams, the dominant models included the medical model, a systems theory approach, a needs-based model and a social, structural model. The researchers summarise the professional models of understanding by suggesting that:

> The existence of internal variations in explanatory models suggests that there are dilemmas for our teams in achieving cohesion, through negotiating shared practice models, while at the same time embracing and celebrating complexity and diversity. (Anning et al. 2010: 58)

Notably though, it was evident that 'each team was … part of a web and network of resources that had a profound impact on their practice' (Anning et al. 2010: 59).

Source: Anning et al. 2010

This chapter now moves on to consider how professionals work and learn together in teams, as part of an interprofessional network.

SOCIAL WORK IN THE INTERPROFESSIONAL TEAM

In Chapter 3 of this book, as part of a discussion about relationships and networking, you read about how multiagency and interprofessional teams are seen as one mode of relationship, amongst others. This was illustrated in Figure 3.2 and you may wish to revise that section before reading further.

Earlier in this chapter, I referred to Whittington's (2003b) ideas about what practitioners need to learn and apply in order to establish effective interprofessional collaboration. According to Whittington, one important area that practitioners need to address is 'how to work together' (Whittington 2003b: 48–9). Through research, it has been recognised that the most effective teams work together by recognising, balancing and transferring between a number of roles (Belbin 1993). Whilst commonly applied in management studies, Belbin's theory of team roles is relevant and applicable to contemporary social work, particularly in helping us to understand the complexity of interprofessional teamworking (Figure 6.3).

Team role	Contribution	Allowable weakness
Plant	Creative, imaginative, unorthodox. Solves difficult problems	Ignores incidentals. Too pre-occupied to communicate effectively
Resource investigator	Extrovert, enthusiastic, communicative. Explores opportunities. Develops contacts	Over-optimistic. Loses interest once initial enthusiasm has passed
Co-ordinator	Mature, confident, a good chairperson. Clarifies goals, promotes decision-making, delegates well	Can be seen as manipulative. Offloads personal work
Shaper	Challenging, dynamic, thrives on pressure. Has the drive and courage to overcome obstacles	Prone to provocation. Offends people's feelings
Monitor evaluator	Sober, strategic and discerning. Sees all options. Judges accurately	Lacks drive and ability to inspire others
Teamworker	Co-operative, mild, perceptive and diplomatic. Listens, builds, averts friction	Indecisive in crunch situations
Implementer	Disciplined, reliable, conservative and efficient. Turns ideas into practical actions	Somewhat inflexible. Slow to respond to new possibilities
Completer finisher	Painstaking, conscientious, anxious. Searches out errors and omissions. Polishes and perfects	Inclined to worry unduly. Reluctant to delegate
Specialist	Single-minded, self-starting, dedicated. Provides knowledge and skills in rare supply	Contributes on only a narrow front. Dwells on technicalities

Figure 6.3   Belbin team roles

Reproduced by kind permission of Belbin Associates (http://www.belbin.com)

There is no space here to describe each of these roles in more detail, but the important learning point is that this theory argues that the success or failure of a team, in this case the interprofessional team, is dependent upon its team role composition: diverse teams, with a balance across these roles, being stronger and more effective. By understanding and being aware of how these roles are enacted within teams, it may also be possible to understand some of the team dynamics, where the team functions well and where its effectiveness is most challenged.

Reflective practice question 6.3

Reflect on times when you have worked as part of a team, either as part of your studies or within your practice learning.

- What role do you take in a team?
- What is your approach to teamworking, your style and behaviour in this setting?
- Can you recognise other roles in the team and who adopted those roles?

COMMENT

You may find it difficult to answer these questions as they require a heightened sense of self-awareness and it can be difficult to reflect retrospectively on your own behaviour. You could always ask your peers, those who were in the team with you, or your practice assessor or colleagues, what their perceptions are of you as part of a team, but be prepared that you may be surprised by their responses! Reflect on these things with caution, though, as you and others that you work with may take on different roles at different times and when working in different teams with different purposes. For more information on Belbin's theory, a description of the team roles and the Belbin team role assessment tool, you can access the 'home to Belbin team roles' at http://www.belbin.com.

As well as this recognition that there are different roles within teams, Øvretveit (1997*a*: 14) has distinguished two different types of multiprofessional teams:

Co-ordinated profession teams: which he defines as 'referral and communication meetings for separately organised and accountable professional services'.

Collective responsibility teams (CRT): which are defined as 'teams in which members are accountable as a group for pooling and using their collective resources in the best way to meet the most pressing special needs of the population they serve'.

Øvretveit's collective responsibility teams are fully integrated teams that are funded and recognised as teams in their own right. The teams that were part of Anning et al.'s (2010) research discussed earlier would fall into this category. Such teams have collective, agreed priorities and

share responsibility with the others for working out how to serve a priority client referred to the team – they cannot opt out because that type of client or need is not a priority for their profession or agency. On the other hand, members of such teams cannot undertake work with a client or patient which they are not competent to do, because they remain accountable as individual professionals for their case work. (Øvretveit 1997*a*: 14–15)

Such cohesion and clarity, however, is not achieved simply by putting together a range of professionals with the skills and abilities to take on Belbin's (1993) roles. You may, for example, have come across the influential work of the educational psychologist, Tuckman (1965), who described how groups move through different stages as they come together, grow and develop. The stages are given memorable names:

Forming: A comfortable first stage where people get to know each other and the task.

Storming: As the team moves to address core issues, minor confrontations and challenges arise.

Norming: Having clarified understanding about roles, responsibilities and tasks, the team settles into a more cohesive and goal-directed mode.

Performing: Tuckman is clear that not all teams will achieve this stage where really effective work takes place. At this stage, there is recognized interdependency, group identity, loyalty and goal focus. (Tuckman 1965)

Reflective practice question 6.4

Building on your reflections from Reflective practice question 6.3, where you considered your role and the roles of others in a team or teams you have had experience of, reflect on how that team worked together, how they achieved their goals and moved forward together:

- Are you able to recognise Tuckman's stages as having occurred in that team?
- What does this mean for interprofessional collaborative practice?

COMMENT

It is likely that you recognised some if not all of the stages outlined by Tuckman (1965). When you next have the opportunity to work in a newly constituted team, you might reflect on Tuckman's stages again and consider how his ideas apply to the team you are in. For interprofessional practice, whether different professionals are coming together as an integrated team or are working together across agencies, Tuckman's stages give some important insights for how these teams might evolve. For example, teams can expect a 'storming' stage as part of their development and growth: if handled constructively, these challenges can be beneficial to the eventual effectiveness of the team. However, so often in practice, team members change through normal career movements or through job-role changes that result in different representation from agencies. When such changes occur, a team may revert to earlier stages in its development, potentially resulting in reduced effectiveness.

The dynamic changes and complexity of collaborative work is captured in the concept of 'knotworking', which arises from Engeström's work on activity theory (Engeström 1999, 2008). In Chapter 3 of this book, you were briefly introduced to how activity theory might help us to describe the processes that occur in interprofessional, collaborative practice. In later work, with new research, Engeström (2008) focuses on how we understand and use teams. He argues that the shape and form of teams is becoming more complex, flexible, transient, self-governing and distributed (Engeström 2008). From these notions of knots and knotworking emerges a description of collaboration that is creative, complex, fluid and yet stable. Importantly, being mindful of earlier discussion in this chapter, the metaphor describes how organisations and professionals as single threads are weak, but collectively knotted together, are very strong even in unstable conditions (Engeström 2008).

Activity 6.3

Return for a short while to Chapter 3 and any notes you made whilst studying that chapter. In Chapter 3, you were introduced to a number of theories, models and frameworks that can help us to understand the

(Continued)

(Continued)

dynamics of collaborative practice. Make some brief notes in response to the questions below. Your work here will supplement and reinforce your understanding of the theoretical perspectives:

- Having read about the concept of 'knotworking', which, as you have seen, emerges from an activity theory perspective, are there other theories (from Chapter 3) that may support, enhance or overlap with this idea?
- Do these other theories help us to understand 'knotworking' in collaborative practice? If so, which theories and how do they aid our understanding?

COMMENT

You may have recognised how some aspects of 'knotworking' may overlap with social exchange theory and Communities of Practice, for example. Social exchange theory could be seen to further the notion of 'knotworking' by describing the specific nature of those knotted relationships within interprofessional practice. Furthermore, Chapter 3 set out how the Communities of Practice are characterised by their collective identity, mutual engagement, joint enterprise and shared repertoire (see Figure 3.3) (Wenger 1998), thus reflecting the strong ties of 'knotworking'. The theory of Communities of Practice emerged from a social-learning theory basis, and thus Communities are seen through engagement and participation to have learning and development embedded within them (Wenger 1998).

As a student social worker on his final practice learning opportunity, Robert attended a care review meeting to discuss George's apparent changing needs. George, aged 61, had been in receipt of a range of care services almost all of his life, having learning difficulties and autism. Robert listened carefully at the review as George's carers from the respite unit, the day centre and the outreach support team explained the issues. After the meeting and following a discussion with his supervisor, Robert contacted George's key worker and suggested a meeting with the clinical psychologist. After some planning, two meetings were held. These meetings were attended by care staff from all of the services that George accessed, including his advocate, a volunteer. At the first meeting, carers discussed their various concerns and the clinical psychologist suggested alternative approaches and strategies to meet George's needs. One example related to George frequently asking different carers the same question. It was apparent that he might receive many different answers or the same answer in different ways. This confused and frustrated George. It was suggested that the staff record these questions and one clear answer, so that all staff could respond with the same clear, consistent answer. At the second meeting, four weeks later, the new ways of working with George were reviewed. It was evident that the shared learning across the carers and the increased consistency in the way they worked with George, had enabled him to be more settled and confident.

CASE STUDY

The example of Robert and George, above, is a good example of how learning together can make a significant difference to practice and the experience of service users. There have been many developments in recent years to encourage and support cross-disciplinary approaches to professional learning, education and training. Loxley (1997: 66) suggests that learning together is 'held as an essential component of collaboration'. For example, within the social work degree, universities have to demonstrate 'that all students undertake specific learning and assessment in the following: partnerships working and information sharing across professional disciplines and agencies' (DoH 2002b: 3–4). Furthermore, the National Occupational Standards for social work require that you can 'work within multi-disciplinary and multi-organisational teams, networks and systems' and that you 'contribute to evaluating the effectiveness of the team, network or system' (Key Role 5). Furthermore, in the Common Core of Skills and Knowledge (DfES 2005) for everyone who works with children, young people and their families, the areas of expertise required include multiagency working and sharing information.

Interprofessional education and training provide the opportunities for different professionals to come together, develop expertise collectively, share knowledge and begin to understand the range of perspectives that individual disciplines may have on a topic. Writing in the context of child protection services, Corby et al. (2009: 77) argue that joint training establishes 'a common purpose and sympathetic evaluation and understanding of each other's roles'. However, whilst there is a continued belief in the efficacy of joint-training initiatives, there is limited understanding about how interagency and interprofessional training influences practice (Charles and Horwath 2009). Loxley (1997) also acknowledges the limitations of interprofessional learning. There does seem, however, to be more research emerging in this area – see, for example, Carpenter et al. (2009) who set out to develop an evidence base for interagency training to safeguard children and undertook their research in study sites across four areas of England. Among the wide-ranging findings, it is clear that training participants had not only increased their knowledge of the topic (i.e. child abuse or domestic violence), but had furthered their confidence in working with service users and other professionals (Carpenter et al. 2009). Similarly, Anning et al. (2010: 86) examined sharing of knowledge across the teams in their research and found that 'multi-professional teamwork offers opportunities for professional knowledge and expertise of individuals to be distributed across the team'.

There is, therefore, a growing body of evidence to support a view that collaborative practice is furthered through learning together. Adding some caution, Loxley argues that interprofessional learning needs

> to be recognised not as an end in itself but as a necessary if insufficient condition for effective collaboration. At one level it should address current service development, emphasising current competence and efficiency, but at another be seen as an ongoing professional education aiming to promote understanding, innovation and effectiveness. (Loxley 1997: 68)

CONCLUSION

Social work has been recognised throughout this chapter as being a distinct profession that can make a significant contribution to interprofessional collaborative practice.

Your learning across this chapter and Chapter 5 has focused on the importance of professional identity and its implications for you as a social worker, for the individuals you work with, and specifically in this chapter, for the wider profession. Through the chapter, you have examined some of the challenges social work faces in collaborative practice, such as professional protectionism, differing discourses, stereotyping and power imbalances. In the latter part of the chapter, you learnt about the ways in which interprofessional teams might work, learn and mature together. Yet, perhaps the biggest question posed here, and admittedly not fully answered, related to the future for social work, its identity and place as a profession, as approaches to practice, service configurations and delivery change. It seems fitting, therefore, for the last words of this chapter to come directly from the document titled *The future of social work in adult services in England* (DoH, ADASS, BASW, SfC and SCA 2010):

> There is a role for social work in a transformed world, where new roles can be developed as well as existing ones strengthened. Social work skills will continue to be important contributions to assessment, care planning and review, but social workers may do more direct social work with a stronger therapeutic element. (DoH, ADASS, BASW, SfC and SCA 2010: 3)

FURTHER READING

Anning, A., Cottrell, D., Frost, N., Green, J. and Robinson, M. (2010) *Developing multiprofessional teamwork for integrated children's services: Research, policy and practice*, 2nd edn (Berkshire: Open University Press).

This book is the result of a substantial research project funded by the Economic and Social Research Council. During this chapter and in earlier chapters, you have been introduced to various elements of this text which reports the research findings in detail. With a strong theoretical basis, the book offers a clear illustration of interprofessional practice in integrated children's teams.

O'Sullivan, T. (2011) *Decision making in social work*, 2nd edn (Basingstoke: Palgrave Macmillan).

I have drawn on O'Sullivan's first edition (1999) and this second edition (2011) at different points in this book. O'Sullivan adopts an interprofessional approach to exploring how social workers make decisions in practice. In this second edition, you will find O'Sullivan's Chapter 4, 'Working together', particularly relevant to support your learning about interprofessional collaboration in social work.

Øvretveit, J. (1997a) 'How to describe interprofessional working', in J. Øvretveit, P. Mathias and T. Thompson (eds), *Interprofessional working for health and social care* (Basingstoke: Palgrave), pp. 9–34.

This first chapter in the edited collection, whilst now becoming quite dated, offers a really clear and comprehensive analysis of different approaches to teamworking in health and social care. This includes helpful diagrams and explanations about a range of approaches to team structures and team processes.

Malin, N. (ed.) (2000) *Professionalism, boundaries and workplace* (Florence, KY: Routledge).

If you are interested to develop further a critical understanding about the complexity of the concepts of professional power, authority and boundaries, this edited collection of chapters examines professionalism, drawing on examples from health and social care. Analysing the inherently political nature of the concept 'professional', the authors suggest that partnerships and participation are appropriate goals for professionalism. In this chapter, I have drawn on Chapter 2 (Deverell and Sharma 2000), however, each chapter of this book is highly relevant to the critical debates about how issues of professionalism impact upon interprofessional collaboration in social work practice.

INTERNET RESOURCES

The Children's Workforce Development Council – http://www.cwdcouncil.org.uk

This site relates specifically to practitioners who work with children, young people and their families across the whole spectrum of the social care workforce. This is a very 'busy' site with a specific area, under the 'Areas of work' tab, dedicated to integrated working. The site has regular updates on the Common Core of Skills and Knowledge and includes policy guidance and real life examples.

Skills for Care – New Types of Worker – http://www.newtypesofworker.co.uk

This site relates specifically to practitioners who work with adult service users across the whole spectrum of the adult social care workforce. As I write this book, the site would be largely of interest to employers as much of the content relates to wider workforce developments. However, it is very likely that as the role of social workers and social care workers more broadly changes and develops, this site will become more relevant to individual workers. That being said, there are a number of links from this site that you may find very useful.

7

INTERPROFESSIONAL PRACTICE IN THE COLLABORATIVE ORGANISATION

Chapter summary

When you have worked through this chapter, you will be able to:

- Describe the organisational context of interprofessional practice.
- Recognise different approaches to structuring and organising interprofessional working, in particular the different forms of organisations that are represented in:

  o Integrated care services.
  o User-led organisations in the collaborative environment.
  o Local Involvement Networks.

- Describe the concept of organisational culture.
- Examine the role of leadership and management in the collaborative organisation.
- Consider how interprofessional practice at the organisational level is evaluated.
- Reflect on some examples of evaluative research into collaborative practice.

INTRODUCTION

As part of your developing knowledge base for practice, you need to gain an understanding of the organisational context of practice, your workplace and the processes that go on within it (Thompson 2010: 139). This chapter will therefore help you to consider the organisational context of interprofessional collaborative practice. As you read this chapter, you will have the opportunity to look at different organisational approaches to meeting the collaborative 'agenda', including integrated care services. You will also learn about the role of service user-led organisations in the collaborative environment. Having considered different organisational structures and forms, you will further your learning from previous chapters with regard to the notion of culture and values: in the case of this chapter, on the subjects of organisational culture and its influence on professional practice. As part of the discussion in this section of the chapter, you will explore ways in which you can influence the culture of organisations that you might work in.

The notion of change and influence is embedded in the chapter, particularly in the section that discusses the roles of leaders and managers in collaborative organisations. This is followed by consideration of how collaborative practice at the organisational level can be evaluated and how services and the practices within them can learn and develop through evaluation. To draw all of this together, at the end of the chapter there are some examples of evaluative research and some fictional case studies of different forms of interprofessional, multiagency partnership. Crucially, though, I conclude the chapter by reinforcing the point that effective interprofessional organisational structures and cultures must enable social workers and other practitioners to focus on the centrality of service users' and carers' needs, wishes and feelings.

THE ORGANISATIONAL CONTEXT OF INTERPROFESSIONAL PRACTICE

As you have seen in the earlier chapters of this book, enhancing and embedding effective interprofessional collaborative working has been an aspiration of national and local health and social care strategy for some decades. As explored in Chapter 2, this aspiration has been driven by a shower of legislation, policy and guidance, which in turn have resulted in different local organisational structures, models and strategies. In this section of the chapter, you will explore variations in the organisational context of interprofessional practice. There may be many ways to understand, categorise or group different approaches to organising multiagency, partnership working: here, I have drawn on three examples.

The first example offers a way of understanding collaborative arrangements between organisations by describing the pattern of relationships between them. The relationship may be coordinated through a hierarchical, a networks or a market model:

- **Hierarchical structures**: These have clear and overt lines of control, accountability and responsibility. Hierarchical collaborative relationships are commonly found in single integrated organisations, with named senior managers and chief officers.
- **Market structures**: Collaborative organisations that depend on market structures separate the functions of purchase from those of provision, or commissioning from those of production. Commonly, the relationships are coordinated through processes which require specifications, contracts or service agreements between the parties.

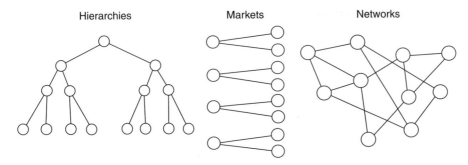

Figure 7.1   Hierarchies, markets and networks

- **Networks**: Collaboration organised by networks reflect a more informal approach, with each professional having connections and mutual engagement with other professionals in the network. This concept is mirrored in the notions of knotworking (Engeström 2008), discussed in Chapter 6, and social exchange theory and Communities of Practice (Wenger 1998) outlined in Chapter 3.

The simple illustrations in Figure 7.1 help to visualise the different relationships explained by these broad concepts. Most clearly, in my view, through the connecting lines, the illustrations show the different dependencies and accountabilities that exist in these relationships. I am not suggesting that one is better than another, merely that these are different approaches to working together. It is suggested, however, that:

> There may be some situations where conceiving of the collaboration as a network may have an advantage over something more contractual, for example scope for immediate flexibility, or innovative responses to change circumstances. This should in no way detract from the importance of partnership agreements, but it does suggest that turning an effective network into a contract or into a hierarchy inevitably alters something profound about the nature of relationships. (Glasby and Peck 2006: 25)

The second example offers a way of thinking about partnerships that is two-dimensional, examining the depth and breadth of the arrangements, as illustrated in Figure 7.2.

The third way of describing different configurations of organisational collaboration arises from research exploring a wide range of multiagency initiatives undertaken by Atkinson et al. (2002, cited in Atkinson et al. 2007). The research found that by identifying organisational form and function, the range of multiagency configurations can be classified into a five-model typology. The five models are summarised below (the authors provide diagrammatic representations of these in their original text):

- **Decision-making groups**: Providing a forum for professionals from different agencies to meet, discuss and make decisions.
- **Consultation and training**: In which professionals from one agency enhanced the expertise of those of another by providing consultation and/or training.

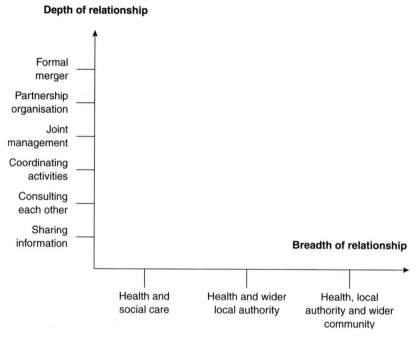

Figure 7.2   The depth and breadth of multiagency partnerships

Source: Glasby and Peck 2006: 14

- **Centre-based delivery**: In which professionals from a range of agencies operated from a single centre to deliver a more coordinated and comprehensive service; they also became more aware of what the roles of other professionals and disciplines entailed.
- **Coordinated delivery**: Where a number of agencies involved in the delivery of services were coordinated by a coordinator with the responsibility for pulling together previously disparate groups.
- **Operational-team delivery**: In which professionals from different agencies worked together on a day-to-day basis to form a multiagency team that delivered services directly to clients. (Atkinson et al. 2002, cited in Atkinson et al. 2007: 18)

These three different ways of explaining and understanding the range of approaches to working together can assist us to think about, reflect on and compare the organisational contexts of practice.

Activity 7.1

Review the reading, Figure 7.1 and Figure 7.2 which outline three different ways of classifying and under-standing interprofessional organisational structures and relationships. Then identify a multiagency service

(Continued)

(Continued)

that you know of, either that you have experience of working in or using, or perhaps that you learnt about through your studies so far:

- Is this service organised as a hierarchy, a market or a network? Note down some of the characteristics of the service or organisation that you feel illustrate this approach.
- Using Glasby and Peck's graph (Figure 7.1), plot where you think that service might be and write a few notes to explain why you think it should be in that position.
- Finally, using the same example, decide which of Atkinson et al.'s (2002, cited in Atkinson et al. 2007) five models you feel is most likely to apply to the form and function of the service, and why.

If you can work on this with a colleague who has knowledge of the same service, that would be interesting, but undertake this activity separately first, before discussing the similarities and differences between your responses.

COMMENT

With regard to the first part of the activity, you may have found it difficult to be clear about how the service is organised. Often it is possible to see all three forms of coordination in operation with, for example, hierarchical structures operating with internal 'markets', but it is also possible to see evidence of more informal networking also taking place. You may recall from your reading of Chapter 3, in particular Figure 3.2, how commonly modes of interaction and, in this case, coordination, are interconnected and may overlap. Crucially, though, it is usually possible to identify that one form or another is more dominant in how the organisation operates and achieves its objectives. For the second part of the activity, Glasby and Peck (2006) suggest that, broadly speaking, adult and children's services may be plotted as being at very different positions on this graph, reflecting their different approaches and starting points. They plot adult services as being at the point between 'formal merger' and 'health and social care' on the lower axis; whilst children's services have wider relationships, being plotted at the further end of the lower axis, but only to the level of 'consulting each other' on the vertical axis. The services that you have in mind may be somewhere in between, of course, and indeed services continue to develop and change so there may be debate about whether Glasby and Peck's placings on the graph remain accurate. With regard to the five models, you will recognise that some of these categories may overlap, for example decision-making groups, and consultation/training may be embedded in practice in one area. These categories are also not specific about how these organisational forms are managed or led, which is an issue that you will read more about later in this chapter.

Particular issues that must be clarified at an organisational level, regardless of the structural arrangements for collaboration, are the processes that impact on finance and budgets, in particular the processes for commissioning or purchasing services. In Chapter 2, you learnt about lead commissioning (section 75 of the NHS Act 2006), being a formal agreement that one of the statutory partners takes responsibility for the strategic activity of commissioning services. This usually includes assessment of need, mapping need in a community or area, having an overview of current services and potential service gaps and making decisions about arranging and paying for service provision. In effect, this means that one organisation, such as the local authority or local NHS Trust, could commission the whole range of services for a specific user group, such as those with learning difficulties or older people, with agreed contributions being paid by the relevant partners. You may also have come across the term 'Joint Commissioning', which refers to a process in which the partners work more collaboratively to achieve this. So, rather than delegation as in 'lead commissioning', this is a joint responsibility. Both of these approaches aim to provide more effective collaborative working, efficient use of resources and an improved overview of services provided, so that service users experience a more coherent service.

Clearly the scope and complexity of the organisational context for collaborative practice is vast. Multiagency collaborations can include organisations that vary greatly in size and emerge from a wide spectrum of backgrounds, with different priorities, funding arrangements, legislative status and regulation. Thus, statutory bodies, private agencies, user-led organisations, voluntary, charitable, social and community groups (often referred to as third-sector organisations) can make up the complex mix of partners in practice. However the multiagency collaboration is configured, it will be attempting to bring together a range of different practices and potentially diverse service users and carers, including, for example, black and minority ethnic groups. This will include each organisation's explicit stated policies, priorities, procedures, processes, values and regulations, alongside those that are more implicit and less tangible. These factors may all make up the unique organisational culture, a topic you will learn more about in the next section of this chapter.

As such, multiagency organisations or even less formalised collaborations may be likened to different forms of communities or populated areas such as cities, towns and villages, each one varying in size, in its history, in its culture, in its politics and in the way it supports and maintains itself, being also made up of different communities and cultures. Cities, towns and villages are frequently identified as having connections to certain industries or trades, or perhaps having a specific function in the wider nation. They often also have particular characteristics. You can develop this metaphor further by considering potential likenesses between collaborative organisations and cities/towns/villages in how they are governed, how decisions are made, how consensus and disagreement are expressed, how growth and development come about and, crucially, how the different components come together to function as a whole. Whittington (2003a) visualises a continuum of collaborative arrangements, with less integrated, ad hoc cooperation at one end and integrated services, such as Care Trusts, at the other.

INTEGRATED CARE SERVICES

Services that are 'integrated' can be seen to be at the furthest point of the models you explored earlier from Glasby and Peck (2006) and Atkinson et al. (2002, cited in Atkinson et al. 2007), where there is depth of collaboration and 'operational-team delivery'. Integrated care is recognised as being a 'core component of health and social care reforms across Europe' (Lloyd and Wait 2006: 5):

> [Integrated care] is a coherent set of methods and models on the funding, administrative, organisational, service delivery and clinical levels designed to create connectivity, alignment and collaboration within and between the cure and care sectors. (Kodner and Spreeuwenberg 2002, cited in Lloyd and Wait 2006: 9)

Thus, integrated services aim for total systemic coherence of procedures, rules, priorities and approaches to governance: 'a single system of needs assessment, service commissioning and/or service provision' (Thistlethwaite 2007, cited in Institute of Public Care 2010: 6). In the UK, the various configurations of care trusts are commonly seen to be the vehicles for the delivery of integrated care services. More recently, as care trusts have become larger and more complex, they have tended to be characterised by vertical integration, bringing together professionals and agencies responsible for different stages and levels of the commissioning and delivery of health and social care. However, where the trust or other collaborative agency brings together professions, services and agencies undertaking similar activities, providing similar stages and levels in the care pathway, this can be described as horizontal integration.

Integrated services result in social workers being increasingly located in large, complex, multipurpose organisations (Cree and Davis 2007; Whittington 2003a). Whilst there are strengths to this 'joined-up' approach, it also begs the question as to whether such large organisations may become like monopolies in the world of business, with all the resultant problems of domination, control and excessive power. The fundamental principle for integrated care is 'to improve the quality and appropriateness of services and support received by users ... and ... service user experience and outcomes' (Thistlethwaite 2007, cited in Institute of Public Care 2010: 6). However, you will recall from your reading of Chapter 4 of this book, how service users may feel disempowered and insignificant when working with professionals from large and complex integrated services. Similarly in Chapters 5 and 6, I referred to the work of Barrett and Keeping (2005) and O'Sullivan (1999), respectively, in highlighting concerns about how professional power, compounded by collective strength (as in integrated organisations), can inhibit collaboration with service users and may be experienced as oppressive.

For individual practitioners, the experience of working in large, multipurpose, integrated services may be very different from working in a uni-professional organisation. Although, the reality may be that as a result of the increasing pace of change, in many areas, practitioners may not be fully familiar with any one form of organisation as, according to Cree and Davis's (2007: 156) research, many staff felt that they were in a 'state of permanent reorganisation'.

Much of the literature that explores the organisational context of collaborative practice refers to the structures, designs and approaches evident in statutory agencies providing health and social care services. Increasingly, particularly with regard to current drives towards personalisation and independent living, user-led organisations are working with statutory, private and other third-sector agencies as key partners in the development and provision of services.

USER-LED ORGANISATIONS IN THE COLLABORATIVE ENVIRONMENT

The Social Care Institute for Excellence (SCIE) describe user-led organisations as being:

> run by and controlled by people who use support services, including disabled people of any impairment, older people, and families and carers. They were set up to promote giving people more choice and control over how their support needs are met. (SCIE 2009)

A national research study, commissioned by the Department of Health, found that there are a range of user-led organisations with different structures, priorities and foci, but commonly they have been established by people with particular impairments for self-help and peer support (Maynard Campbell et al. 2007: 43). Some user-led organisations serve to meet the needs of particular minority groups, some are affiliated to larger organisations, whilst others are small social enterprises and others have charitable status, yet overall the majority consider themselves to be service providers (Maynard Campbell et al. 2007: 43). They may, for example, provide advocacy, peer support (particularly with regard to individual budgets or direct payments), information, advice and training. Further to this, it is worth noting that as the landscape of practice changes, increasing numbers of newly qualified social workers are working within the voluntary and charitable sector, including in social enterprise settings and user-led organisations.

User-led organisations therefore make important contributions to multiagency collaborations. They commonly focus on local issues and have specialist insight into how the needs of the particular group of service users can most effectively be met. 'They are a local un-tapped source of knowledge about access, participation and empowerment issues' as 'users have more vision and more experience (in their condition, coping, support, self help). They have shared knowledge and experiences that unite them' (Maynard Campbell et al. 2007: 68). However, the research indicates that user-led organisations may struggle to develop fully effective collaborative relationships due to competitive environments operating in health and social care (Maynard Campbell et al. 2007: 68).

Similar to user-led organisations are the English Local Involvement Networks (LINks), which you read about in Chapter 4. These are community-led groups which are made up of members of the public who may or may not be current users of services, their aim being to support service providers to enhance services by informing them about what the local community likes and dislikes about local services. LINks rely heavily on volunteers undertaking different aspects of the LINk activities. Indeed, many of the organisations that you may work with in the collaborative environment may draw upon the skills and resources of volunteers to widen the scope of their work. As such, you need to be aware that interprofessional practice in social work will require you to work not only with other employed professionals and those who use services, but also with volunteers.

The contribution of user-led organisations to the collaborative environment is an important aspect of your studies and, as such, it is recommended that you undertake further reading in this area. There is a vast body of literature and research available on the subject of community development that considers the practices, values and processes that support working with diverse ranges of community groups. You should give particular consideration to the specific needs, interests and contribution of all diverse groups. For example, you may wish to explore further how to develop effective collaborative working with black and minority ethnic (BME) voluntary and community organisations. You could start your further studies in this area by visiting http://www.thecompact.org.uk, which is a website that explores shared principles and guidelines for effective partnership working between government and the third sector in England. Additionally, you can freely download from this site the 'Black and Minority Ethnic Voluntary and Community Organisations Compact Code of Good Practice' (Commission for the Compact 2001).

So far in this chapter, you have read about the ways in which organisations respond to the drive for effective interprofessional, interagency, collaborative working. Apparent throughout this discussion is the need for full engagement with the diverse range of stakeholders, drawing on the range of expertise, skills and knowledge available. If you refer back to Chapter 1 in this book, where you identified the possible stakeholders and partners in collaborative practice, the possibility of working across organisations and individuals with a variety of values, priorities and perspectives is readily apparent. This complexity is also evident if you think back to my description earlier in the chapter, of collaborative organisations as being analogous to different types of communities, towns, cities and villages. Furthermore, as you learnt in earlier chapters, moves towards co-production, personalisation and increased interprofessional practice are leading to new ways of working, 'new types of workers' (see the Children's Workforce Development Council (CWDC) website at http://www.cwdcouncil.org.uk and the New Types of Worker website at http://www.newtypesofworker.co.uk), alongside new organisational forms and structures as discussed here. Crucially then, services must be proactive in ensuring that organisational cultures and structures are responsive to the diverse range of stakeholders, the changing environment and the needs of vulnerable people. In this way, organisations can harness what is known as the 'social capital', wherein the overall efficiency, coordination and standard of the service are improved through effective participation, engagement, interaction and networking. Thus, whilst the structures and models to which organisations are configured are important, organisational culture may be even more significant in determining the success of collaborative working endeavours.

ORGANISATIONAL CULTURE

In Chapters 5 and 6, the notion of professional culture was referred to. In Chapter 6, for example, you learnt how professional identities arise from the wider professional culture and how these cultures can potentially result in barriers or drivers to effective collaborative practice. In a similar way, organisations can be seen to have particular cultures.

Activity 7.2

- How would you describe what is meant by 'organisational culture'?

You may also find it helpful to look back at Chapters 5 and 6 where professional culture is discussed:

- How far are the same concepts transferable to organisations?
- Write down some of the core characteristics of an organisation that you think might be reflected in its culture.

You may find it helpful to imagine an organisation you have experience of working in, or studying in:

- If someone new to the organisation asked you 'What's the organisational culture like?' how would you reply?

COMMENT

Thompson (2010: 140) states that 'the notion of organisational culture is captured in the phrase "the way we do things round here"'. If you looked back at Chapters 5 and 6, you will have been reminded that professional cultures are linked to education, knowledge base, values, rules and constraints. In a similar way, organisational cultures reflect the organisation's history, its values, the professional knowledge base, the legal and policy context and dominant practices. Organisational cultures can also be seen to be made up of a number of intersecting cultures, including different team and professional cultures that operate within organisations. Additionally, much like professional cultures, cultures in organisations may change over time and are manifested in particular embedded ways of working, much as Thompson's phrase above suggests.

O'Sullivan (1999: 37) also links organisational culture to values and routines. As you may recall from your reading of Chapter 5 of this book, one of the characteristics of a profession or discipline is having a common set of explicit values. Similarly, for effective interprofessional collaboration, having a shared set of values is seen as essential (Davis and Sims 2003). The core values for interprofessional practice that you identified and read about in Chapter 5 will also impact on organisational culture, as they will result in attitudes that respect and appreciate difference and seek constructive resolutions to disagreement (Loxley 1997). Importantly, the culture of an organisation may significantly affect the way in which it views and engages in collaborative practice.

To some extent, the General Social Care Council (GSCC) has attempted to influence the values, culture and practices of organisations that employ social care workers by producing a Code of Practice for Employers of Social Care workers, which supports the Codes of Practice for Social Care Workers (GSCC 2002: 5):

To meet their responsibilities in relation to regulating the social care workforce, social care employers must:

- Make sure people are suitable to enter the workforce and understand their roles and responsibilities;
- Have written policies and procedures in place to enable social care workers to meet the General Social Care Council Code of Practice for Social Care Workers;
- Provide training and development opportunities to enable social care workers to strengthen and develop their skills and knowledge;
- Put in place and implement written policies and procedures to deal with dangerous, discriminatory or exploitative behaviour and practice; and
- Promote the GSCC's codes of practice to social care workers, service users and carers and co-operate with the GSCC's proceedings.

The culture and priorities of organisations are, to some degree, also influenced by the mandatory legal, policy and regulatory context in which they operate. Any organisation that provides social work or social care services, however large or small, will be subject to a range of compulsory, legislative requirements and policy drivers, many of those related to collaborative practice being outlined in Chapter 2 of this book. Commonly, organisations respond by developing local practices, some of which will be enshrined in formalised local policies and procedures.

Thus, 'the way we do things round here' (Thompson 2010: 140) may be locally accepted, often dominant practices, which can be seen both to facilitate and potentially constrain effective collaborative working. Agreed, inclusive policies and practices can ensure a consistent approach to working with service users, with effective, aligned methods of assuring standards and quality. It is also apparent from research that where there is a history of working together, collaborative ventures are more likely to succeed (Glasby and Peck 2005; Stewart et al. 2003). This may in part be the consequence of developed shared practices, but may also be the result of long-standing personal relationships building trust between agencies and individual practitioners, which according to social exchange theory is an important component of effective collaboration. Wenger (1998: 85), in his work on Communities of Practice that you read about in Chapter 3, argues that sustained engagement in shared practices reinforces interpersonal relationships and shared knowledge, but is not without potential problems. Dominant practices are not always 'best practices' and where such practices are deeply embedded in the culture of an organisation, they can reinforce resistance to change and creative thinking. Once you understand the culture and context of an organisation, you can begin to consider how it might be influenced, changed or enhanced.

Reflective practice question 7.1

This chapter focuses on professional practice in the collaborative organisation. Therefore, reflecting on your learning from the chapter, note down some thoughts about how, as an interprofessional practitioner, you might influence the organisational context of your practice. For example, think about an organisation that you have worked in, perhaps as part of a practice learning opportunity, or the organisation where you study:

- What part can you play in bringing about change and enhancing the collaborative culture?

COMMENT

You may feel that you have little power or influence to change anything in relation to an organisation's culture. Yet, 'culture is learnt, shared and transmitted' by those who work within organisations (Hafford-Letchfield 2009: 10), as it relates to a set of habits that 'only persist(s) if reinforced' (Thompson 2010: 144). So, organisational cultures and approaches can change and develop. Later in this chapter, you will learn about what it means for an organisation to be a 'learning organisation', one that is open to change and development. As an individual social worker working in an organisations, you can be a conduit for change, by challenging poor practice, asking questions, sharing your knowledge and skills and modelling effective interprofessional practice.

Petch (2008: 6) discusses the way in which individuals can be 'catalyst(s) for change' and develops the notion of 'champions', 'who will secure progress despite traditional bureaucratic and hierarchical systems' (Petch 2008: 6). However, whilst not explicit in the text, this concept does appear to relate to individuals who are in more senior leadership roles. Thompson offers a potentially more accessible approach in his notion of 'organisational operators' as people within organisations:

> who have the knowledge, skills and commitment to making a positive difference within their organization … somebody who plays a part in shaping the culture, helping to move away from destructive aspects … focusing on developing a more value-driven form of professional practice within the organization. (Thompson 2010: 150)

You may also recall from Chapter 4 of this book that I introduced briefly the idea of 'boundary spanners' (Kessler and Bach 2007, cited in Hudson and Henwood 2009) as practitioners who work across the boundaries of organisations, disciplines and/or user groups. Boundary spanners are also sometimes known as 'change agents' as they are instrumental in facilitating change within organisations. However, whilst there is a lack of clarity about the role and status of people who act as boundary spanners, Caldwell (2003, cited in Hudson and Henwood 2009: 82) proposes that they need skills, knowledge and expertise in:

- Understanding the relevant topic and substance of change.
- Project management.
- Communication, team building, negotiating and influencing others.
- 'Backstage activities' as in dealing, fixing and trade-offs.

The need to 'span boundaries' connects with systems theory thinking. You may recall from your learning in Chapter 3 how systems are perceived as 'entities with boundaries within which physical and mental energy are exchanged internally more than they are across the boundary' (Payne 2005: 144). Boundary spanners have a pivotal role in bringing about an increase in the flow of physical and mental energy across the boundaries.

Reflective practice question 7.2

Reflect on your own skills, knowledge and values as a developing interprofessional social worker. Where you have experience of working in practice, reflect upon that experience and the roles you undertook. Ask yourself:

- Have you acted as a boundary spanner at any time in your career or studies?
- Do you have the skills, knowledge and values necessary to be a boundary spanner?
- Can you identify who might be boundary spanners in organisations that you have experience of working in, perhaps from your practice learning or other work experiences?

COMMENT

As the readership of this book is likely to consist of students and practitioners at different points in their careers and study, it may be that you have not yet had the opportunity to undertake practice in a social care setting, but are in the process of developing the skills, knowledge and confidence to practice in this way. In the next chapter of this book, you will have more opportunities to reflect on your professional development. The literature that explores the role of boundary spanners and what it takes to be one, highlights a range of skills and ways of working that are deemed necessary. In my view, these are largely the same range of attributes necessary for all interprofessional practitioners. Williams (2002) highlights the importance of boundary spanners having the relational and interpersonal attributes needed to build social capital. He goes on to emphasise the importance of communication, political skills, building cultures of trust, understanding complexity and working effectively within a myriad of power relationships (Williams 2002). Trevillion (1991, cited in Williams 2002) views boundary spanners as 'cultural brokers' who need to understand other organisations and to 'make a real effort to empathise with, and respect anothers' values and perspectives'. Hence, such roles necessitate taking knowledge out and bringing knowledge back into the organisation (moving energy across the boundaries of the system) through facilitation, negotiation, coordination and brokerage.

You may feel that this role, with its complex set of skills, is a leadership or management role. However, I would argue that every social worker and interprofessional practitioner can act as a boundary spanner for parts of the time, in some aspects of their practice. For example, when attending interagency meetings, or liaising with colleagues from other organisations or professional disciplines, you can model the values and attitudes that will foster effective collaboration, sharing knowledge and taking knowledge back into your team and organisation. In some small way, then, you are 'spanning the boundary'. That being said, the roles and responsibilities of leaders and managers are critical to taking collaborative practice forward. Research findings support the view that 'effective leadership is crucial in providing an environment that values and celebrates the diversity of different professionals' (Anning et al. 2010: 105). As a result, organisational culture is shaped and nurtured by management and leadership functions (Hafford-Letchfield 2009), and it is to this subject that the chapter now turns.

LEADERSHIP AND MANAGEMENT IN THE COLLABORATIVE ORGANISATION

It is evident that a number of public inquiries and Serious Case Reviews have highlighted the need for good management and leadership, particularly in respect of partnership working (Lambley 2009). The concepts of leadership and management may encompass different roles, functions and responsibilities. Hafford-Letchfield (2009: 25) states that 'management is mainly to do with planning and organising, whereas leadership is associated with creating, coping and helping to adapt to change'. In reality though, managers have to lead and leaders have to manage, and the two are arguably difficult to differentiate. Furthermore, it is argued that all social workers have to lead and manage in respect of their work with service users, carers and other professionals (Coulshed and Mullender 2001). What is clear, however, is that effective leadership and management in organisations that provide social work services requires the skills to motivate, manage change, communicate and negotiate with others, develop and take forward strategy and vision and model good interprofessional practice. Some leaders will have specific responsibilities for developing and promoting the overall approach, values, policies and objectives of the organisation, within the financial, legal and policy context. These strategic managers can be particularly influential in shaping the culture, philosophy and style of the organisation.

The literature on management and leadership in organisations, particularly that which explores social work services, offers a wider discussion on different approaches to management, styles of leadership and models for tackling the range of managerial tasks. It is not possible in this book to discuss all of these areas, so if you are interested in taking this aspect of your studies further, I have included some useful texts in the Further Reading section at the end of this chapter. However, with specific reference to leadership and management in the context of collaboration and integration in practice, there is significance in the debate that I set out in Chapter 2 related to approaches to management that are underpinned by a neoliberalist philosophy, emphasising regulation, measurable performance, 'league tables' and statistical indicators, these approaches being known as 'managerialist' or 'new public management'. These are often bureaucratic, with a focus on inspection and accountability in one organisation. As such, these 'government-driven managerial methods and their effects' can sit in tension with imperatives to multiagency, interprofessional practice (Whittington 2003b: 45).

Further to this, Biggs (1997) progresses a debate about professionalism, the role of management and the increasing role of quality control and standards in the development of effective service provision. Biggs concludes by drawing out the importance of a focus of a tripartite partnership between services users, professionals and managers:

> Future efforts towards interprofessional collaboration must build on the strengths of management coordination, professional expertise and increased user-participation. It will then become both efficient and effective and might even be able to deliver services that people need in ways that they want. (Biggs 1997: 199)

Leaders and managers also have responsibility for managing diversity within organisations, ensuring that practices and processes are anti-discriminatory by embedding equality throughout their work. You might expect that, given the value base of the profession, leaders and managers in social work organisations would not find this challenging. However, as organisational structures change to facilitate collaborative working, as set out in the first part of this chapter, so the context of managing diversity becomes more complex. Additionally, the Equality Act 2010, which draws together previous equality legislation from the past thirty years or so, also sets out new requirements and possibilities that organisations and their managers will need to embrace.

Earlier in this section, you read about how the role of leadership is associated with change (Hafford-Letchfield 2009). This is worthy of further exploration given that, as you have seen throughout this book, collaborative social work practice is characterised by constant change. Therefore, you need to prepare yourself to work within the ever-changing context of professional practice.

Reflective practice question 7.3

Identify a time when you have had to deal with change. This might be in a practice setting or perhaps in your personal life. Reflect on how you felt about the change, what you did and why. As you look back on this change, would you now do anything differently, and if so, why?

COMMENT

Whilst it is, of course, impossible for me to know about the change you reflected on here, or the ways in which you reacted to that change, there are likely to be some common reactions. Those reactions may also differ, depending on whether the change was expected, unexpected, desired or undesired. People often resist change and the processes associated with change (Coulshed and Mullender 2001; Lambley 2009). There is little doubt that change takes time and effort, not only for those leading it, but also for those who are affected by it. Change can be associated with loss and related stages of the grieving process: denial, anger, bargaining, depression and acceptance (Kubler-Ross 1969, cited in Lambley 2009). Whilst you may not have used these exact words in your reflections on a change that you experienced, you may recognise some similar feelings and behaviours.

Organisational change in the context of social care is about doing things differently to improve outcomes for service users and carers. Some changes can be quite small and perhaps incremental, but are nonetheless significant, such as a new training course or development opportunity. Other changes might be more radical, resulting in major restructures and procedural overhauls. One approach to visualising and analysing the factors that may facilitate or hinder change is to conduct a 'force field analysis' (Lewin 1951, cited in Coulshed and Mullender 2001: 72). As shown in Figure 7.3, through identifying the different forces that may influence the change process, an illustration of this type assists in planning and predicting the process of change. When using force field analysis to depict a particular change process, the specific hindering and driving forces would be identified with the force arrows being made thicker or thinner, according to the perceived strength of that force. You could go back to your earlier reflections and,

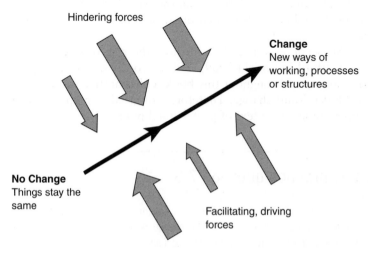

Figure 7.3   Force field analysis

using the diagram in Figure 7.3 as a starting point, add in the driving and hindering forces that influenced your response to that change. You could then reflect upon whether your force field analysis is representative of the way in which the change you experienced occurred.

EVALUATING INTERPROFESSIONAL PRACTICE AT THE ORGANISATIONAL LEVEL

Evaluating interprofessional practice is a process of assessing, appraising, asking questions, examining and investigating that practice based on particular objectives, criteria or desired features. The main aim of evaluation is to provide an evidence base for continued development, progress and quality enhancement of that which is being evaluated. Evaluations can indicate the level of success achieved by a service, project or programme, and provide the opportunity to explore, record and learn from aspects that have been less successful:

> Evaluation is now a vital ingredient in the recipe for the health and long-term survival of projects working to make a difference in people's lives. (Hoggarth and Comfort 2010: 14)

Typically, evaluations take place at predetermined intervals, although an ongoing or 'process evaluation' is more akin to action research in that it allows for learning to take place and changes to be made as the service or project progresses. With the aim of continuous enhancement, evaluations need to be self-critical and reflective. Evaluating organisational, collaborative practice is likely to focus on two key aspects: first, the processes, communications, relationships and procedures that create practice in that organisation; and second, the impact on, or outcomes for, those who use the service. To aid enquiry into the former, the following evaluation questions might therefore also be asked:

- What is the status of the partnership – i.e. is there a form of formalised agreement or does the service come together through informal networking arrangements?
- What forms of funding and resourcing arrangements are in place?
- How do different parts of the organisation communicate with each other on a daily basis? How effective is that communication?
- How are activities allocated and prioritised?
- Do policies and clear procedures exist? Are they understood and followed across all parts of the organisation?
- How are processes, communications and relationships managed in this organisation?
- How are decisions made? Who is involved in the decision-making processes?

The second key aspect of evaluations is the question about whether the service makes a difference for service users, which is a question about the outcomes of the service:

> Outcomes are the changes or benefits for individuals, families, communities or organisations – whether changes in knowledge, attitudes, practical skills, behaviour, health and wellbeing, or the capacity to cope. (Hoggarth and Comfort 2010: 21)

This focus on outcomes has become more established in recent years as is demonstrated, for example, through the government's attention to outcomes for children (DfES 2003) and for adults (DoH 2006). Whilst the complexity of measuring outcomes is recognised (Eccles 2008), it is argued that this focus on outcomes provides a powerful approach that is clear and straightforward to communicate to all stakeholders. It also makes the participation of service users and carers in evaluation all the more central (Glasby and Dickinson 2008). It is evident, for example, that the five key outcomes from the Every Child Matters programme (DfES 2003) have become embedded across all services that work with children and their families. Moreover, it is argued that 'health and social care outcomes are interdependent' (Lloyd and Wait 2006: 12).

There are a number of tools or instruments available to facilitate evaluation; some are freely available, whilst others involve commercial software. Cheminais argues that 'evaluation of multi-agency provision should combine quantitative and qualitative approaches' (2009: 117), and proceeds to offer a number of examples of tools and models for evaluating outcomes of multiagency partnership working in education settings and children's centres. Within this, Cheminais cites a framework for evaluation developed by Thorlby and Hutchinson (2002, cited in Cheminais 2009: 119):

> A framework for evaluating multi-agency partnerships using four key dimensions:
>
> **Rationale:** Do the multi-agency partnership's vision and aims match the needs identified? Is the programme of intervention and support appropriately targeted? Are conditions and contexts changing, and if so, is there a need for the intervention and support programme to change?
> **Effectiveness:** What outputs have been delivered? How do they compare with the multi-agency partnership's aims and objectives? How effective has the partnership been?
> **Cost-effectiveness:** Compare inputs and outputs. What are the unit costs? Does this represent value for money?
> **Impact and significance:** Who is benefiting and how? What is the nature and extent of the impact and how does this compare with local conditions? What difference has the programme of intervention and support made?

It is also important to remember that theory can aid our understanding and evaluation of collaborative practice. You will recall from your learning in Chapter 3 of this book how, for example, systems theory can help to identify informal and formal networks and systems, their interconnections, the strength of those interconnections, the types of boundaries that exist and the purposes that each might have. Similarly, organisational theory can support an analysis of bureaucracy, organisational behaviour, interrelationships and managerial approaches (Crowther and Green 2004). You have seen, for example, extracts from the evaluative research undertaken by Anning et al. (2010) which was informed and underpinned by

Wenger's theory of 'Communities of Practice' (1998) and Engeström's Activity Theory (1999); again, both of these are discussed further in Chapter 3 of this book.

At the beginning of this section of the chapter, it was clear that the overall aim of evaluating organisational practice is for the organisation to learn and develop as a result. It is therefore worth putting evaluation into the context of what is known as the 'learning organisation'. This term is commonly attributed to the work of Senge (1990: 5), who contrasts learning organisations with 'traditional authoritarian "controlling organizations"', defining the learning organisation as:

> an organization that is continually expanding its capacity to create its future. (1990: 14)

> where people continually expand their capacity to create the results they truly desire, where new and expansive patterns of thinking are nurtured, where collective aspiration is set free, and where people are continually learning how to learn together. (1990: 3)

There are clear links here to the importance of interprofessional education which you read about in Chapter 6 of this book.

Learning organisations are characterised by being evidence-based, with clear informed processes of decision-making. They tend to be proactive in their approach to service development and delivery, rather than being reactive, defensive and inward looking. Thus, learning organisations are responsive, outward-looking and open to constructive critique, change and development. They learn from past experience, with everyone engaging with knowledge-informed, evidence-based practice and lifelong learning. Furthermore, proactive agencies tend to be structured around the needs of the population they serve. Øvretreit (1997c: 37) is clear that 'the preferable and ideal approach to planning teams is ... to start with an analysis of needs and finish up with the details of team organisation'.

There is a two-way dynamic relationship between people and the organisations they work in. Organisations are made up of people, and it is the quality, abilities and skills of those people that are directly reflected in the quality, creativity and success of the organisation. Yet, it is acknowledged that 'good social work has to have an organisational context that allows it to thrive' (Cree and Davis 2007: 156). Hudson and Henwood are clear that:

> Whilst there has been much policy and political rhetoric about the virtues of partnership and integration, it remains the case that the bulk of services and support is planned, commissioned and delivered on a mono-organisational basis. If this is to change, there will be implications for workforce development at all levels. (Hudson and Henwood 2009: 80)

EXAMPLES OF EVALUATIVE RESEARCH

As you have now developed your understanding about the organisational context of collaborative practice and processes of evaluation, you may find it helpful to read through the following examples of evaluative research. Both of these examples are outline summaries from more detailed journal articles.

'DELIVERING EFFECTIVE MULTI-AGENCY WORK FOR VICTIMS AND WITNESSES OF CRIME'

The article by Fleming et al. (2006), 'Delivering effective multi-agency work for victims and witnesses of crime', was written after an evaluation of a multi-agency group, the Victims and Witnesses Action Group, in Leicester in 2005. The article details the strategic aims and goals of the group and sets the discussion in the context of political and policy changes with regard to meeting the needs of victims and witnesses of crime. This group is made up of a number of separate organisations who maintain their individual identities, but work together at a policy and strategic level. The evaluation set out to assess strategic impact (influence on the policy and practice of relevant organisations), and service provision impact (influence on how services are provided), so there was no intention to evaluate outcomes for service users in this evaluation. The evaluation drew on interviews, focus groups, and scrutiny of documents. Findings related to funding and sustainability issues, information sharing, communication and overall effectiveness. Importantly, as would be expected from any evaluation, the article closes with a section headed 'lessons for the future'.

'EVALUATING PARTNERSHIPS: A CASE STUDY OF INTEGRATED SPECIALIST MENTAL HEALTH SERVICES'

The article by Freeman and Peck (2006), 'Evaluating partnerships: A case study of integrated specialist mental health services', reports on an evaluation of a case study of integrated mental health services in the UK. The authors set out the context for the integration of services, including the legislative, policy and structural developments that enabled the case study services to integrate. Drawing on the perspectives of users, carers, managers and practitioners, through focus groups, interviews and questionnaires, the evaluation sought to discover the perceived impact of partnership working in integrated mental health provision. Detailed findings are reported under key headings: pressures for fragmentation and integration; benefits and difficulties for staff; user and carer perspectives; and staff experiences. This is followed by a comprehensive 'discussion' section, which not only explores the themes arising from the findings, but also evaluates the evaluation processes themselves. The evaluation raises debate about the complexity of evaluating partnerships involving social interventions in a turbulent policy context.

To consolidate, revise and summarise your learning about the organisational context of collaborative practice, read the following fictional case studies and then work through the activity that follows.

Case studies (fictional)

1. Chrysalis: A user-led organisation

Chrysalis is a user-led social enterprise that has been established and is run by people who use or have used mental health services. They have developed an expertise in advocacy, tenancy sustainment and supporting people to gain independence through key life skills. Chrysalis has developed a collaborative partnership with the local Mental Health Trust to provide support to people accessing the early intervention team's service. The expertise that Chrysalis staff have complements and supports the work of the Trust. Chrysalis employs a number of part-time care support workers and has a service that is staffed by volunteers. For its part, the Trust agreed to support Chrysalis with training, some supervision and opportunities for its trustees to be involved in developments within the Mental Health Trust.

2. Rivenport team for older people

Rivenport health and social care community established an integrated assessment and intake team to enable quick and appropriate responses to meet the needs of local older people. An advisory group of older people were involved throughout the development and implementation of the project. The Primary Care Trust and Local Authority Social Services set up a pooled budget arrangement to support the implementation of this project. The multi-disciplinary team included district nurses, social workers and a range of workers with specialism in welfare rights, housing and leisure services. Collaborative arrangements with voluntary sector and community development workers ensured access to advice and support. Finding a suitable location for the team was difficult, meaning that the team could not initially be co-located, although later in the project this was achieved. Each agency had been using different ICT systems and it became impossible, due to costs and technological barriers, to align these. As the team began to develop team policies and procedures, other challenges arose, including recognition that the different agencies categorised 'older people' in different ways, had different criteria for service provision and had traditionally worked within slightly different geographical boundaries.

3. Fenlandshire extended general practitioner (GP) practice project

The Fenlandshire project brought together the East Fenlandshire County Council and the Fenlandshire Primary Care Trust in an agreement to locate social workers within general practitioner (GP) practices. The project was part of a wider initiative by the Trust to extend the range of services provided directly in GP practices, including holistic therapies, more community nurses and mental health services. The social workers remained employed and managed by East Fenlandshire County Council, but were based in local GP practices. The social workers received referrals and met with service users in the practices to undertake initial assessments, to inform decisions about next steps and for possible onward referral decisions to specialist teams. Despite the seeming simplicity of this collaborative arrangement, it was extremely complex to establish. The GPs had concerns about social workers having access to patient information in the practice and sought clarity about use of space, cost of overheads and so forth. There were also anxieties from the social work teams about their status and role in the project, how they would seek support, and how these arrangements might change the nature of local social work. As the project was implemented, there were ongoing concerns to address, particularly about the way in which co-location began to change the nature of the relationship between the practice staff, including the GPs, and the social work team.

Activity 7.3

Read the three fictional case studies above. For each case study, consider the following questions:

- Look back at the early part of this chapter and the three ways to categorise or understand different approaches to organising collaborative working. Attempt to categorise each of the case studies using these approaches:

  o Hierarchies, markets and networks (Figure 7.1).
  o Depth and breadth of partnerships (Glasby and Peck 2006).
  o Five-model typology (Atkinson et al. 2002, cited in Atkinson et al. 2007).

- How will the partners know if this project is a success and if they should look to expand this work to other areas?
- How could such an organisation or partnership evaluate the impact of these arrangements on those who use its services?
- In what ways might the approach taken in the case study to collaborative working change the experience of service users?
- How might this collaboration be developed to enhance further the experience of service users?

COMMENT

The purpose of this activity is to encourage you to look back over the chapter to apply your learning to examples that mirror real situations in practice. These case studies are by their very nature brief and only 'part of the story', but I hope that they will have given you a focus upon which to think about or perhaps discuss with a fellow student or colleague the ideas raised in the chapter, although there is no one clear, correct answer for any of the questions in the activity.

CONCLUSION

This chapter has focused on how organisations are responding to the collaborative 'agenda' and how that impacts on collaborative working practices. You have had the opportunity to explore organisational structures and cultures, management and leadership in collaborative practice, leading change and how organisations learn from evaluations of practice. Importantly, though, I hope you will study this chapter, in the context of this whole book, as just one aspect of interprofessional collaboration. Thus, whilst organisational issues are important in terms of the context of your practice, you must remain ever-mindful that the core focus and purpose of interprofessional social work is to support, empower and meet the needs and wishes of service users and carers. A suitable closing sentence for this chapter is provided by Whittington (2003b: 57), who argues that effective interprofessional and multiagency practice 'is realized by involvement of service users and by the collaboration of organizational leaders, middle managers and front-line staff across the shifting boundaries of professions and organizations, and in the spaces between'.

FURTHER READING

Cheminais, R. (2009) *Effective multi-agency partnerships: Putting every child matters into practice* (London: Sage Publications).

This book offers practical advice and guidance on establishing and managing effective multi-agency partnerships. Of particular relevance to your learning in this chapter, Cheminais' Chapter 3 considers partnership agreements and models of leadership, whilst Chapter 6 provides guidance on evaluating the impact and outcomes of partnership working.

Glasby, J. and Peck, E. (2006) *We have to stop meeting like this: The governance of inter-agency partnerships*, Discussion Paper (London: Integrated Care Network, available at http://www.icn.csip.org.uk).

This relatively short (31 pages) discussion paper focuses on governance in interagency collaboration. The authors explore issues such as decision-making, leadership, roles and accountability in interagency partnerships.

Hafford-Letchfield, T. (2009) *Management and organisations in social work*, 2nd edn (Exeter: Learning Matters).

This text explores different approaches to management and leadership, considering, amongst other topics, the management of change.

Institute of Public Care (IPC) (2010) *From the ground up: A report on integrated care design and delivery* (Oxford: IPC).

This report was commissioned by Community Health Partnerships and the Integrated Care Network and compiled by the Institute of Public Care, Oxford Brookes University. The report explores the benefits of integration and reinforces the two key components of strong local leadership and sound organisational approaches. The report includes some interesting case studies and a range of useful Internet links.

INTERNET RESOURCES

Smarter Partnerships – http://www.lgpartnerships.com

The Employers' Organisation for local government (EO) has established this website to support learning and skills development in effective collaborative working. The site offers a range of interactive resources, including 'toolkits' to help you assess the strengths and needs, including learning and skills needs, of a particular partnership. There are also a number of case studies, a checklist and other resources relevant to developing partnerships and the skills for collaborative working.

8

ENHANCING INDIVIDUAL PRACTICE IN THE COLLABORATIVE ENVIRONMENT

Chapter summary

When you have worked through this chapter, you will be able to:

- Reflect on the core themes of this book. This will enable you to do the following.
- Critically discuss how participation in the collaborative environment may be experienced by service users and carers.
- Evaluate the place, contribution and significance of social work as a profession in the collaborative environment.
- Identify the skills, knowledge, research and values that you will apply in your developing interprofessional practice, including ways in which you might source ongoing development and support.
- Identify a range of strategies, guidance and tools that will assist you in taking your learning forward beyond this text and into interprofessional social work practice.
- Devise your own action plan for sourcing ongoing development and support.

INTRODUCTION

Interprofessional collaboration in social work is fundamentally about relationships and, as I have argued throughout the chapters in this book, like all other relationships, collaborative practice needs constant attention, development, sensitivity, energy, motivation and common purpose. This final chapter is specifically dedicated to helping you think through and plan how you will develop and enhance your practice to harness the necessary knowledge, skills, attributes and values. Key Role 6 of the National Occupational Standards for Social Work requires that you 'demonstrate professional competence in social work practice' and within this that you 'work within agreed standards of social work practice and ensure own professional development' (Unit 19, TOPSS UK Partnership 2002). It is intended that after working through this chapter, you will be able to critically evaluate and reflect on the implications of collaboration, cooperation and integrated working on your individual practice. You have already started doing this, not only through reading the chapters, but through the activities and questions throughout the book. Thus, here you will consolidate your learning and plan for future learning through a range of reflective practice questions, activities and practical tasks, supported by strategies, guidance and tools that will assist you in taking your learning forward beyond this text and into interprofessional social work practice.

In Chapter 1, you were introduced to the key themes that underpin and are threaded throughout each part of this book. I hope that as you studied the text, you were able to identify these themes and their significance. This chapter is structured around the three themes, although there is deliberately more emphasis on the last theme as this reflects the overall purpose of this particular chapter. The themes that make up the sections of this chapter are:

- The experience and participation of service users and carers in the collaborative environment.
- The place, contribution and significance of social work as a profession in the collaborative environment.
- The skills, knowledge, research and values that will underpin your effective interprofessional practice, including ways in which you might source ongoing development and support.

This chapter also provides a summary of the book, not chapter by chapter but, through its thematic structure, by highlighting the key themes and how they have been addressed.

THE EXPERIENCE AND PARTICIPATION OF SERVICE USERS AND CARERS IN THE COLLABORATIVE ENVIRONMENT

In setting the context of collaborative practice in the first part of this book, Chapter 2 in particular raised the point of how the experience and position of service users and carers and user-led organisations has changed, with more importance and effort being given to ensuring meaningful participation and control. This discussion was supported in Chapter 3, where it was examined through different theoretical lenses, for example where users are centralised in Whittington's model (2003a) and in looking at how social exchange theory can aid our understanding of the nature of the interrelationship with service users. It is in Part 2 of the book, however, particularly in Chapter 4, where the experience and participation of service users in the collaborative environment is most sharply focused. Chapter 4 revisits the concept of change in how users experience collaboration, but also balances this with consideration of how power impacts on relationships. Using literature that has emerged from service users, the chapter explores the important concepts of partnership and participation, it also draws on the current drive towards personalisation, user-controlled services and co-production as setting the future landscape for collaborative practice with service users and carers. Later, in Chapter 7 where the organisational context of professional practice is examined, the important contribution of user-led organisations is discussed.

Reflective practice question 8.1

Reflect on service users' and carers' experiences of interprofessional collaboration, drawing on your notes and reading from the chapters in this book, your wider studies and any practice experience you may have.

- Make a note of the things that you will do differently to improve service users' experiences, to empower individuals and promote meaningful participation in the complex environment of collaborative working.

COMMENT

After you have responded to this question, you would find it useful to go back to Chapter 4 and your notes on that chapter if you have them. Crucially, at the end of that chapter, I reinforce the importance of empowerment, addressing imbalances of power and supporting service users in their interactions with your colleagues in the interprofessional arena. Minhas (2009), in the article that I recommend to you at the end of Chapter 4, draws out some personal attributes that he suggests are fundamental to user empowerment – these include honesty, trust, justice, care and respect.

THE PLACE, CONTRIBUTION AND SIGNIFICANCE OF SOCIAL WORK AS A PROFESSION IN THE COLLABORATIVE ENVIRONMENT

The National Occupational Standards for Social Work require that you can 'work within multi-disciplinary and multi-organisational teams, networks and systems' and that you 'contribute to evaluating the effectiveness of the team, network or system' (Key Role 5, in TOPSS UK Partnership 2002). This will require knowledge of the range of skills, experiences and knowledge that other professionals can bring to meeting the needs of service users and their carers, but also a clear understanding of the role of social work and its contribution to the 'collaborative table'. The place of the profession of social work was outlined at the beginning of the book in Chapter 2, where you learnt about the historical, political, legal, policy, social and economic imperatives for interprofessional social work. More specifically, in Part 2 of the book, Chapters 5 and 6 helped you to develop your understanding of how social work's professional identity, value base, culture, and knowledge base contribute to interprofessional and interagency work. Your learning in Chapter 5 was focused on what this all means for you as a social worker, whilst in Chapter 6 you learnt about the identity of social work as a whole profession and the contribution it makes to interprofessional teamworking. Moreover, in Chapter 6, you were encouraged to reflect on the value of the many different perspectives, forms of knowledge and theoretical views that all stakeholders bring to interprofessional practice. Chapter 6 also drew your attention to the importance of values in interprofessional practice, with Chapter 7 explaining how values are also influenced by organisational priorities, culture and practice.

Thus, the complexity of interprofessional practice is not only about skills, knowledge and theory, but very importantly is hinged on professional values, as 'values and ethics lead directly into principles of practice and rules for good practice' (Davis and Sims 2003: 96). Therefore, practice, and the implications of practice, are an integration of all these complex aspects. The diagram in Figure 8.1 illustrates how these elements come together to inform our practice, but importantly for each discipline or profession you work with, the types of skill, knowledge and values that make up each of the spheres will differ.

Figure 8.1   Knowledge, skills and values in interprofessional practice

Source: Crawford 2006: 141

Davis and Sims (2003) discuss the place of values and ethics in collaborative practice, drawing on research, the history of particular professions' developments and on particular examples of professional codes of practice. One of the main threads in their discussion is that differences in professional values, cultures and ethics that are not recognised and valued can hinder effective collaborative working. Each agency, each discipline, each service user and carer will have their own value base, their own beliefs, their own experiences, attitudes and culture to bring into the 'social exchanges' that make up the collaborative and integrated professional encounters. Furthermore, it cannot be denied that all of those stakeholders (including yourself) also have assumptions, perceptions, prejudices, stereotypes, experiences and beliefs with regard to the other agencies and disciplines – these also contribute to the 'social exchange'. It is necessary, in my view, to 'forefront' or make explicit these values and beliefs, in order to discuss openly and use them to ensure that professional diversity and the significance of each person's contribution is acknowledged and valued. Thus, collaborative practice could be seen to be most effective where we do not expect everyone else in practice to be like ourselves to adopt our values and views, but where we seek to highlight, value and draw attention to the diversity, using it to maximise the effectiveness of collaborative and interprofessional working practice for the benefit of those who use services.

Reflective practice question 8.2

Consider the questions below, with regard to any experiences you have of working across disciplines, professions or agencies. This may have been as part of your studies or during a practice learning opportunity. Make a note of your thoughts and reflections in response to each question. You would find it useful, if you are able, to discuss your reflections with colleagues who also undertake this activity, particularly if they are studying a different professional programme.

- Have you ever discussed professional values and/or ethics with colleagues from other disciplines or agencies? If so, what did you learn? If not, why do you think this has never occurred?
- Have you ever discussed organisational or agency values with colleagues who work, or who have experience of working, in other agencies? If so, what did you learn? If not, why do you think this has never occurred?
- When working with other professionals, in what ways have you attempted to understand their role, their specialist skills and their responsibilities? Have they attempted to learn about you as a professional in the same way? If so, what was learnt and what difference has this made? If not, why do you think this has never occurred?
- Have you participated in joint training or education with colleagues from other professional disciplines? In what ways do you feel that the 'jointness' may have facilitated or hindered further collaborative work?

COMMENT

As stated at the outset of the above activity, it would potentially be very useful to share and discuss this activity with a colleague, particularly, if possible, with a colleague from another discipline. It would be very interesting to see where your responses are similar and where they differ, and to try and understand why this might be the case. Each person reading and working through this book will have different experiences of collaborative working, either in an educational setting or in practice, and thus responses will greatly vary. Other students completing this activity have often reflected on how challenging discussions with other disciplines about values, skills and roles can be, but also how learning from these interactions can lay strong foundations for effective working together. What is clear is that however collaborative work is configured or whatever the setting, it is not enough simply to require that people work together or create multidisciplinary teams. Whittington (2003a: 29) argues that the competencies of collaboration require a 'particular blend of values and practice'. Hence, at the level of individual practice, there is a fundamental need for well-organised and established communication; valuing of professional difference; overcoming of ignorance and prejudice about each other's professions; defining of common goals; well-developed local relationships; and clearly agreed and defined functions, purposes and tasks.

THE SKILLS, KNOWLEDGE, RESEARCH AND VALUES THAT WILL UNDERPIN YOUR EFFECTIVE INTERPROFESSIONAL PRACTICE, AND WAYS OF SOURCING ONGOING DEVELOPMENT AND SUPPORT

Having established the significance of the skills, knowledge and value base that professional social work contributes to interprofessional practice, this last of the three core themes in the book draws attention to your learning needs and how you can further your development as an interprofessional social worker. One of my aims in writing this book is that it should enable you to critically evaluate and reflect on the implications of interprofessional collaborative working on individual practice, particularly on your practice. This theme is embedded in every chapter of the book, specifically through the reflective practice questions, activities and my comments that follow them. This section of this final chapter is primarily intended to be a further resource for you, with activities, ideas and strategies, starting by highlighting the skills and knowledge for interprofessional practice and moving on to explore how critical reflection can support your development. Essentially, in my view, if I had to state in one phrase what the fundamental essence of this book is, I would say that it is about critical, reflective, collaborative practice. Hence, this seems an appropriate time to reiterate, highlight and further develop the notion of reflection and critical approaches to practice. At the end of the section, there are a number of links to organisations that develop and share knowledge about interprofessional practice, followed by some revision exercises linked to each chapter of the book.

Activity 8.1

- Make a list of the skills and knowledge which you can evidence as having acquired that you bring to your collaborative working practices.
- Make a second list of the skills and knowledge that you feel you need to develop in order to enhance your collaborative practice.

COMMENT

It is possible that you have not stopped to think about this before or to make your thinking and reflections on this explicit, hence this is a useful exercise in bringing that thinking to the surface. McCray (2007: 133–4) offers a useful list of actions and skills that are involved in collaborative working. These are given in the extract that follows. Does this list mirror your list of skills or have you thought of a range of other skills? The difference, if there is one, may reflect the specific details of any practice experience you may have had, or your learning from specific modules on your programme of study. Also, in this extract, McCray does not set out to consider the knowledge base for interprofessional practice, but focuses on skills and activities:

- Making time to get to know other professionals and their roles and how they may be evolving in new contexts.
- Thinking about language and terms used and their relevance and meaning to other professionals or workers.
- Exploring your own prejudices about other professional groups and their models of practice.
- Reflecting on values and not making assumptions about shared beliefs or views.
- Being clear about resources and their impact on collaboration.
- Being confident about your professional practice and ability in the collaborative working role.
- Being credible – delivering as promised to action plans and keeping others involved of progress.
- Gaining consensus on leadership and accountability in a specific practice situation. (McCray 2007: 133–4)

Consider the following extract from Hammick et al. (2009: 23), who suggest that as an interprofessional practitioner you need the following knowledge, skills and attitudes:

- Knowledge

  ○ Understand the role and working context of other practitioners and begin to identify how these relate.
  ○ Recognise the range of knowledge and skills of all other colleagues.
  ○ Understand the principles and practice of effective teamwork.

- Skills

  - Apply sound verbal and written communication methods with colleagues from other work settings.
  - Identify situations where collaboration is helpful or essential.
  - Work collaboratively with service users and carers.
  - Use interprofessional learning in work settings.

- Attitudes

  - Appreciate the value of interprofessional collaboration.
  - Acknowledge and respect others' views, values and ideas. (Hammick et al. 2009: 23)

Do the two extracts together cover all the skills and knowledge that you felt you either have or need to develop? You may find it useful to look back at your notes from Chapter 5, particularly Activity 5.4 and Figure 5.1, as here we discussed the concept of skills and different types of skills required for effective practice. However, as I read these two extracts, what I felt was missing was the importance of professional confidence, which Loxley (1997) associates with professional identity. You read about professional identity in Chapters 5 and 6 of this book. Barrett and Keeping (2005: 20) are clear that 'confidence and competence are crucial to interprofessional working'. They move on to cite the work of Molyneux who 'found that professionals who were confident in their own role were able to work flexibly across professional boundaries without feeling jealous or threatened' (2001, cited in Barrett and Keeping 2005: 20). Hence, the knowledge and skills you acquire are not only a crucial contribution to interprofessional practice, but your awareness of them will enhance your confidence in collaborative work.

The discussion about skills and knowledge cannot, however, be a static one. You will be aware, from your studies so far, that interprofessional work may be very different in different areas of practice, with different service-user groups and services and at different levels of the services. However, what might be argued as being universally true is that 'the range of professional networks and the nature of partnerships for collaboration are shifting, and require new ways of working' (McCray 2007: 131).

Activity 8.2

Think about why McCray (2007) would argue that collaborative working requires new ways of working. Make a list of the reasons why you feel that working in partnership collaboratively across professions, agencies and services, might require new knowledge and new skills.

COMMENT

If you have an understanding of why new knowledge and skills might be necessary to developing effective collaborative practice, you will be more able to reflect upon your own practice with regard to the enhancement of the skills and knowledge necessary. As partnerships, roles, policies and organisational structures change constantly, it is necessary to meet the challenges that this presents and to ensure that service delivery is responsive, continually enhanced and that service users' needs and perspectives are kept at the forefront. You will recall discussion in Chapter 4 about how drives towards the personalisation agenda will require practitioners to develop new skills and knowledge, and then in Chapter 6 about how new ways of working are resulting in new types of workers. Reflection on practice within yourself, with your supervisor and with your colleagues and peers is the key 'tool' to ensure that you can meet these challenges.

Throughout this book, you have been asked to reflect upon your understanding, your practice and your values in relation to collaborative practice and I have set out some very practical ways in which you can reflect. In Figure 8.2 I illustrate more practical reflective activities that you can engage in as part of your studies and practice to develop and evidence your ability to enhance your practice through reflection. Figure 8.2 is framed around Kolb's cycle of experiential learning; this model describes a cyclical process of learning and improved practice, through reflection on practice (1984, cited in Crawford 2006).

Reflection is an important element in enhancing professional practice and should be ongoing, recurring and developmental. Using the knowledge you have built up over your studies and, if you have it, practice experience, and drawing on the ideas in Figure 8.2, work through Activity 8.3.

Activity 8.3

Make a list of the strategies and mechanisms that you have in place, or may wish to have in place in future practice, to support you as a reflective practitioner.

COMMENT

The contents of your list will vary according to whether you have had practice experience, the type of practice in which that experience took place and where you are in the progress of your studies. There are, however, some clues in the sentence that precedes the Activity box, in that reflection is more effective when it is articulated and shared and when further reflection on those discussions takes place. Indeed, there are a number of possible strategies that you can 'bring into play' to support you to reflect upon your practice when working with others to ensure that you are developing and enhancing your skills, knowledge and values in practice. Here are some examples:

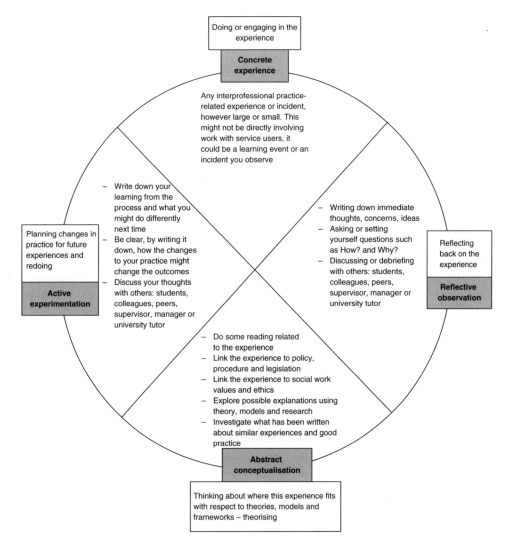

Figure 8.2 Examples of practical reflective practice activities associated with Kolb's experiential learning cycle

Source: Crawford 2006: 141

- Supervision with your line manager or nominated supervisor.
- Supervision with your practice assessor or day-to-day supervisor when in a practice learning situation.
- Maintaining a reflective learning journal or log.
- Using tutorials or academic support processes to discuss your reflections on the interface between your developing formal knowledge base and your practice experience.

- Discussions with other students or in your team at team meetings or other appropriate fora.
- Discussions with other professional colleagues to share concerns, good practice, knowledge of each other's roles and responsibilities and particular practice situations.
- Undertaking student research projects or practitioner research (see Crawford 2006: 143) to explore further issues that arise from your reflections on collaboration in practice.
- Extending your reading, keeping up to date with recent research, academic texts and policy changes to support your reflections.
- Attending further training and education programmes, particularly those in which a range of professionals participate.

As you can see from Figure 8.2, to be really effective reflection needs to draw on different perspectives, including where possible the literature and feedback from colleagues and service users. Reflections also need to be open to learning from areas of practice that were less effective as well as those that were successful. All of this means that reflection must be 'critical': open, honest and thoughtful. Essentially, then, throughout the whole book you have been encouraged to take a critical, reflective perspective on your learning. It is important to realise that to develop as a critical, reflective practitioner, you need to acquire and hone the skills of critical thinking and reflection on practice.

Reflective practice question 8.3

Think about a case situation, either one you have read about during your studies or in this book or from a practice experience, where collaborative working was a key feature. Write down the situation briefly – just a paragraph should suffice (if you are reflecting on an example from a practice experience, you must anonymise the details when making notes). Reflecting on that case situation, make a note of your responses to the following questions:

a   Who were the other professionals involved (not by name, but by job title)?
b   What was the purpose of their involvement? Why were you or other social workers working with them?
c   What did you or could you learn from professional colleagues in this situation?
d   Can you identify factors that facilitated and enhanced the collaboration? If so, what were they?
e   Can you identify factors that may have hindered the collaboration? If so, what were they?
f   If the service user and their carer had kept a reflective journal during their experiences of the collaborative services, what sort of reflections and thoughts might they have recorded? How do you think they would express their experiences?
g   What elements of your practice would you want to replicate or might you do differently?

COMMENT

Of course, I cannot 'second guess' your responses to the above activity, but wonder, for example at point (b), whether you considered the policy and legislative framework for their involvement as well as the practical aspects of what they could contribute to the service? Also, at point (c), did you think widely about this? So, apart from gaining practical learning about the service user's situation, what could you learn about the other's professions, their constraints and their employing organisation? I also wonder if your notes at points (d) and (e) reflect any of the barriers and drivers discussed throughout this book, and if so, it would be good to note down the reference and page number as you may want to refer back to these points later in your studies. There are so many interconnected facets and complexities to interprofessional practice that you may have identified others, so it would be interesting to expand your reading and explore what research and literature has to say about those issues. I think point (f) is particularly interesting and if you have the opportunity and it is appropriate, you should discuss this with the service user, ask their views and then reflect upon what this means for your practice. If this is not possible, consider for a moment what you can base your response to on point (f): is it on things that a user has said or an evaluation tool they have completed? Is it by attempting to 'put yourself in their shoes', and is that at all possible? Is it from reading a review report or being at a review where the user was present? Is your response based on your own values? How valid and genuine is the basis for your response to point (f), given the impact of power on relationships, discussed in Chapter 4 of this book? Here, I am asking you to reflect more deeply on the way in which you develop and frame your reflections and on what you perceive as meaningful user participation and co-production.

Service-user experiences and views are a crucial element of the knowledge base for practice and for your critical reflections. Additionally, as mentioned earlier, reflection becomes more critical and more effective where it also takes account of research and literature-based knowledge, asking what is known about this situation or form of practice. You may find it helpful, therefore, to explore the work of some of the easily accessible organisations that provide research and knowledge related to interprofessional collaborative social work practice. The organisations detailed here with their Web addresses supplement those provided in the Internet resources sections at the end of Chapters 2 through to 7 of this book. These should serve as a starting point for your own research as this list is not exhaustive and you will find many more. Furthermore, you should always undertake this work with caution, for example by checking the relevance, particularly in terms of time and place, of the organisation you are looking at in relation to your own practice; in other words, ensure it is relevant to contemporary practice in your country.

Activity 8.4

Read through the annotated list offered below and, when you have access to the Internet, explore their Web pages. My brief descriptions are largely taken from the website's home pages. Make notes about the orientation of each agency, in particular who provides funding for the organisation, the main area of practice that they address and what resources are offered from these organisations in respect of collaborative practice. Consider the ways in which the work of these organisations can inform effective collaborative practice. This work, your reflections and evaluation of the information provided and your related notes may prove helpful to your further studies.

The National Mental Health Development Unit (NMHDU)

The National Mental Health Development Unit (NMHDU) (http://www.nmhdu.org.uk), launched in April 2009, consists of a small central team and a range of programmes funded by both the Department of Health and the NHS to provide national support for implementing mental health policy by advising on national and international best practice to improve mental health and mental health services. The site has a useful downloads and resources section and a page with further relevant links.

Higher Education Academy Social Policy and Social Work Subject Centre (SWAP)

The website of the Social Policy and Social Work Subject Centre of the Higher Education Academy (SWAP) (http://www.swap.ac.uk) has a range of resources, including project reports and help sheets to support interprofessional learning and collaborative working. SWAP will close towards the end of 2011 but their work will be incorporated into the work of the Higher Education Academy centrally (http://heacademy.ac.uk).

Improvement and Development Agency (IDEA)

The Improvement and Development Agency (IDEA) (http://www.idea.gov.uk) was established by and for local government in April 1999. The organisation works by providing practical solutions to help local councils improve their services. The IDEA is a knowledge resource applicable across all council services, but in relation to social care, it is a useful reference point for adult social care, education and children's services in particular.

Intute

Intute was formerly known as the Resource Discovery Network (RDN) (http://www.intute.ac.uk) and offers a range of resources, not specifically related to social work, but more broadly about social research. Within the social sciences, social welfare section of the website, you will find many useful resources, including tutorials on research skills, Web links, blogs, papers, articles and reports.

Making Research Count (MRC)

Making Research Count (MRC) (http://www.makingresearchcount.org.uk) was established in 1998 to promote knowledge-informed practice. It is a national, collaborative research dissemination initiative currently run by ten regional centres based in universities. The partnership promotes knowledge-informed practice and improved services in social work and social care and its interface with health.

The Social Research Unit

The Social Research Unit (http://www.dartington.org.uk) is an independent charity dedicated to improving the health and development of children, primarily in Europe and North America. Much of their work has a clear outcomes focus, as discussed in Chapter 7 of this book. Again, on this site there are numerous resources, blogs, interactive features and downloads.

Research in Practice

Research in Practice (http://www.rip.org.uk) is the largest children and families research implementation project in England and Wales. Their mission is to promote positive outcomes for children and families through the use of research evidence. This busy website provides access to research resources, an 'evidence bank' and a range of research and publication updates.

Research in Practice for Adults (RiPfA)

Research in Practice for Adults (RiPfA) (http://www.ripfa.org.uk) describes itself as 'a national research utilisation organisation for adult social care'. Their mission is to promote the use of evidence-informed practice in the planning and delivery of adult social care services. The website provides access to publications, policy updates and research links.

Shaping Our Lives

On the home page of their website (http://www.shapingourlives.org.uk), the national user network, Shaping Our Lives, explains that it is an independent user-controlled organisation that started as a research and development project and became an independent organisation in 2002. Through the website, you can download publications and information about projects on user participation and related research.

The King's Fund

The King's Fund (http://www.kingsfund.org.uk) is an independent charitable foundation whose goal is to improve health care. The King's Fund undertakes research and studies in health and social care, particularly in mental health, doing a considerable amount of work that involves service users and their carers.

The UK Centre for the Advancement of Interprofessional Education (CAIPE)

The UK Centre for the Advancement of Interprofessional Education (CAIPE) (http://www.caipe.org.uk) is a national and international resource for interprofessional education in both universities and the workplace across health and social care, and they have a close association with the *Journal of Interprofessional Care*. The website provides information and advice, bulletins, papers and links.

You are now coming towards the end of your studies through this book. To help you revise and consolidate your notes from each chapter, undertake the activities in Activity 8.5.

Activity 8.5

Revision and consolidation

- Reflect on the historical and political imperatives which drive collaborative working and organisational change in the statutory, voluntary and independent sectors (you read about these in Chapter 2 and its supporting texts). Write a few paragraphs that reflect your thoughts on the implications of these imperatives for your developing practice.
- Reflect on the legal, policy, social and economic imperatives which drive collaborative working and organisational change in the statutory, voluntary and independent sectors (you read about these in Chapter 2 and its supporting texts). Write a few paragraphs that reflect your thoughts on the implications of these imperatives for your practice.
- Reflect on the theoretical frameworks that were discussed in Chapter 3. Select two of the theories and write a few paragraphs to show how you can use them to analyse the interrelationships between professionals and organisations in your area of practice.
- Consider service users' and carers' experiences of interprofessional, collaborative practice. In particular, revise your learning from Chapter 4 and make notes on how different approaches to working together might impact on users' experiences. What are the key issues to take account of and how might they impact on your practice?
- Reviewing your learning across Chapters 5 and 6, write down how your professional identity as a social worker or student social worker impacts on your practice in the collaborative environment. Within this, consider the specific contribution that you, as a social worker, make to interprofessional practice and some of the challenges you might face.
- In Chapter 7 of this book, you examined the organisational context of interprofessional practice. Following your studies in that chapter, write a summary of how the structure, culture and leadership in an organisation, in which you might work, could influence your effectiveness as an interprofessional social worker. Also, in your summary, make note of what you might do to influence the culture and practices within the organisation.

COMMENT

The last activity was essentially a revision activity through all of the chapters and the fundamental underpinnings of this book. However, I would acknowledge that suggesting a very structured activity like this may make it appear as though reflective collaborative practice is easy. The reality is, of course, that reflection on practice, particularly collaborative practice, in this ever-changing and developing context of social work is not straightforward. You certainly cannot do it once and consider it done! So, as a summarising revision activity, consider what the key learning points are for you from working through this chapter and this book.

Activity 8.6

As a final activity for this book, draw up your own action plan of practical ways in which you can and will develop your skills, knowledge and values to become a more effective, reflective, interprofessional social worker. Be specific about how you will take those learning actions forward.

COMMENT

You may have found it helpful to look back over your notes from previous chapters and the activities and questions in this chapter as you consider this activity. The starting point might be to consider how you can be proactive in your work with others to ensure that ignorance and prejudices about the values, ethics, roles and responsibilities of other professions are eradicated. Perhaps you have considered ways to facilitate open dialogue about these issues with colleagues or students both within your own discipline/agency and beyond its boundaries, including ways in which you might share professional knowledge. Perhaps you have thought of ways in which you might work with others to define common goals in practice, articulating the centrality of the user and their needs, including ensuring a common language and balancing power relationships both with service users and across hierarchical structures. It is important to note, too, that your studies on interprofessional practice will connect with other areas of your studies and these new skills, ideas and knowledge will be transferable, just as the learning from other areas of study will have relevance to your studies here. A starting point for your action plan could be to share your learning from this book with fellow students and, if you have practice experience, your colleagues from practice; this interaction in itself will further your development and learning (Wenger 1998).

CONCLUSION

Here, in the final chapter of this book, I deliberately set out to enable you to summarise and consolidate your learning from across the chapters. This has been achieved through a focus on the key themes that are threaded throughout the book, supported by an emphasis on reflective practice questions, activities, practical tasks, tools and guidance for you, the reader. If there has to be one core message running through this book, then it is this: interprofessional, collaborative social work does not simply happen by putting professionals together or demanding that they work to particular processes; effective collaborative partnerships, that involve users as equal partners, take time and resources to develop, maintain and grow. As a developing interprofessional social worker, you need to be prepared to reflect continually and be attentive to your professional learning and working relationships.

GLOSSARY OF TERMS AND ABBREVIATIONS

The following glossary highlights some of the key terms and abbreviations used in this book. However, many terms are given detailed descriptions within the chapters and are therefore either not included in this glossary or are given only brief outlines here with reference to the relevant chapter. Please also note that with ongoing changes in governmental structures and the Internet sources that reflect them, the Web links provided here may change and you may be redirected to other relevant sites.

Activity theory	Activity theory, also known as Cultural Historical Activity Theory (CHAT), is a theory that describes the behaviour and approaches of professionals as integral to the social, cultural, historical and institutional context in which they practice. Activity theory is discussed in more detail in Chapter 3
BASW	British Association of Social Workers
CAF	Common Assessment Framework
CAFA	Common Assessment Framework for Adults
Care Council for Wales	The social care workforce regulator in Wales (http://www.ccwales.org.uk)
Care Programme Approach (CPA)	The CPA provides a framework for care planning and coordination in mental health services. The Care Programme Approach Association (CPAA) provides details about the background, the process and implementation differences across the countries of the UK on its website at http://cpaa.co.uk/thecareprogrammeapproach
Children's Workforce Development Council (CWDC)	The CWDC is a government-sponsored, executive, non-departmental public body. The organisation leads on reform of the children and young people's workforce, drawing on the concerns, experiences and views of a range of stakeholders. Its website is http://www.cwdcouncil.org.uk

(Continued)

(Continued)

Collaboration	The activity of working together with others towards meeting shared objectives which benefit all parties. The joint, cooperative effort brings together a range of skills and knowledge to achieve collective outcomes, which are substantially greater than each individual could achieve alone
Common Assessment Framework (CAF)	The CAF is a standardised approach to conducting holistic assessments of children's additional needs and, through integrated working, deciding on how these needs should be met by coordinated service provision
Common Assessment Framework for Adults (CAFA)	Following the Single Assessment Process for older people (SAP) and the Common Assessment Framework (CAF) for children, the CAFA aims to improve information sharing across organisations for multidisciplinary assessment, care and support planning
Communities of Practice	This concept stems from the work of Wenger (1998) and describes a group of people who interact and learn through having a shared and common purpose or concern. Communities of Practice are characterised by collective identity, mutual engagement, joint enterprise and shared learning. Communities of Practice are discussed in more detail in Chapter 3
eCAF	National electronic Common Assessment Framework system
General Social Care Council (GSCC)	The social care workforce regulator in England, available at http://www.gscc.org.uk
ICN	Integrated Care Network
ICS	Integrated Children's System
ICT	Information and communication technologies
IFSW	International Federation of Social Workers
Individual budgets	Individual budgets are a new way of providing personalised support with the underpinning ethos of empowering service users to take control and have more choice and power in the decisions about the care that they receive. Individual budgets are a development from 'personal budgets' and 'direct payments', in that they go beyond the allocation of funding to users after assessment, by including a range of funding streams beyond social care. Individual budgets are discussed in more detail in Chapter 4

(Continued)

(Continued)

Integrated Care Network (ICN)	The ICN provides information and support to organisations and seeks to improve the quality of provisions to service users, patients and carers by integrating the planning and delivery of services. The ICN facilitates communication between agencies and government so that policy and practice inform each other. Its website is http://www.dhcarenetworks.org.uk/icn/
Integrated Care Services	Through total systemic coherence of procedures, rules, priorities and approaches to governance, previously separate services and professionals work together in a newly formed collaborative organisation. Integrated Care Services are discussed in more detail in Chapter 7
Integrated Children's System (ICS)	A conceptual framework and practice tool which generates and collates information about children in need and their families. It set out to improve outcomes for children and their families whilst supporting multiagency planning and information sharing. For a more detailed discussion about the ICS, see Chapter 5
Integration	The coming together or combining of separate parts or entities to form one new whole entity. In the context of interprofessional collaboration in social work practice, integration normally refers to integrated services and integrated care, which are discussed in more detail in Chapter 7
Interdisciplinary	Where different disciplines work together and there is a collaborative relationship between them
International Federation of Social Workers (IFSW)	'A global organisation striving for social justice, human rights and social development through the development of social work, best practices and international co-operation between social workers and their professional organisations.' Its website is http://www.ifsw.org
Interprofessional	Where different professionals work together and there is a collaborative relationship between them
Lead professional working	Lead professionals work with children with additional and complex needs to coordinate the provision of integrated frontline services. The lead professional acts as a single point of contact for the child and family. A copy of national guidance for practitioners can be downloaded from http://www.cwdcouncil.org.uk
Local Involvement Networks (LINks)	Local Involvement Networks have been established in England to give people a stronger voice in how their health and social care services are delivered. They are organised and managed by local people, groups and communities who can use their powers to hold services to account

(Continued)

(Continued)

Local Safeguarding Boards (LSB)	Statutory, interagency forums for agreeing how the relevant organisations in each local area will cooperate to safeguard and promote the welfare of individuals and ensure the effectiveness of what they do. They are responsible for developing, monitoring and reviewing relevant policies, procedures and practice and for providing interagency training. There are LSBs for children and for adults. Details of the roles and responsibilities of Local Safeguarding Children's Boards form Chapter 2 of the *Working together to safeguard children* guide (DCSF 2010)
Multiagency	Involving many organisations or services, but they may be working independently or in parallel and whilst coordinated, may interact on a limited basis
Multidisciplinary	Involving many different disciplines, but they may be working independently or in parallel and whilst coordinated, may interact on a limited basis
Multi-professional	Involving many different professionals, but they may be working independently or in parallel and whilst coordinated, may interact on a limited basis
National Service Frameworks (NSF)	Policy documents that set standards, principles and objectives to improve health and social care services, in specific service areas, nationally. NSFs are discussed in detail in Chapter 1
Networking (in social work practice)	The contacts and negotiations that take place as part of the social work processes and procedures, for example through referral, planning, intervention and evaluation
New types of worker (NToW) programme	Creative approaches to workforce developments to meet changes in the way social care services are provided (or planned, commissioned or monitored), specifically to provide more user-led, collaborative approach to services. Its website is http://www.newtypesofworker.co.uk
Northern Ireland Social Care Council (NISCC)	NISCC is the regulatory body for the Northern Ireland social care workforce. Its website is http://www.niscc.info
Partnership	Partnership indicates a formal union, arrangement or process, whereby two or more individuals or organisations form an agreement to work together towards agreed goals and objectives. Partnerships are characterised by shared and negotiated decision-making. The concept of partnership working is discussed in more detail in Chapters 1 and 4

(Continued)

(Continued)

Personalisation	Personalisation provides service users with more choice, flexibility and control to be creative about how their needs are met. On the basis of multidisciplinary, holistic assessments and plans, personalised provision aims to be truly service user-led. For some users, this means having total control by being provided with the money to arrange and commission services themselves. For other users, Individual Support Funds will enable them to leave the money with the funder, whilst maintaining control and choice about the form and provision of support. Personalisation is discussed in more detail in Chapter 4
Quality Assurance Agency (QAA)	The QAA safeguards quality and standards in UK higher education. It provides a reviewing function, publishing reports on the quality of learning opportunities and the academic awards offered by institutions providing higher education. Its website is http://www.qaa.ac.uk
Scottish Social Services Council (SSSC)	SSSC is the regulatory body for the Scottish Social Services workforce. Its website is http://www.sssc.uk.com
Single Assessment Process (SAP)	First introduced in the National Service Framework for Older People (DoH 2001*b*), the SAP set out standards to ensure effective and coordinated interprofessional assessment and care planning. Building on this initiative, a Common Assessment Framework for adults (CAFA) is being piloted
Skills for Care	Skills for Care is part of the sector skills council and is an independent registered charity that works with adult social care employers to develop and support the sector standards and qualifications. Its website is http://www.skillsforcare.org.uk
Systems theory	A broad, cross-disciplinary theory that describes society and relationships within it as a complex set of interrelating, interacting and interdependent subsystems and components within subsystems. Systems theory and its main principles are discussed in more detail in Chapter 3
Team Around the Child (TAC)	Supporting the Common Assessment Framework (CAF) for children and young people, and the lead professional worker role, the 'Team Around the Child' is a model of service provision that aims to provide a more integrated approach within existing resources. The TAC brings together parents and practitioners into a specific team for each particular child who has been identified as having additional needs

(Continued)

(Continued)

Whole systems working/ approach	Underpinned by the principles of systems theory (see Chapter 3), the whole systems approach adopts a holistic perspective across the complexity of all services and professionals relevant to meeting the needs of a particular service-user group. It is inclusive, in that it involves all stakeholders and the search for synergies across the various components of the 'whole system'

REFERENCES

Anning, A., Cottrell, D., Frost, N., Green, J. and Robinson, M. (2010) *Developing multiprofessional teamwork for integrated children's services: Research, policy and practice*, 2nd edn (Berkshire: Open University Press).

Arnstein, S.R. (1969) 'A ladder of citizen participation in the USA', *Journal of the American Institute of Planners*, 35(4): 216–24.

Atkinson, M., Jones, M. and Lamont, E. (2007) *Multi-agency working and its implications for practice: A review of the literature* (CfBT Education Trust, available at http://www. cfbt.com).

Audit Commission (1986) *Making a reality of community care* (London: Her Majesty's Stationery Office).

Barrett, G. and Keeping, C. (2005) 'The processes required for effective interprofessional working', in G. Barrett, D. Sellman and J. Thomas (eds), *Interprofessional working in health and social care: Professional perspectives* (Basingstoke: Palgrave Macmillan), pp. 18–31.

Barrett, G., Sellman, D. and Thomas, J. (eds) (2005) *Interprofessional working in health and social care: Professional perspectives* (Basingstoke: Palgrave Macmillan).

Barton, C. (2003) 'Allies and enemies: The service user as care co-ordinator', in J. Weinstein, C. Whittington and T. Leiba (eds), *Collaboration in social work practice* (London: Jessica Kingsley Publishers), pp. 103–20.

Beckett, C. (2006) *Essential theory for social work practice* (London: Sage Publications).

Belbin, R. (1993) *Team roles at work* (Oxford: Butterworth-Heinemann).

Belbin Team Roles (accessed 20 March 2010) (available at http://www.belbin.com).

Beresford, P. (2005) *Developing knowledge-based practice – Context and background*, Presentation to a symposium of the British Society of Gerontology Annual Conference, Keele University, 15 July (available at http://www2.warwick.ac.uk/fac/soc/shss/mrc/older people/bsg/beresford.pdf).

Beresford, P. and Trevillion, S. (1995) *Developing skills for community care: A collaborative approach* (Aldershot: Arena).

Beveridge, Sir W. (1942) *Social insurance and allied services* (Beveridge Report) (London: His Majesty's Stationery Office).

Biggs, S. (1997) 'Interprofessional collaboration: Problems and prospects', in J. Øvretveit, P. Mathias and T. Thompson (eds), *Interprofessional working for health and social care* (Basingstoke: Palgrave Macmillan), pp. 186–200.

Brandon, M., Howe, A., Dagley, V., Salter, C. and Warren, C. (2006) 'What appears to be helping or hindering practitioners in implementing the Common Assessment Framework and Lead Professional Working?' *Child Abuse Review*, 15(6): 396–413.

Braye, S. and Preston-Shoot, M. (2010) *Practising social work law* (3rd edn) (Basingstoke: Palgrave Macmillan).

Brown, H. and Barrett, S. (2008) 'Practice with service-users, carers and their communities', in S. Fraser and S. Matthews (eds), *The critical practitioner in social work and health care* (London: Sage Publications), pp. 43–59.

Brown, K. and White, K. (2006) *Exploring the evidence base for integrated children's services* (Scottish Executive Education Department, available at http://www.scotland.gov.uk/publications).

Butler, G. (2007) 'Reflecting on emotion in social work', in C. Knott and T. Scragg (eds), *Reflective practice in social work* (Exeter: Learning Matters), pp. 30–142.

Cambridge Dictionaries Online (accessed 23 March 2010 available at http://dictionary.cambridge.org).

Canavan, J., Coen, L., Dolan, P. and Whyte, L. (2009) 'Privileging practice: Facing the challenge of integrated working for outcomes for children', *Children and Society*, 23: 377–88.

Carnwell, R. and Carson, A. (2009) 'The concepts of partnership and collaboration', in R. Carnwell and J. Buchanan (eds), *Effective practice in health, social care and criminal justice: A partnership approach* (Berkshire: Open University Press), pp. 3–21.

Carpenter, J., Hackett, S., Patsios, D. and Szilassy, E. (2009) *Outcomes of interagency training to safeguard children: A report to the Department for Children, Schools and Families and Department of Health* (Department for Children, Schools and Families, available at http://www.dcsf.gov.uk/research).

Carr, S. (2008) *Personalisation: A rough guide* (London: Social Care Institute for Excellence).

Carr, S. (2009) *The implementation of individual budget schemes in adult social care*, Research Briefing No. 20 (London: Social Care Institute for Excellence).

Charles, M. and Horwath, J. (2009) 'Investing in interagency training to safeguard children: An act of faith or an act of reason?' *Children and Society* 23: 364–76.

Cheminais, R. (2009) *Effective multi-agency partnerships: Putting every child matters into practice* (London: Sage Publications).

Children's Workforce Development Council (CWDC) (2009) *Coordinating and delivering integrated services for children and young people: The team around the child (TAC) and the lead professional – a guide for practitioners* (Leeds: CWDC, available at http://www.cwdcouncil.org.uk).

Children's Workforce Development Council (CWDC) (2010) *The common core of skills and knowledge* (Leeds: CWDC, available at http://www.cwdcouncil.org.uk).

Clarke, J. and Glendinning, C. (2002) 'Partnership and the remaking of welfare governance', in C. Glendinning, M. Powell and K. Rummery (eds), *Partnerships, New Labour and the governance of welfare* (Bristol: Policy Press), pp. 33–50.

Commission for the Compact (with Compact Voice, Office of the Third Sector, and the Local Government Association) (2001) *Black and Minority Ethnic Voluntary and Community Organisations Compact Code of Good Practice*, (Birmingham: Commission for the Compact, available at http://www.thecompact.org).

Corby, B., with Young, F. and Coleman, S. (2009) 'Interprofessional communication in child protection', in R. Carnwell and J. Buchanan (eds), *Effective practice in health, social care and criminal justice: A partnership approach* (2nd edn) (Berkshire: Open University Press), pp. 65–79.

Coulshed, V. and Mullender, A. (2001) *Management in social work* (Basingstoke: Palgrave Macmillan).

Crawford, K. (2006) *Social work and human development: Reflective reader* (Exeter: Learning Matters).

Crawford, K. and Walker, J. (2008) *Social work with older people* (2nd edn)(Exeter: Learning Matters).

Cree, V.E. (2009) 'The changing nature of social work', in R. Adams, L. Dominelli and M. Payne (eds), *Social work themes, issues and critical debates* (3rd edn) (Basingstoke: Palgrave Macmillan), pp. 26–36.

Cree, V.E. and Davis, A. (2007) *Social work voices from the inside* (Abingdon: Routledge).

Crowther, D. and Green, M. (2004) *Organisational theory* (London: Chartered Institute of Personnel Development).

Daly, G. and Davis, H. (2002) 'Partnerships for local governance: citizens, communities and accountability', in C. Glendinning, M. Powell and K. Rummery (eds), *Partnerships, New Labour and the governance of welfare* (Bristol: Policy Press), pp. 97–112.

Daniels, H., Edwards, A., Engeström, Y., Gallagher, R. and Ludvigsen, S.R. (eds) (2009) *Activity theory in practice: Promoting learning across boundaries and agencies* (London: Routledge).

Davis, J. and Sims, D. (2003) 'Shared values in interprofessional collaboration', in J. Weinstein, C. Whittington and T. Leiba (eds), *Collaboration in social work practice* (London: Jessica Kingsley Publishers), pp. 83–99.

Department for Children, Schools and Families (DCSF) (2008a) *Information sharing: Guidance for practitioners and managers* (DCSF Publications, available at http://www.dcsf.gov.uk/everychildmatters/resources-and-practice/IG00340).

Department for Children, Schools and Families (DCSF) (2008b) *Making it happen: Working together for children, young people and families* (DCSF Publications, available at http://www.dcsf.gov.uk/everychildmatters/resources-and-practice/Ig00130).

Department for Children, Schools and Families (DCSF) (2009a) *Information sharing: Further guidance on legal issues* (DCSF Publications, available at http://www.dcsf.gov.uk/everychildmatters/resources-and-practice/IG00340).

Department for Children, Schools and Families (DCSF) (2009b) *The protection of children in England: Action plan – The government's response to Lord Laming* (Norwich: The Stationery Office).

Department for Children, Schools and Families (DCSF) (2009c) *Social Work Task Force: Building a safe, confident future – The final report of the Social Work Task Force* (London: DCSF, available at http://publications.dcsf.gov.uk).

Department for Children, Schools and Families (DCSF) (2010) *Working together to safeguard children: A guide to inter-agency working to safeguard and promote the welfare of children* (Nottingham: DCSF Publications, available at http://publications.dcsf.gov.uk).

Department for Education and Employment (DfEE) (1998) *Meeting the childcare challenge: A framework and consultation document* (Suffolk: DfEE publications, available at http://www.dcsf.gov.uk/everychildmatters/research/publications/surestartpublications/523/).

Department for Education and Skills (DfES) (2003) *Every child matters*, Cm. 5860 (London: The Stationery Office, available at http://www.everychildmatters.gov.uk).

Department for Education and Skills (2004) *Every child matters: Change for children* (Nottingham: DfES).

Department for Education and Skills (DfES) (2005) *Common core of skills and knowledge for the children's workforce* (London: DfES).

Department for Education and Skills (DfES) (2006) *The common assessment framework for children and young people: Practitioners' guide* (available at http://www.everychildmatters.gov.uk/caf).

Department for Education and Skills (DfES) and Department of Health (DoH) (2004) *The national framework for children, young people and maternity services* (London: DoH).

Department of Health (DoH) (1989) *Caring for people: Community care in the next decade and beyond*, Cm. 849 (London: Her Majesty's Stationery Office).

Department of Health (DoH) (1997a) *The new NHS: Modern, dependable* (London: Her Majesty's Stationery Office).

Department of Health (DoH) (1997b) *Report on the review of patient-identifiable information* (Report of the Caldicott Committee) (DoH, available at http://www.dh.

gov.uk/prod_consum_dh/groups/dh_digitalassets/@dh/@en/documents/digitalasset/dh_4068404.pdf).

Department of Health (DoH) (1998) *Modernising social services: Promoting independence, improving protection, raising standards*, Cmnd. 4169 (London: Her Majesty's Stationery Office).

Department of Health (DoH) (1999a) *Planning for health and health care: Incorporating guidance for health and local authorities on health improvement programmes, service and financial frameworks, joint investment plans and primary care investment plans*, Circular HSC 1999/244:LAC(99)39 (London: DoH).

Department of Health (DoH) (1999b) *A national service framework for mental health* (London: DoH).

Department of Health (DoH) (2000a) *The NHS plan: A plan for investment, a plan for reform: A summary* (London: DoH, available at http://www.nhs.uk/nhsplan).

Department of Health (DoH) (2000b) *Framework for the assessment of children in need and their families* (London: The Stationery Office).

Department of Health (DoH) (2000c) *No secrets: Guidance on developing and implementing multi-agency policies and procedures to protect vulnerable adults from abuse* (London: The Stationery Office).

Department of Health (DoH) (2001a) *Valuing people: A new strategy for learning disability for the 21st century* (London: Her Majesty's Stationery Office).

Department of Health (DoH) (2001b) *The National Service Frameworks for older people* (London: DoH).

Department of Health (DoH) (2002a) *Keys to partnership: Working together to make a difference in people's lives* (London: DoH).

Department of Health (DoH) (2002b) *Requirements for social work training* (London: DoH).

Department of Health (DoH) (2004) *Single assessment process (SAP) implementation guidance* (London: The Stationery Office).

Department of Health (DoH) (2006) *Our health, our care, our say: A new direction for community services*, Cm. 6737 (Norwich: The Stationery Office, available at http://www.dh.gov.uk/publications).

Department of Health (DoH) (2007) *Putting people first: A shared vision and commitment to the transformation of adult social care* (available at http://www.dh.gov.uk/prod_consum_dh/groups/dh_digitalassets/@dh/@en/documents/digitalasset/dh_081119.pdf).

Department of Health (DoH) (2008) *Refocusing the care programme approach: Policy and positive practice guidance* (London: DoH).

Department of Health (DoH) (2009a) *Careers in social work* (London: DoH).

Department of Health (DoH) (2009b) *Common assessment framework for adults: A summary of the consultation on proposals to improve information sharing around multi-disciplinary assessment and care planning* (London: DoH).

Department of Health (DoH) (2009c) *Integrated care pilots: An introductory guide* (London: DoH, available at www.dhcarenetworks.org.uk_library/Resources/ICP/ICP-intro.pdf).

Department of Health (DoH) (2009d) *Valuing people now: A new three-year strategy for people with learning disabilities* (London: DoH).

Department of Health (DoH), the Association of Directors of Adult Social Services (ADASS), the British Association of Social Workers (BASW), Skills for Care (SfC) and the Social Care Association (SCA) (2010) *The future of social work in adult services in England* (DoH, ADASS, BASW and SfC and SCA, available at http://www.dh.gov.uk/en/SocialCare/DH_098322).

Department of Health and Social Security (DHSS) (1990) *People first: Community care in Northern Ireland for the 1990s* (Her Majesty's Stationery Office, available at http://www. dhsspsni.gov.uk/people_first.pdf).

Deverell, K. and Sharma, U. (2000) 'Professionalism in everyday practice: Issues of trust, experience and boundaries', in N. Malin (ed.), *Professionalism, boundaries and workplace* (Florence, KY: Routledge), pp. 25–46.

Dickinson, A. (2006) 'Implementing the single assessment process: Opportunities and challenges', *Journal of Interprofessional Care*, 20(4): 365–79.

Dowling, B., Powell, M. and Glendinning, C. (2004) 'Conceptualising successful partnerships', *Health and Social Care in the Community*, 12(4): 309–17.

Eby, M. and Gallagher, A. (2008) 'Values and ethics in practice', in S. Fraser and S. Matthews (eds), *The critical practitioner in social work and health care* (London: Sage Publications), pp. 114–31.

Eccles, A. (2008) 'Single shared assessment: The limits to "quick fix" implementation', *Journal of Integrated Care*, 16(1): 22–30.

Emerson, R.M. (1976) 'Social exchange theory', *Annual Review of Sociology*, 2: 335–62.

Engeström, Y. (1999) 'Activity theory and individual and social transformation', in Y. Engeström, R. Miettinen and R.-L. Punamäki (eds), *Perspectives on activity theory* (Cambridge: Cambridge University Press), pp. 19–39.

Engeström, Y. (2001) 'Expansive learning at work: Toward an activity theoretical reconceptualization', *Journal of Education and Work*, 14(1): 133–56.

Engeström, Y. (2008) *From teams to knots: Activity-theoretical studies of collaboration and learning at work* (Cambridge: Cambridge University Press).

Etzioni, A. (ed.) (1969) *The semi-professions and their organization* (London: Collier-Macmillan).

Fleming, J., Goodman, H., Knight, V. and Skinner, A. (2006) 'Delivering effective multi-agency work for victims and witnesses of crime', *Practice*, 18(4): 265–78.

Flynn, M. (2007) *The murder of Steven Hoskin: A Serious Case Review, Executive Summary* (Cornwall Adult Protection Committee, available at http://www.towerhamlets. gov.uk).

Freeman, T. and Peck, E. (2006) 'Evaluating partnerships: A case study of integrated specialist mental health services', *Health and Social Care in the Community*, 14(5): 408–17.

General Social Care Council (GSCC) (2002) *Codes of practice for social care workers and employers* (London: GSCC, available at http://www.gscc.org.uk).

General Social Care Council (GSCC) (2008) *Social work at its best: A statement of social work roles and tasks for the 21st century* (London: GSCC).

Gilligan, P. and Manby, M. (2008) 'The common assessment framework: Does the reality match the rhetoric?' *Child and Family Social Work*, (13): 177–87.

Glasby, J. (2003) 'Bringing down the Berlin Wall: The health and social care divide', *British Journal of Social Work*, 33(7): 969–75.

Glasby, J. and Dickinson, H. (2008) *Partnership working in health and social care* (Bristol: Policy Press).

Glasby, J. and Littlechild, R. (2004) *The health and social care divide: The experiences of older people* (Bristol: Policy Press).

Glasby, J. and Littlechild, R. (2006) 'An overview of the implementation and development of direct payments', in J. Leece and J. Bornat (eds), *Developments in direct payments* (Bristol: Policy Press), pp. 19–32.

Glasby, J. and Peck, E. (2005) *Partnership working between health and social care: The impact of Care Trusts* (Health Services Management Centre, University of Birmingham, available at http://www.hsmc.bham.ac.uk).

Glasby, J. and Peck, E. (2006) *We have to stop meeting like this: The governance of inter-agency partnerships*, Discussion Paper (London: Integrated Care Network, available at http://www.icn.csip.org.uk).

Glendinning, C., Powell, M. and Rummery, K. (eds) (2002) *Partnerships, New Labour and the governance of welfare* (Bristol: Policy Press).

Glendinning, C., Hudson, B., Hardy, B. and Young, R. (2004) 'The Health Act 1999 section 31 partnership "flexibilities"', in J. Glasby and E. Peck (eds) *Care trusts: Partnership working in action* (Abingdon: Radcliffe Medical Press).

Griffiths, R. (1988) *Community care: Agenda for action: A report to the Secretary of State for Social Services* (Griffiths Report) (London: Her Majesty's Stationery Office).

Hafford-Letchfield, T. (2009) *Management and organisations in social work* (2nd edn) (Exeter: Learning Matters).

Hammick, M., Freeth, D., Copperman, J. and Goodsman, D. (2009) *Being interprofessional* (Cambridge: Polity Press).

Haringey Safeguarding Children Board (2009) *Serious Case Review: Baby Peter, Executive Summary* (available at http://www.haringeylscb.org/executive_summary_peter_final.pdf).

Hart, R. (1992) 'Children's participation: From tokenism to citizenship', Innocenti Essay No. 4 (Florence: UNICEF International Child Development Center, available at http://www.unicef-irc.org/cgi-bin/unicef/download_insert.sql?ProductID=100).

Hean, S., Macleod Clark, J., Adams, K. and Humphris, D. (2006) 'Will opposites attract? Similarities and differences in students' perceptions of the stereotype profiles of other health and social care professional groups', *Journal of Interprofessional Care*, 20(2): 162–81.

Heenan, D. and Birrell, D. (2005) 'The nature and context of cross-border social work in Ireland', *European Journal of Social Work*, 8(1): 63–77.

Henwood, M. (2004) 'Reimbursement and delayed discharges discussion paper for the Integrated Care Network' (Leeds: Integrated Care Network, available at http://www.dhcarenetworks.org.uk/).

Her Majesty's Government (HMG) (2009) *Shaping the future of care together* (Norwich: The Stationery Office).

Hoggarth, L. and Comfort, H. (2010) *A practical guide to outcome evaluation* (London: Jessica Kingsley).

Hornby, S. and Atkins, J. (2000) *Collaborative care: Interprofessional, interagency and interpersonal* (Oxford: Blackwell).

Horner, N. (2009) *What is social work? Context and perspectives* (3rd edn) (Exeter: Learning Matters).

Howe, D. (1987) *An introduction to social work theory* (Aldershot: Wildwood House).

Howe, D. (2009) *A brief introduction to social work theory* (Basingstoke: Palgrave Macmillan).

Hudson, B. (2002) 'Interprofessionality in health and social care: The Achilles' heel of partnership?' *Journal of Interprofessional Care*, 16 (1): 7–17.

Hudson, B. (2006) *Whole systems working: A guide and discussion paper* (Leeds: Integrated Care Network).

Hudson, B. and Henwood, M. (2009) *Working for people: The workforce implications of putting people first: A report for the Department of Health* (Northamptonshire: Melanie Henwood Associates, available at http://www.melaniehenwood.com/documents/WorkingforPeople.pdf).

Hudson, B., Hardy, B., Glendinning, C. and Young, R. (2002) *Use of the Section 31 Partnership Flexibilities in the Health Act 1999, final project report: Executive Summary 27* (National Primary Care Research and Development Centre, available at http://www.npcrdc.ac.uk/Publications/EXECSUM27.pdf).

Hugman, R. (2009) 'But it is social work? Some reflections on mistaken identities', *British Journal of Social Work*, 39(6): 1138–53.

Hunter, S. and Ritchie, P. (2007) 'Introduction – With, not to: Models of co-production in social welfare', in S. Hunter and P. Ritchie (eds), *Co-production and personalisation in social care: Changing relationships in the provision of social care* (London: Jessica Kingsley), pp. 9–18.

Individual Budgets Evaluation Network (IBSEN) (2008) *Evaluation of the individual budgets pilot programme final report* (York: Social Policy Research Unit, University of York, available at http://www.york.ac.uk/spru).

Institute of Public Care (IPC) (2010) *From the ground up: A report on integrated care design and delivery* (Oxford: IPC).

Integrated Care Network (2004) *Bringing the NHS and local government together: Integrated working: A guide* (Exeter: Integrated Care Network).

International Federation of Social Workers (IFSW) (2000) (accessed 13 March 2010 at http://www.ifsw.org/f38000041.html and available at http://www.ifsw.org).

Johnson, N. (1999) 'The personal social services and community care', in M. Powell (ed.), *New Labour, New Welfare State?* (Bristol: Policy Press), pp. 77–100.

Johnson, T.J. (1972) *Professions and power: Study in sociology* (London: Palgrave Macmillan).

Lambley, S. (2009) *Proactive management in social work* (Exeter: Learning Matters).

Laming, H. (2003) *The Victoria Climbié inquiry report*, Cm. 5730 (London: The Stationery Office, available at http://www.victoria-climbie-inquiry.org.uk).

Laming, H. (2009) *The protection of children in England: A progress report*, HC330 (London: The Stationery Office).

Larson, M.S. (1977) *The rise of professionalism: A sociological analysis* (Berkeley, CA: University of California Press).

Leadbetter, C. (2004) *Personalisation through participation: A new script for public services* (London: Demos).

Leadbetter, J., Daniels, H., Edwards, A., Martin, D., Middleton, D., Popova, A., Warmington, P., Apostolov, A. and Brown, S. (2007) 'Professional learning within multi-agency children's services: Researching into practice', *Educational Research*, 49(1): 83–98.

Leathard, A. (2003) 'Models for interprofessional collaboration', in A. Leathard (ed.), *Interprofessional collaboration from policy to practice in health and social care* (Hove: BrunnerRoutledge), pp. 93–119.

Leiba, T. and Weinstein, J. (2003) 'Who are the participants in the collaborative process and what makes collaboration succeed or fail?' in J. Weinstein, C. Whittington and T. Leiba (eds), *Collaboration in social work practice* (London: Jessica Kingsley Publishers), pp. 63–82.

Leicester, Leicestershire and Rutland Safeguarding Adults Board (2008) *Executive summary of Serious Case Review in relation to A and B* (available at http://www.leics.police.uk/files/news/Final%20_full%20doc_%20%20LLR%20SAB%20SCR%20A%20%20B.pdf).

Lishman, J. (2009) *Communication in social work* (2nd edn) (Basingstoke: Palgrave Macmillan).

Lloyd, J. and Wait, S. (2006) *Integrated care: A guide for policymakers* (London: Alliance for Health and the Future).

Loxley, A. (1997) *Collaboration in health and welfare: Working with difference* (London: Jessica Kingsley).

Lymbery, M. (2006) 'United we stand? Partnership working in health and social care and the role of social work in services for older people', *British Journal of Social Work*, 36(7): 1119–34.

Lymbery, M. and Millward, A. (2009) 'Partnership working', in R. Adams, L. Dominelli and M. Payne (eds), *Practising social work in a complex world* (2nd edn) (Basingstoke: Palgrave Macmillan), pp. 167–78.

McCray, J. (2007) 'Reflective practice for collaborative working', in C. Knott and T. Scragg (eds), *Reflective practice in social work* (Exeter: Learning Matters), pp. 30–142.

Malin, N. (ed.) (2000) *Professionalism, boundaries and workplace* (Florence, KY: Routledge).

Manthorpe, J. and Stanley, N. (eds) (2004) *The age of the inquiry* (London: Routledge).

Masson, J. (2006) 'The Climbié Inquiry – Context and critique', *Journal of Law and Society*, 33(2): 221–43.

Mathews, I. and Crawford, K. (2011) *Evidence-based practice in social work* (Exeter: Learning Matters).

Maynard Campbell, S., Maynard, A. and Winchcombe, M. (2007) *Mapping the capacity and potential for user-led organisations in England: A summary of the main findings from a national research study* (Department of Health, available at http://www.dh.gov.uk/prod_consum_dh/groups/dh_digitalassets/documents/digitalasset/dh_078532.pdf).

Minhas, A. (2009) 'On the receiving end: Reflections from a service user', in R. Carnwell and J. Buchanan (eds), *Effective practice in health, social care and criminal justice: A partnership approach* (2nd edn) (Berkshire: Open University Press), pp. 251–62.

Mur-Veeman, I., van Raak, A. and Paulus, A. (2008) 'Comparing integrated care policy in Europe: Does policy matter?' *Health Policy*, 85: 172–83.

Needham, C. (2009) *Co-production: An emerging evidence base for adult social care transformation*, Research Briefing 31 (London: Social Care Institute for Excellence).

Newman, T., Moseley, A., Tierney, S. and Ellis, A. (2005) *Evidence-based social work: A guide for the perplexed* (Lyme Regis: Russell House Publishing).

NHS Modernisation Agency (2004) *Improvement leaders' guide to working in systems*, Series 3 (Leicester: NHS Modernisation Agency).

NHS National Centre for Involvement (2008) *Local involvement networks: Working with volunteers*, Guide No. 13 (London: NHS Centre for Involvement).

Office for Standards in Education (Ofsted), with Audit Commission and Social Services Inspectorate (2003) *The Children's Fund: First Wave Partnerships*, HMI 585 (Ofsted Publications Centre, available at http://www.ofsted.gov.uk/Ofsted-home/Publications-and-research/Browse-all-by/Education/Extended-services/The-Children-s-Fund-first-wave-partnerships).

O'Sullivan, T. (1999) *Decision making in social work* (Basingstoke: Palgrave Macmillan).

O'Sullivan, T. (2011) *Decision making in social work* (2nd edn) (Basingstoke: Palgrave Macmillan).

Øvretveit, J. (1997a) 'How to describe interprofessional working', in J. Øvretveit, P. Mathias and T. Thompson (eds), *Interprofessional working for health and social care* (Basingstoke: Palgrave), pp. 9–34.

Øvretveit, J. (1997b) 'How patient power and client participation affects relations between professionals', in J. Øvretveit, P. Mathias and T. Thompson (eds), *Interprofessional working for health and social care* (Basingstoke: Palgrave), pp. 79–102.

Øvretveit, J. (1997c) 'Planning and managing interprofessional working and teams', in J. Øvretveit, P. Mathias and T. Thompson (eds), *Interprofessional working for health and social care* (Basingstoke: Palgrave), pp. 34–52.

Parker, P.J. (2009) *Professional boundaries in social work: A qualitative study* (London: General Social Care Council).

Parton, N. (2004) 'From Maria Colwell to Victoria Climbié: Reflections on public inquiries into child abuse a generation apart', *Child Abuse Review*, 13(2): 80–94.

Payne, M. (2005) *Modern social work theory* (3rd edn) (Basingstoke: Palgrave Macmillan).

Petch, A. (2008) *Health and social care: Establishing a joint future?* (Edinburgh: Dunedin Academic Press Ltd).

Pincus, A. and Minahan, A. (1973) *Social work practice: Model and method* (Itasca, IL: F.E. Peacock Publishers).

Pithouse, A., Hall, C., Peckover, S. and White, S. (2009) 'A tale of two CAFs: The impact of the electronic common assessment framework', *British Journal of Social Work*, 39(4): 599–612.

Powell, M. and Glendinning, C. (2002) 'Introduction', in C. Glendinning, M. Powell and K. Rummery (eds), *Partnerships, New Labour and the governance of welfare* (Bristol: Policy Press), pp. 1–14.

Quality Assurance Agency (QAA) (2008) *Subject benchmark statements for social work* (Mansfield: QAA, available at http://www.qaa.ac.uk/academicinfrastructure/benchmark/statements/socialwork08.pdf).

Quinney, A. (2006) *Collaborative social work Practice* (Exeter: Learning Matters).

Radford, J. (2010) *Serious Case Review under chapter VIII 'Working together to safeguard children' in respect of the death of a child: Case number 14* (available at http://www.lscbbirmingham.org.uk/downloads/Case+14+New.pdf).

Reder, P. and Duncan, S. (2004) 'Making the most of the Victoria Climbié Inquiry Report', *Child Abuse Review*, 13: 95–114.

Reder, P., Duncan, S. and Gray, M. (1993) *Beyond blame: Child abuse tragedies revisited* (London: Routledge).

Ritchie, J.H., Dick, D. and Lingham, R. (1994) *Report of the inquiry into the care and treatment of Christopher Clunis* (London: Her Majesty's Stationery Office).

Robinson, R. (2006) *Report of the independent inquiry into the care and treatment of John Barrett* (London: NHS).

Schön, D. (1983) *The Reflective Practitioner: How professionals think in action* (London: Temple Smith).

Scottish Executive (2007) *National guidance on self-directed support*, Circular No. CCD 7/2007 (Edinburgh: Scottish Executive Primary and Community Care Directorate).

Seden, J. (2008) 'Innovation still needed? Service user participation in social care services and practice-led management', *Innovation Journal: The Public Sector Innovation Journal*, 13(1): 5.

Seebohm, F. (1968) *Report of the Committee on Local Authority and Allied Personal Social Services* (Seebohm Report) (London: Her Majesty's Stationery Office).

Senge, P.M. (1990) *The fifth discipline: The art and practice of the Learning Organization* (London: Century Business/ Random House).

Shaw, I., Bell, M., Sinclair, I., Sloper, P., Mitchell, W., Dywon, P., Clayden, J. and Rafferty, J. (2009) 'An exemplary scheme? An evaluation of the integrated children's system', *British Journal of Social Work*, 29(4): 613–26.

Social Care Institute for Excellence (SCIE) (2007) *Developing social care: Service users driving culture change*, Knowledge Review 17 (London: SCIE, available at http://www.scie.org.uk/publications/knowledgereviews/kr17.pdf).

Social Care Institute for Excellence (SCIE) (2009) *At a Glance 15: Personalisation Briefing – Implications for User Led Organisations* (London: SCIE, available at http://www.scie.org.uk/publications/ataglance/ataglance15.pdf).

Social Exclusion Task Force (2008) *Think family: Improving the life chances of families at risk* (London: Cabinet Office, available at http://www.cabinetoffice.gov.uk).

Stanley, N. and Manthorpe, J. (2001) 'Reading mental health inquiries: Messages for social work', *Journal of Social Work*, 1(1): 77–99.

Stanley, N. and Manthorpe, J. (2004) 'Introduction: The inquiry as Janus', in N. Stanley and J. Manthorpe (eds), *The age of inquiry: Learning and blaming in health and social care* (London: Routledge), pp. 1–16.

Stewart, A., Petch, A. and Curtice, L. (2003) 'Moving towards integrated working in health and social care in Scotland: From maze to matrix', *Journal of Interprofessional Care* 17(4): 335–50.

Thompson, N. (2010) *Theorizing social work practice* (Basingstoke: Palgrave Macmillan).

Thompson, T. and Mathias, P. (1997) 'The World Health Organization and European Union: Occupational, vocational and health initiatives and their implications for cooperation amongst the professions', in J. Øvretveit, P. Mathias and T. Thompson (eds), *Interprofessional working for health and social care* (Basingstoke: Palgrave Macmillan), pp. 201–25.

TOPSS UK Partnership (2002) *National Occupational Standards for Social Work* (available at http://www.skillsforcare.org).

Trevillion, S. (2007) 'Critical commentary: Health, disability and social work: New directions in social work research', *British Journal of Social Work*, 37(5): 937–46.

Tuckman, B. (1965) 'Developmental sequence in small groups', *Psychological Bulletin*, 63(6): 384–99.

Weinstein, J., Whittington, C. and Leiba, T. (eds) (2003) *Collaboration in social work practice* (London: Jessica Kingsley Publishers).

Wenger, E. (1998) *Communities of practice: Learning, meaning, and identity* (Cambridge: Cambridge University Press).

West, M.A. and Poulton, B.C. (1997) 'A failure of function: Teamwork in primary health care', *Journal of Interprofessional Care*, 11(2): 203–16.

White, V. and Harris, J. (2001) 'Changing community care', in V. White and J. Harris (eds), *Developing good practice in community care: Partnership and participation* (London: Jessica Kingsley).

Whittington, C. (2003a) 'Collaboration and partnership in context', in J. Weinstein, C. Whittington and T. Leiba (eds), *Collaboration in social work practice* (London: Jessica Kingsley Publishers), pp. 13–38.

Whittington, C. (2003b) 'A model of collaboration', in J. Weinstein, C. Whittington and T. Leiba (eds) *Collaboration in Social Work Practice* (London: Jessica Kingsley), pp. 39–62.

Williams, P. (2002) 'The competent boundary spanner', *Public Administration*, 80(1): 103–24.

World Health Organization (WHO) (2006) *Working together for health: The World Health Report 2006* (Geneva: WHO).

World Health Organization (WHO) (2010) *Framework for action on interprofessional education and collaborative practice* (Switzerland: WHO Health Professions Network Nursing and Midwifery Office, available at http://www.who.int/hrh/nursing_midwifery/en/).

Younghusband, E. (Chair) (1959) *Report of the Working Party on Social Workers in the Local Authority Health and Welfare Services* (London: Her Majesty's Stationery Office).

Zastrow, C. (2009) *Introduction to social work and social welfare: Empowering people* (10th edn) (Belmont: Cengage Learning).

INDEX